NEXT STEPS

NEXT STEPS

New Directions for/in Writing about Writing

EDITED BY
**BARBARA BIRD
DOUG DOWNS
I. MORIAH MCCRACKEN
JAN RIEMAN**

UTAH STATE UNIVERSITY PRESS
Logan

© 2019 by University Press of Colorado

Published by Utah State University Press
An imprint of University Press of Colorado
245 Century Circle, Suite 202
Louisville, Colorado 80027

All rights reserved

 The University Press of Colorado is a proud member of the Association of University Presses.

The University Press of Colorado is a cooperative publishing enterprise supported, in part, by Adams State University, Colorado State University, Fort Lewis College, Metropolitan State University of Denver, University of Colorado, University of Northern Colorado, Utah State University, and Western State Colorado University.

ISBN: 978-1-60732-841-4 (paperback)
ISBN: 978-1-60732-842-1 (ebook)
DOI: https://doi.org/10.7330/9781607328421

Library of Congress Cataloging-in-Publication Data

Names: Bird, Barbara (Professor of English), editor. | Downs, Doug (Douglas P.), editor. | McCracken, I. Moriah, editor. | Rieman, Jan, 1967– editor.
Title: Next steps : new directions for/in writing about writing / edited by Barbara Bird, Doug Downs, I. Moriah McCracken, Jan Rieman.
Description: Logan : Utah State University Press, [2019] | Includes bibliographical references and index.
Identifiers: LCCN 2018056063 | ISBN 9781607328414 (pbk.) | ISBN 9781607328421 (ebook)
Subjects: LCSH: English language—Rhetoric—Study and teaching (Higher) | Academic writing—Study and teaching (Higher) | Writing—Study and teaching (Higher)
Classification: LCC PE1404.N54 2019 | DDC 808.06/6378—dc23
LC record available at https://lccn.loc.gov/2018056063

Cover illustration © patrimonio designs ltd/Shutterstock

*We dedicate this book to all writing teachers who use any version of writing about writing: you play an important role in the writing studies community to which you belong. And your commitment to the ideals of WAW—promoting students' writerly identities, processes, and engagement—has far-reaching effects on your students.
This book is for you.*

CONTENTS

Preface xi

Introduction
Barbara Bird, Doug Downs, I. Moriah McCracken, and Jan Rieman 3

1. Writing about Writing: A History
   Barbara Bird, Doug Downs, I. Moriah McCracken, and Jan Rieman 13

   PART I: WRITERLY IDENTITIES

2. Threshold Concepts as a Foundation for "Writing about Writing" Pedagogies
   Elizabeth Wardle and Linda Adler-Kassner 23

3. Writing about Writing in the Disciplines in First-Year Composition
   Rebecca Robinson 35

4. STUDENT VOICE: Reflections on Our Freshman Writing Course
   Emma Gaier and Megan Wallace 47

5. (Dis)Positioning Writing Confidence, Reflecting on Writer Identity: A Writing about Writing Curriculum Aimed at Knowledge Transfer
   Lisa Tremain 56

6. STUDENT VOICE: Writing about Writing: Leading to New Perspectives
   Hiroki Sugimoto 68

7. VIGNETTE: WAW-Professional Writing for STEM Co-op Students
   Joy Arbor 71

8. "I Am Seen; I Am My Culture; and I Can Write": How WAW Returns Multilingual Learners to Voice, Building Self-Efficacy and Rhetorical Flexibility
   Christina Grant 75

9. VIGNETTE: *El Ensayo*: Latinxs Writing about Writing
   Nancy Wilson, Rebecca Jackson, and Valerie Vera   88

10. VIGNETTE: "Writing Is Like Shaping a Bonsai Tree": Writing about Writing and Culture in a Developmental Composition Course
    Gwen Hart   97

11. Why I Keep Teaching Writing about Writing in Qatar: Expanding Literacies, Developing Metacognition, and Learning for Transfer
    Mysti Rudd   101

12. Next Steps, or Rather, One Step at a Time: A How-To Guide for Implementing Writing about Writing
    Kristen di Gennaro   112

13. Developing a Writing about Writing Curriculum
    Cat Mahaffey and Jan Rieman   123

PART II: PROCESS

14. VIGNETTE: Community College Composition, Critical Literacy, and the Writing about Writing Curriculum
    Shawn Casey   137

15. VIGNETTE: FYC Students as Writing Studies Scholars: Promoting Procedural Knowledge through Participation
    Andrew Ogilvie   143

16. VIGNETTE: Processes of Engagement: A Community College Perspective
    Olga Aksakalova and Dominique Zino   146

17. VIGNETTE: Engineering Writing about Writing in Engineering: Experiments in Technical Writing and Collaborative Design
    Andrew Lucchesi   150

18. VIGNETTE: Writing about Writing Pedagogy in a Mixed Major/Nonmajor Professional Writing Course
    Gabriel Cutrufello   155

19. Negotiating WAW-PW across Diverse Institutional Contexts
    Sarah Read and Michael J. Michaud   159

20. VIGNETTE: A Unique Pair: Pairing WAW in a First-Year Writing Sequence as the First Step in Academic Research
    Frances Johnson   172

21. VIGNETTE: Researching about Research, Writing about Writing from Sources
    Elizabeth Kleinfeld   177

22. VIGNETTE: The FYW WAW Composition Classroom Reimagined: Threshold Concepts through Gamification
    Samuel Stinson   180

23. Curricular Review in WAW: Involving Alumni, Students, and Faculty in Writing about Writing in Technical Fields
    Jennifer deWinter   187

    PART III: ENGAGEMENT

24. Transfer of Writing-Related Learning
    Rebecca S. Nowacek   201

25. STUDENT VOICE: Writing about Writing Focus: A Roundtable
    Kimberly Hoover with Elle Limesand, Maggie Hammond, and Max Wellman   209

26. Finding a Way into WAW: Extending Invitations across Disciplinary Lines
    Matthew Bryan, Kevin Roozen, and Nichole Stack   220

27. Digital Composing in WAW: What Students Learn through Infographics
    Christy I. Wenger   234

28. STUDENT VOICE: Podcasting and Protocols: An Approach to Writing about Writing through Sound
    Christian Smith with Gabrielle Frick and Patrick Siebel   252

29. Play the Game but Refocus the Aim: Teaching WAW within Alternative Pedagogies
    Katie Jo LaRiviere   261

Conclusion: Afterwards and Forwards
*Barbara Bird, Doug Downs, I. Moriah McCracken,
and Jan Rieman*   271

List of Contributors   281
Index   287

PREFACE

Putting together a book like this is a long-term project. All four of us brought unique perspectives and expertise; all four of us had seasons where we really leaned on the others to continue the work; all four of us had the same level of passion for this project. Our working relationship was characterized by the best teamwork: we supported each other, contributed equally, critiqued our collective work, and worked so well together that we cannot determine who "composed" what. (While at the same time we can also point to distinctive moments and breakthroughs by each of us that are responsible for the current shape of the book.) But of course, a legion more people were involved in the creation of this collection.

This book was initially inspired by discussions among the teachers and researchers who participate in the Writing-about-Writing Standing Group of the Conference on College Composition and Communication. In its yearly meetings at the CCCC convention and in its electronic communications throughout the year, the standing group strongly encourages its members to take on research projects that will let teachers employing various writing about writing designs test their efficacy and provide educators with descriptions of effective curricula that can be explored in other sites. Our editorial team emerged from rounds of such conversations in September 2014. It's fair to say that without the standing group's organization and push for research, this project would not have gotten under way. (Which itself seems to be solid validation for CCCC's idea of standing groups.)

As we worked on conceptions for this collection, editors at several presses helped us both imagine and articulate a project that would attract the kinds of contributions we wanted and be most workable for publication. Key among these advisors were David Blakesley at Parlor Press and Susan McLeod at the WAC Clearinghouse. We thank them both for their valuable perspective and generous advice.

Without question, our best motivator and advisor on the project was Michael Spooner, our first editor at Utah State University Press. His willingness to meet with us at CCCC 2015 to hear ideas and speculate about the book, his guidance in every stage of the process to help four scholars who had never edited a collection before, and his wisdom in framing and explaining the book, both to potential contributors and to his colleagues at USUP, were simply irreplaceable. So too were his patience and encouragement in understanding and working with peer reviews of the collection. We hope this collection is one more credit in a huge list of them for Mike, as he retired from USUP while we were in process on this book.

We were admittedly apprehensive to meet our new editorial contact at USUP, but Rachael Levay and Laura Furney immediately put us at ease with their terrific helpfulness, wonderful enthusiasm, and an infectious confidence in the project. Their work, along with that of the rest of the USUP and UPC production staffs, made us feel we were in excellent hands all the way through the publication process.

Our research assistant, Kayla Sulewski, who was a writing and rhetoric major at St. Edward's University, was invaluable in our efforts to construct a first manuscript draft for peer review. We are grateful she was willing to intern for Moriah and put so much effort into compiling and copyediting our first manuscript.

We thank our anonymous peer reviewers, who tackled a massive draft manuscript and whose frank suggestions and encouraging feedback (along with Michael Spooner's assistance in interpreting them) were key to a major turning point in the book's development.

We each also wish to thank our respective institutions for their continuing support of our research, and for ensuring that both the scholarship of teaching and learning and the collaborative editing of a major collection of other voices are counted as important research contributions.

Finally, and most of all, a huge thank-you to each of the smart, adaptable, and patient contributors to this collection. Their willingness to work to our timelines, templates, and revision needs, and their goodwill in shaping their ideas to enable coherence across so large a collection has been the heart of this project. We are humbled, and encouraged, to see so many wise and good-hearted teachers committed both to the kind of teaching this book describes and to sharing their experiences and analyses of that teaching with the field. It's been a privilege to work with each of them.

NEXT STEPS

INTRODUCTION

Barbara Bird, Doug Downs,
I. Moriah McCracken, and Jan Rieman

This book captures a representative variety of "writing about writing" (WAW) approaches to teaching writing that composition teachers are currently using. The authors of this book do not offer a singular set of practices or assignments or readings. We are deliberately calling WAW an *approach*, not a "pedagogy," since pedagogy may elicit thoughts of techniques or practices in a classroom. Similarly, we have chosen *approach* over "curriculum," since this term may leave readers asking for reading assignments and writing assignments. Though pedagogical techniques and the curricular design are here, our guiding purpose has been to help our readers, and us, see the breadth of current WAW approaches.

The approaches the field generally recognizes as "writing about writing" are founded on three *principles* for writing instruction, not a singular class or set of assignments (for example, ones mirroring those outlined by Doug Downs and Elizabeth Wardle in 2007). The first and foundational principle of the WAW approach is making writing itself the object of study in the writing classroom, regardless of course level. WAW courses study writing—in all its forms and with all its related concepts, including rhetoric, discourse, and literacy—as *the content* of the course, the subject of pieces students write. The content of WAW matters because it is in wrestling with writing concepts (both threshold and other key concepts) that students think deeply about what writing is, does, and means to them, and it is in writing about these concepts that students form their writer identities and develop deep writing knowledge. Writer identities and writing concept knowledge tends to result in an improved ability to discern what each new writing situation requires. In this way, WAW courses aren't interested in telling students *how* to write or *what* to write. Instead, they invite students into deep, meaningful conversations about writing and reflection on themselves as writers.

Part of the effectiveness of these writing concept conversations and writerly self-reflections stems from the second WAW principle: students are viewed as writers, not *student* writers. WAW acknowledges that no one is ever done learning to write, and by centering conversations around what scholars in writing know about writing—the research findings, terms and concepts, and effective practices—we explore what is still unknown with our students, who bring new experiences and practices into the classroom each semester. This is why WAW courses position students as novices, or individuals just beginning their study of writing as an artifact and studyable subject; and as novices, students are positioned in WAW courses as advancing along a continuum, not toward mastery but instead toward emerging expertise.

The third WAW principle is that WAW instructors want to advance writing knowledge *with* students. WAW asks students to be scholars with us; for ten or fifteen weeks, WAW instructors ask students to wrestle with ideas of what it means to be a reader, a writer, a literate citizen in the twenty-first century. What is most important in this reorientation toward students as novice scholars of writing knowledge is that WAW teachers want to discover this knowledge *with* students, not *for* them. WAW instructors, in other words, act precisely like the best faculty in general education courses across the rest of the curriculum: asking students for a moment to become practitioners of (rather than merely bodies acted upon by) a discipline that is not "theirs" but in which some fluency will be of great value to any educated individual. Using writing as the object of study and bringing students into the conversation with us about what we know about how writing works, focusing on how writing works *for each student*, is a key feature of WAW courses.

Instructors and students from a wide range of institutions composed the chapters and vignettes included here, and these voices and examples reveal how instructors and students collaborate to define more specifically what WAW means in local contexts. Because these contextualized settings play a large role in why and how each author developed his or her particular WAW approach, we preface chapters that discuss a specific classroom instantiation with a box listing a set of institutional context variables. In courses across the range of settings featured in this book, the three principles continually reemerge: writing is the content, students are writers, and instructors discover new knowledge with and not for student writers. A key result is that this use of declarative knowledge about writing to support students' identities as writers enables them to evidence understanding and choice in their own procedural approaches to writing.

Our initial call for contributions to this book was a very broad question: how are you using WAW? As we began to carefully listen to the descriptions of WAW submitted by our contributors, we eventually realized that the diverse WAW approaches might best be arranged by the three most common outcomes of these WAW practices: sharpened writerly identities, extended writing processes, and deeper writer engagement.

PART I: WRITERLY IDENTITIES

Treating students as writers, explicitly equipping them to develop their own writerly identities, requires us to process with them knowledge about writing, for all identities can only be developed after knowing something about that with which we want to identify. Though our students engage with multiple writerly communities just in their college courses alone, the most effective foundation for all of these communities is the sense of *being* a writer since it is writers who construct knowledge and ask questions. By treating students as writers, a WAW course helps students learn how to become agile and adaptive writers who know what questions to ask when moving into any writing situation and who feel confident in their abilities to figure out how to do the work required in each situation. We share writing knowledge resources with our students as those who have a bit more established writer identities, attempting to shift the culture of first-year writing toward a mentoring system: teachers *and students* talking about writing as writers, encouraging students to own their writer identities. This explicit invitation and equipping helps students move from *doing* writing to *being* a writer.

In this section, authors examine writerly identities from several perspectives, starting with a foundation for creating writerly identities: threshold concepts about writing. In "Threshold Concepts as a Foundation for 'Writing about Writing' Pedagogies," Elizabeth Wardle and Linda Adler-Kassner note that there *are* core principles and concepts that form the foundation of a WAW curriculum and upon which individual instructors can build when they construct courses *about* writing as a subject of study. Wardle and Adler-Kassner demonstrate how those principles and concepts are linked to our discipline's knowledge base—the "threshold concepts" of writing studies—and their work on threshold concepts is particularly important for this collection because research suggest that threshold concept knowledge results in a level of learning that "reflects identity-changing embodiment," which is best studied through multiple data points, such as those offered here.

Rebecca Robinson opens this discussion about research into WAW classrooms in her chapter, "Writing about Writing in the Disciplines in First-Year Composition," which uses a single WAW-focused assignment to help students retheorize writing as a way to understand key threshold concepts—not simply transmit information. This teacher-research discussion is followed by a student voice chapter, "Reflections on Our Freshman Writing Course," in which Emma Gaier and Megan Wallace, two dual-enrollment students, discuss how they each used writing concepts to join communities of practice by engaging in conversations, not reporting on their learning. In "(Dis)Positioning Writing Confidence, Reflecting on Writer Identity: A Writing about Writing Curriculum Aimed at Knowledge Transfer," Lisa Tremain draws connections between literate identity, self-efficacy, writing development, and transfer. Her classroom research suggests that self-efficacy and writer identity are inextricable from how writing transfer is successfully enacted—a claim in conversation with another student voice piece as well as a vignette. In "Writing about Writing: Leading to New Perspectives," Hiroki Sugimoto, a student enrolled in a WAW course, notes how particular class readings and his understanding of discourse communities helped him develop his own relationship to writing. In Joy Arbor's "WAW-Professional Writing for STEM Co-op Students" vignette, we learn how a WAW course helps students write about their process of writing and reflect on themselves as writers in order to facilitate self-teaching. That is, Arbor's students become more explicitly aware of themselves as professional writers, which helps them transform general principles to multiple situations.

The contributions in this writerly identities section also offer insight into how WAW courses can serve the complex needs of multilingual writers. In "'I Am Seen; I Am My Culture; and I Can Write': How WAW Returns Multilingual Learners to Voice, Building Self-Efficacy and Rhetorical Flexibility," Christina Grant suggests that a WAW course design helps multilingual students reestablish their voices and roles in academic writing, integrate the rhetorical traditions of their mother tongue, and make progress on becoming confident, multidimensioned, linguistically hybrid thinkers and writers. In their coauthored vignette, "*El Ensayo*: Latinx Writing about Writing," Nancy Wilson, Rebecca Jackson, and Valerie Vera demonstrate how a WAW approach with Latinx writers can help encourage students to become aware of the "interconnections between their academic identity and language experiences" and to use such interconnections as writing strategies for college writing expectations. In her vignette, "'Writing Is Like Shaping a Bonsai Tree': Writing about Writing and Culture in a Developmental Composition Course," Gwen Hart keeps with the WAW principle that students are writers within a community of learners. Hart's WAW course develops students' understandings of writing and aspects of their home cultures by asking students to think about how they understand writing through comparison. By linking writing to another familiar activity, Hart creates opportunities for students to think about their writing processes in a nonthreatening way so that they can examine the strengths and weaknesses of their current approaches to writing.

Mysti Rudd's chapter, "Why I Keep Teaching Writing about Writing in Qatar: Expanding Literacies, Developing Metacognition, and Learning for Transfer," explores the use of WAW in classrooms abroad. Rudd guides her students through an exploration of their identities as writers and transfer-inspired reflections about the usefulness of the premises they previously held about academic writing and reading. The work on reflection and writerly identities is then picked up by Kristen di Gennaro's "Next Steps, or Rather, One Step at a Time: A How-To Guide for Implementing Writing about Writing." Using her class as an example, di Gennaro suggests that while WAW writing tasks might draw on students' observations and reflections, WAW, as envisioned by di Gennaro, is not simply "writing about my writing." This section of the book closes with another chapter dealing with the programmatic role of WAW. In "Developing a Writing about Writing Curriculum," Cat Mahaffey and Jan Rieman suggest that WPAs who aim to develop a WAW program start with teacher identity. Mahaffey and Rieman argue that it is the shift in teacher identity that WAW prompts that enables student identities to shift. Engaged instructors who "own" the curriculum focus on the identity of the instructors and what that identity requires of them.

PART II: PROCESS

Like most writing teachers, WAW instructors do not view process as a list of practices to be completed in a particular order, like a checklist. More specifically, though, process in WAW classrooms is tied to who students are as writers and as knowledge makers since writing processes do not entail simply generating a draft or product but, more important, are a way to get to knowledge. Though most writing instructors want process made visible to their students, for many writers it isn't visible, at least not in the traditional way of viewing "the writing process." Some writers think and even "write" multiple drafts before putting hands to a keyboard; some writers keyboard only to discover their thinking after their third or tenth draft. WAW, like many writing approaches, invites students to engage in their own unique processes; but unlike other writing approaches, WAW invites students to *study* writing processes: what do *they* do and why? What have other writers done and why? How does writing-thinking work and why? These kinds of metacognition engage our WAW writers in reflective, rhetorical decision making.

Chapters included in this section reveal how, in WAW classrooms, process is not only tied to who students are as writers but also functions *in service of identity*. This identity-focused writing process perspective results from WAW instructors inviting students to connect who they are to all aspects of their writing, including their writing process. WAW emphasizes helping student writers know *how* they got to their final draft and learn how to replicate whatever process is successful for them. Emphasizing the effective and even ineffective processes students bring into classrooms helps WAW teachers to make explicit their goal of inviting writers to adapt and adopt cognizant practices for greater rhetorical understanding and greater content learning in any writing situation in or beyond school.

This section opens with Shawn Casey's vignette, "Community College Composition, Critical Literacy, and the Writing about Writing Curriculum." Casey's WAW students develop a more sophisticated understanding of the expanding literacies in our world, and by recognizing and writing about how literacy is learned, or not learned, Casey's students begin to build a context for understanding why so much emphasis is placed on "processes" in their later courses. Andrew Ogilvie also sees his students as novice writers, and he invites them to use that position to explore disciplinary genres. In his vignette, "FYC Students as Writing Studies Scholars: Promoting Procedural Knowledge through Participation," Ogilvie explores how his WAW course helps students think about how they approach writing, aiming to move students recursively between knowing *what* and knowing *how* with an end goal of helping them learn how to write themselves into a discourse community by exploring writing as ecology. Olga Aksakalova and Dominique Zino also want to help their students think differently about their processes, but their course focuses more directly on dispelling the myth that good writers don't need a writing process. To do this, Aksakalova and Zino give students the tools for navigating problems in their own writing process, showing students that expert writers also struggle and helping students verbalize their own difficulties. Aksakalova and Zino end their vignette, "Processes of Engagement: A Community College Perspective," by noting how they offer students strategies to analyze themselves as writers.

The idea of students exploring discourse communities also appears in Andrew Lucchesi's vignette, "Engineering Writing about Writing in Engineering: Experiments in Technical Writing and Collaborative

Design." In this WAW course, students read professional texts on writing as engineers, and they conduct primary research into their own writing processes. In teaching his students genre and discourse community concepts, Lucchesi helps his engineering students gain career writing knowledge that can be directly applied to themselves as novice engineers. Gabriel Cutrufello's vignette, "Writing about writing Pedagogy in a Mixed Major/Nonmajor Professional Writing Course," uses genres rather than discourse communities to introduce students to writing studies terminology, critical perspectives, and research activities. These elements help his students construct a meaningful understanding of writing, fostering a metacognitive awareness. Cutrufello's specific WAW content is business writing genres and activities—the context of his students' chosen fields and careers.

Sarah Read and Michael Michaud explore how WAW can work in discipline-focused settings in their full-length chapter, "Negotiating WAW-PW across Diverse Institutional Contexts." Read and Michaud begin with their belief that students learn disciplinary knowledge from scholarly articles about professional writing, which situates students as professional researchers, or what they refer to as knowledge transformers. They then discuss their process of helping students situate themselves in their professions. Frances Johnson is also asking students to view themselves as researchers, not just students. In her vignette, "A Unique Pair: Pairing Writing about Writing in a First-Year Writing Sequence as the First Step in Academic Research," Johnson discusses her major assignment, an auto-ethnography as a writer, which requires original research, analysis of peers as writers, and an analysis of scientific discourse. Johnson has found that this WAW approach helps students view themselves more explicitly as writers engaging in discourse community writing and genres. Elizabeth Kleinfeld picks up the conversation about research, arguing that it can help students understand the complexity of source use in her vignette, "Researching about Research, Writing about Writing from Sources." Kleinfeld uses WAW to guide her students through a study of their own writing as an artifact, an approach that helps students understand source use through a consideration of their own past use of sources.

Samuel Stinson's vignette, "The FYW WAW Composition Classroom Reimagined: Threshold Concepts through Gamification," shifts the conversations of process to threshold concepts. Stinson explores how the WAW process of exposing threshold concepts of writing in the service of teaching declarative knowledge about writing led him to develop a procedural method to engage these threshold writing concepts:

gamification. Jennifer deWinter explores the relationship between process and threshold concepts for students and instructors. In "Curricular Review in WAW: Involving Alumni, Students, and Faculty in Writing about Writing in Technical Fields," deWinter explores how a revised curriculum (moving to WAW) helped students gain a more complex, "nuanced" understanding of writing processes; in fact, the students she studied understood the value of writing as a discipline and the methods of research it involves by the end of her course. She also reveals how her curriculum redesign led to faculty in her writing program increasing their own knowledge of writing threshold concepts and research in writing studies in general.

PART III: ENGAGEMENT

WAW approaches to teaching writing not only invite students to develop their own writerly identities and develop metacognitive awareness of their processes, they also encourage student writers to deeply engage with themselves as writer-learners and engage with whatever content they are learning—in and out of the school setting. Of course we recognize that all writing teachers want their students to engage themselves as writers and engage the content. However, we have found that what most engages students as writers is the combination of the three key distinctions of a WAW approach: (1) using writing as content of the course, (2) viewing students as writers, and (3) instructors explicitly discovering new writing knowledge with their students. Each of these aspects of WAW invites deep engagement as writers: students are invited to give their perspectives on the content, are treated as writers above and beyond being students, and are co-learners with instructors. When students are asked their views and treated as writers and co-learners, especially in a classroom community, it leads to a powerful incentive for deep engagement.

Chapters in this section reveal how WAW approaches can and should move beyond typical FYC topics, which are often limited to academic genres and activities. Thus, the authors in these chapters explore wider WAW approaches with an eye on how these newer approaches reinforce the three principles of WAW while also broadening WAW approaches; thus, the authors in this section look at WAW courses from different angles, helping us to better understand how and why our students engage writing and themselves as writers.

Since this level of student engagement is foundational to any kind of transfer, we begin this section with a look at writing transfer. In "Transfer of Writing-Related Learning," Rebecca Nowacek argues that "we have not, as a field, sufficiently grappled with the question of what types of writing–related learning transfer." Nowacek's chapter also addresses key concepts and other writing knowledge and dispositions that most effectively lead to transferable or transformable writing practices.

We have found that WAW teachers do not aim to have students transfer writing *skills* but instead seek the transfer of deeper writing-related learning. The chapters that follow this theoretical opening to our engagement section position student writer engagement in the context of transfer. That is, the deeper writer-related learning that transfers, WAW teachers believe, is just the kind of learning that engages student writers since this learning is necessarily personal (identity-oriented) and intimately connected to their own processes. This conclusion is exemplified by "Writing about Writing Focus: A Roundtable" conducted by Kimberly Hoover with Elle Limesand, Maggie Hammond, and Max Wellman, three undergraduate students. Hoover's discussion of WAW highlights a significant outcome of WAW based on studies and program assessments: students' deep writing content knowledge, personal identification as writers, and strategies for addressing audiences.

In "Finding a Way into WAW: Extending Invitations across Disciplinary Lines," Matthew Bryan, Kevin Roozen, and Nichole Stack acknowledge that WAW requires a shift in our thinking and values. This chapter focuses on how WAW instructors articulate the value of WAW to other stakeholders, many of whom have little or no understanding of WAW principles and who have a range of disciplinary backgrounds, in order to productively engage a variety of stakeholders in conversations about writing instruction and literacy learning. In "Digital Composing in WAW: What Students Learn through Infographics," Christy I. Wenger turns the focus from instructors to students, articulating how WAW helps students become reflective consumers and producers of digital genres by increasing metaknowledge of audience and multimodality. This approach is useful for navigating the digital turn in FYW, but "trappings of expertise" can make WAW resistant to digital composing; thus, Wenger suggests that a digitally focused WAW course aim for mindfulness, not expertise. Also aiming for mindfulness is a student voice chapter, "Podcasting and Protocols: An Approach to Writing about Writing through Sound," written by Christian Smith with Gabrielle Frick and Patrick Siebel. Together, the voices of Smith, Frick, and Siebel suggest ways to improve WAW approaches using multimodal listening via think-aloud protocols. Smith contends that multimodal listening has made students more attentive to their own writing process by making that process "strange," which leads to a new WAW approach as "sonic composing."

Closing out this section, "Play the Game but Refocus the Aim: Teaching WAW within Alternative Pedagogies," Katie Jo LaRiviere creates the concept of "double pedagogy," which she developed as her way into WAW within an argument-focused approach with a specified set of readings that must be taught. Her double pedagogy helps other instructors teaching within a restricted writing program to create WAW approach values within any program. LaRiviere's double pedagogy highlights what she sees as WAW's greatest virtue: its focus on actively and consistently promoting metacognitive thinking about writing and the self as writer.

AFTERWARDS: NEXT STEPS

We conclude with a reflective chapter considering implications for further development of writing about writing approaches based on the state of WAW teaching described throughout the book. What questions have these contributions answered about WAW approaches? What questions have they opened or created? In what ways have WAW approaches established a comfortable center of gravity that might continue to characterize a writing about writing ethos in college writing instruction, and in what ways do the descriptions here leave us, as researchers and teachers of WAW approaches, wanting more or feeling the need to strike out in new directions? What do the pieces in this book suggest is clearly possible, and what possibilities do they leave us only to imagine?

1
WRITING ABOUT WRITING
A History

Barbara Bird, Doug Downs,
I. Moriah McCracken, and Jan Rieman

The central strategy of writing about writing curricula—the element that unites the many approaches to writing instruction described in this book—is the course's focus *on writing*. The object of study in the course, the subject that students' writing focuses on, is some aspect of writing, writers, discourse, literacy, rhetoric, or related subjects. Since contemporary discussion on this approach to writing began in the mid-2000s, that has been the primary insight or innovative factor in this approach to writing instruction.

Yet, as in seemingly every aspect of composition pedagogy, the field has walked this way before, or, what's old(er) is new(er): WAW approaches are only the latest iteration of pedagogies with the insight that students would benefit from direct access to discussion about writing. Throughout modern composition studies (usually dated from 1963), theorists and teachers in our field have repeatedly raised the question, or offered the insight, of what could be learned if we taught not simply *how* to write but *about* writing through the eyes of practitioners and researchers.

ALL THE WAY BACK

It's easy to overlook the fact that the most central works of rhetorical antiquity were effectively writing about writing approaches, focused on student discussion of primary texts on rhetorical discourse. Though we tend to see Aristotle's *On Rhetoric* as a text that discusses his rhetorical theory, the fact that it is actually compiled from *his students' notes* makes clear that Aristotle's mode of teaching rhetoric was not simply to show his students how to compose and deliver good speeches, but to make the course *about* rhetoric. Isocrates assigned texts on rhetoric, a pattern that also inhered in Quintilian's pedagogy, as he assigned his students Cicero's *De oratore*, the leading scholarly work on rhetorical theory of the day. This pattern of assigning students rhetorical texts to discuss continued through the Middle Ages, as demonstrated when Robert of Basevorn's *The Form of Preaching* (one of the early genre studies) was assigned to students not only to help them practice but to study the methodology and invention of sermons. Other rhetorical theory studied by students of rhetoric in Renaissance times included Cypriano Suarez's Jesuit rhetorical text *De arête rhetorica* (Abbott 2001) and Thomas Wilson's *The Arte of Rhetorique* (Herrick 2009). One of the most widely used primary texts of this time was Erasmus's *Copia*, which included not simply advice on "how to invent and compose" but also extensive, cutting-edge rhetorical theory. Moving into the eighteenth and nineteenth centuries, widely popular works such as George Campbell's (1776) *Philosophy of Rhetoric*, Hugh Blair's (1783) *Lectures on Rhetoric and Belles Lettres*, George Jardine's (1825) *Outlines of Philosophical Education*, and Richard Whately's (1834) *Elements of Rhetoric* and (1827) *Elements of Logic* and demonstrate a rich heritage of rhetoric and writing teachers making original rhetorical theory the content that students read, discussed, listened to, and wrote about.

These works were not simply "rhetorics" as we think of the contemporary textbook genre, which is largely understood as *abstracting* much older scholarly study of rhetorical theory and writing research into boiled-down *how-to* advice: no longer scholar-to-scholar communication that directly generates the knowledge driving the field. Rather, they *were* the primary texts that themselves developed and asserted state-of-the-art knowledge of rhetorical interaction. Students were encountering primary "research" (new philosophies of rhetoric and communication and observed results). This is the crucial distinction that the current turn in writing about writing pedagogy makes: the studied subject of the course is *the work of people making knowledge—whether by reporting thoughtfully and deliberately on their own practices or by researching and theorizing others' practices through firsthand observation*. In contemporary terms, this move from a text like *The St. Martin's Guide to Writing* (Axelrod and Cooper 1997) to a text like Donald Murray's "All Writing Is Autobiography" is a shift from presenting students with the second- or thirdhand reduction of existing knowledge to presenting them with the in-the-moment primary generation of knowledge. In a sense, then, this move returns students to the classical roots of and strategies for rhetorical instruction. The continuing principle is that students need to study—read, discuss, and write about—the *what* of rhetoric and writing to be fully equipped as an empowered rhetor.

CONTEMPORARY COMPOSITION STUDIES

Modern composition studies date from three sources: the advent of the Conference on College Composition and Communication (1950); rigorous research methods, such as those pioneered by Richard Braddock and George Hillocks, on the nature of writing and the effectiveness of various approaches to writing instruction (the early 1960s); and the expressivist and process movements in composition pedagogy (mid/late 1960s), including Rohman and Wlecke's 1964 insights on prewriting.

Particularly stemming from those expressivist and process movements, numerous calls for writing students to attend to public statements of practicing writers about the nature and activity of writing peppered the 1970s, 1980s, and 1990s. Donald Murray's *A Writer Teaches Writing* (1968), Ken Macrorie's *Uptaught* (1970), and Peter Elbow's *Writing without Teachers* (1973) all insist, in some measure, that if writers learn from the articulated experience of other writers it will take them much farther than pronouncements from rhetorics and teachers who propound rules. By the end of the 1980s and beginning of the 1990s, Elbow and Pat Belanoff's *A Community of Writers* (1989) and *Nothing Begins with N* (1991) echoed these calls, stressing the value of writing students encountering what practicing writers have to say about the act of writing and their strategies for it. Writing professors throughout this time brought the occasional texts from burgeoning research on writing into classrooms—in our own writing classes as college students, for example, Macrorie, Richard Ohmann's (1979) *College English* classic "Use Definite, Specific, Concrete Language," and Winston Weathers's (1976) work on Grammar A and Grammar B. The approach to writing instruction that featured writers talking about writing found apexes in 1999 and 2001, with Wendy Bishop's *The Subject Is Writing* and Bishop and Pavel Zemliansky's *The Subject Is Research*. These texts featured writers and researchers penning pieces written specifically to and for undergraduate readers on various challenges and issues related to writing and researched writing. These were followed by one of the fullest textbook instantiations of WAW pedagogy to date, Elizabeth Sargent and Cornelia Paraskevas's 2005 *Conversations about Writing: Eavesdropping, Inkshedding, and Joining In*. This collection anthologized significant writers-on-writing statements *and* researchers-on-writing articles to offer students a full spectrum of discussion about various aspects of writing.

Another line of reasoning that developed throughout the 1990s and early 2000s was less interested in writers talking about their own writing processes and more interested in creating encounters for writing students with various apparatuses for theorizing and researching writing that had emerged over the preceding thirty years in composition studies. This movement is actually traceable to a literary approach to composition: Bartholomae and Petrosky's (1986) *Facts, Artifacts, and Counterfacts: Theory and Method for a Reading and Writing Course*. In it and the resulting *Ways of Reading: An Anthology for Writers*, the two scholars argued that even developmental writers could manage, and would benefit from, direct encounters with very difficult texts, including scholarly texts that perform criticism of complicated literary texts. In creating a successful and widely used composition curriculum based on these principles, Bartholomae and Petrosky articulated an enduring principle eventually embodied in the current turn of writing about writing approaches: that students can, and should, engage directly with scholarship on the studied subject of a writing course. (This ethic then emerged in already-mentioned WAW texts by Bishop and by Sargent and Paraskevas.)

One of the first scholars to articulate a similar value for composition studies research itself was David Russell, in Joseph Petraglia's (1995) collection arguing against general writing skills instruction. Russell reasoned that most college composition courses, with the institutional mandate of teaching students "how to write" *universally*, were doomed (by the rhetorical principle stating that writing is situated within specific communities and varies widely across them) to fail unless they stopped trying to teach *how to* write and instead studied the theory and research of the field *about* writing in order to help students better understand the nature of writing and what they would need to learn in future writing settings in order to write successfully. Russell, though, proposed no specific curriculum for such a course. Anne Beaufort came closer in her 1999 study *Writing in the Real World: Making the Transition from School to Work*, identifying five specific knowledge domains in which students could learn concrete findings from composition and rhetoric that demonstrably aid college graduates in new writing situations: discourse community, subject matter, genres, rhetorical situation, and writing process knowledge. Beaufort demonstrated the power of mindful rhetorical articulation of declarative knowledge in these domains for boosting transfer, and was one of the earliest to advocate for teaching such knowledge directly and explicitly in order to foster learning transfer. And in 2003, John Trimbur's *Composition Studies* article "Changing the Question: Should Writing Be Studied?" suggested that composition pedagogy as a field had moved from the questions "Can writing be taught?" and "How can writing be learned?" to "Should writing be studied?"

essentially a movement "from the workshop to the seminar room" (23). In Trimbur's terms, "The historical and theoretical construction of the first-year course, with all of its debates about literacy, rhetoric, culture, and technology . . . laid the groundwork for a curriculum devoted to the study of writing" that would serve as "an intellectual resource for undergraduates" (23).

Indeed, after early moves in the 1990s, in the early/mid-2000s many members of the field were creating curriculum and texts for students that materialized the value of our field's knowledge for students. Linda Flower's (1993) *Problem-Solving Strategies for Writing* articulated her and others' work at Carnegie Melon, offering students the language of her socio-cognitive understanding of writing. Bonnie Sunstein and Elizabeth Chiseri-Strater's (2001) *Fieldworking* textbook brought professional research methods to an audience of first-year composition students even more accessibly than Mary Sue MacNealy's (1998) already usable *Strategies for Empirical Research in Writing*. Both works not only invited but *expected* students to use the methods of writing researchers to build their own knowledge of writing. Nancy DeJoy's 2004 *Process This: Undergraduate Writing in Composition Studies* explicitly described an approach to writing instruction in which students learned about writing by research and writing into the field. While that book was in press, Debra Frank Dew's 2003 *WPA: Writing Program Administration* article "Language Matters: Rhetoric and Writing I as Content Course" was articulating the value of writing about writing composition courses for raising students' awareness of *the existence of* a field of professionalized writing research. By 2009, Laurie Grobman's "The Student Scholar: (Re)Negotiating Authorship and Authority" theorized students as "new, emerging writers, not outsiders begging to be let into a community that needs them as outsiders to function" but *insiders* (188).

FINDING OUR WAYS TO WAW

Variously, these scholarly and teacherly conversations brought each of us editors to explore WAW approaches in our own classrooms. Based on Jardine's "First Philosophy" course, Barbara initially attempted an updated version drawing on contemporary writing theory in the fall of 2003. Meanwhile, in 2002 Doug was working from Russell's challenge to reframe FYC as disciplinary guidance on (essentially) how to learn to write *later*, and Bartholomae and Petrosky's evidence that first-year students could thrive on complex disciplinary readings to develop a spring 2003 pilot of the course he eventually described in his and Elizabeth Wardle's *CCC* article (2007). That article caught the attention of the field as a comprehensive articulation of a range of principles of which many had been more individually articulated in the works previously cited. Jan learned of the approach in conversations with other writing scholars who were considering it (Mark Hall and Tony Scott) and, coming from a PhD in modern British literature, her gradual shift to feeling like and being a rhetoric and composition specialist coincided with her introduction to a WAW curricular approach. Moriah became aware of WAW pedagogy from a presentation on an MA student's instantiation of a WAW curriculum that led to FYC student writing that amazed her. For her, the combination of Grobman's, Russell's, and Trimbur's articulation of the reality of, and need for, this shift in pedagogy, which make students participants in developing knowledge about the nature of writing and its workings, was persuasive.

While many faculty who are currently employing WAW pedagogies in their own courses and in their writing programs might point to Downs and Wardle's research as a motivator for their work, in fact the intellectual roots of writing about writing run long and deep in the field, and as we have found in our own paths to WAW and as many of the pieces in this collection suggest, the progenitors of what we are currently calling WAW are widely varied and diverse, tracing from many areas of the field. That diversity was reflected in early research on contemporary WAW approaches conducted in 2009 and 2010 by Downs and Wardle (2012). Survey responses led them to a three-category taxonomy of major WAW approaches, emphasizing literacy and discourse, language and rhetoric, and writers and their practices (140). Several years later, our work in compiling this collection suggests that so much diversity exists in course designs and purposes that it might be impossible to taxonomize. Newer scholarship on transfer and "teaching for transfer" (Yancey, Robertson, and Taczak 2014) as well as on threshold concepts (Adler-Kassner and Wardle 2015) are motivating approaches as well, as chapters in this book demonstrate. So too is composition's turn to translingualism and its increasing awareness of multimodality.

Among reasons for the current wide implementation of WAW approaches—and for the breadth of approaches to writing instruction that find their way under its umbrella—is this deep and rich history, from antiquity and through every decade of composition studies' modern existence, of calls, theories, and curricula that pull our attention from "how-to" instruction to study "about" writing and rhetoric.

REFERENCES

Abbott, Don Paul. 2001. "Rhetoric and Writing in Renaissance Europe and England." In *Short History of Writing Instruction*, edited by James Murphy, 124–44. New York: Routledge.

Adler-Kassner, Linda, and Elizabeth Wardle, eds. 2015. *Naming What We Know: Threshold Concepts of Writing Studies*. Logan: Utah State University Press.

Axelrod, Rise B., and Charles R. Cooper. 1997. *The St. Martin's Guide to Writing*. 5th ed. Boston: St. Martin's.

Bartholomae, David, and Anthony Petrosky. 1986. *Facts, Artifacts, and Counterfacts: Theory and Method for a Reading and Writing Course*. New York: Heinemann.

Bartholomae, David, and Anthony Petrosky. 1987. *Ways of Reading: An Anthology for Writers*. Boston: Bedford/St. Martin's.

Beaufort, Anne. 1999. *Writing in the Real World: Making the Transition from School to Work*. New York: Teachers College Press.

Elbow, Peter, and Pat Belanoff. 1989. *Community of Writers*. New York: McGraw-Hill Companies.

Belanoff, Pat, Peter Elbow, and Sheryl I. Fontaine, eds.1991. *Nothing Begins with N: New Investigations of Freewriting*. Carbondale and Edwardsville: Southern Illinois University Press.

Bishop, Wendy. 1999. *The Subject Is Writing*. 2nd ed. New York: Heinemann.

Bishop, Wendy, and Pavel Zemliansky. 2001. *The Subject Is Research: Processes and Practices*. Portsmouth, NH: Boynton-Cook.

Blair, Hugh. 1783. *Lectures on Rhetoric and Belles Lettres*. Delmar, NY: Scholars' Facsimiles & Reprints, 1993.

Campbell, George. 1776. *The Philosophy of Rhetoric*. Carbondale and Edwardsville: Southern Illinois University Press, 1963.

DeJoy, Nancy. 2004. *Process This: Undergraduate Writing in Composition Studies*. Logan: Utah State University Press.

Dew, Debra Frank. 2003. "Language Matters: Rhetoric and Writing I as Content Course." *WPA: Writing Program Administration* 26 (3): 87–104.

Downs, Douglas, and Elizabeth Wardle. 2007. "Teaching about Writing, Righting Misconceptions: (Re)Envisioning 'First-Year Composition' as 'Introduction to Writing Studies.'" *College Composition and Communication* 58:552–82.

Downs, Doug, and Elizabeth Wardle. 2012. "Reminagining the Nature of FYC: Trends in Writing-about-Writing Pedagogies." In *Exploring Composition Studies: Sites, Issues, and Perspectives*, edited by Kelly Ritter and Paul Kei Matsuda, 123–44. Logan: Utah State University Press.

Elbow, Peter. 1973. *Writing without Teachers*. New York: Oxford University Press.

Flower, Linda. 1993. *Problem-Solving Strategies for Writing*. 4th ed. New York: Harcourt.

Grobman, Laurie. 2009. "The Student Scholar: (Re)Negotiating Authorship and Authority." *College Composition and Communication* 61:175–96.

Herrick, James A. 2009. *The History and Theory of Rhetoric*. 4th ed. Needham Heights, MA: Pearson.

Jardine, George. 1825. *Outlines of Philosophical Education, Illustrated by the Method of Teaching the Logic Class in the University of Glasgow; Together with Observations on the Expediency of Extending the Practical System to Other Academical Establishments, and on the Propriety of Making Certain Additions to the Course of Philosophical Education in Universities*. Glasgow: Glasgow University Press.

MacNealy, Mary Sue. 1998. *Strategies for Empirical Research in Writing*. New York: Pearson.

Macrorie, Ken. 1970. *Uptaught*. New York: Hayden.

Murray, Donald. 1968. *A Writer Teaches Writing*. New York: Houghton Mifflin.

Murray, Donald M. 1991. "All Writing Is Autobiography." *College Composition and Communication* 42 (1): 66–74.

Ohmann, Richard. 1979. "Use Definite, Specific, Concrete Language." *College English* 41: 390–97.

Rohman, D. Gordon, and Albert O. Wlecke. 1964. "Pre-Writing: The Construction and Application of Models for Concept Formation in Writing." ERIC. ED001273.

Russell, David. 1995. "Activity Theory and Its Implications for Writing Instruction." In *Reconceiving Writing, Rethinking Writing Instruction*, edited by Joseph Petraglia, 51–78. Mahwah, NJ: Lawrence Erlbaum.

Sargent, M. Elizabeth, and Cornelia C. Paraskevas, eds. 2005. *Conversations about Writing: Eavesdropping, Inkshedding, and Joining In*. Toronto: Nelson.

Sunstein, Bonnie Stone, and Elizabeth Chiseri-Strater. 2001. *Fieldworking: Reading and Writing Research*. Boston: Bedford/St. Martin's.

Trimbur, John. 2003. "Changing the Question: Should Writing Be Studied?" *Composition Studies* 31 (1): 15–23.

Weathers, Winston. 1976. "Grammars of Style: New Options in Composition." *Freshman English News* 4 (3): 1–4, 12–18.

Whately, Richard. 1827. *Elements of Logic*. Boston: James Munroe and Co., 1856.

Whately, Richard. 1834. *Elements of Rhetoric*. Nashville, TN: Southern Methodist Publishing House, 1861.

Yancey, Kathleen Blake, Liane Robertson, and Kara Taczak. 2014. *Writing across Contexts: Transfer, Composition, and Sites of Writing*. Logan: Utah State University Press.

PART I

Writerly Identities

2
THRESHOLD CONCEPTS AS A FOUNDATION FOR "WRITING ABOUT WRITING" PEDAGOGIES

Elizabeth Wardle and Linda Adler-Kassner

"Writing about writing" courses enact a foundational principle: that "our field has particular research- and theory-based views of writing, how it works and gets accomplished. Some of that research and theory can and should be taught to undergraduates, . . . and learning *about* writing in this way has a positive impact for student writers" (Wardle and Downs 2013). This approach extends from three premises: (1) postsecondary institutions are constituted, in part, by the disciplines within them; (2) disciplinary identities are constituted when individuals participate in a shared knowledge base and shared practices (i.e., ways of defining and investigating questions, and ways of representing what is learned) related to the development and interrogation of that base; and (3) courses *in* disciplines engage students in exploration of both knowledge and practices from that discipline.

While there is no single writing about writing curriculum, there *are* core principles and concepts that extend from these premises that form the foundation of a curriculum and upon which individual instructors build when they construct courses *about* writing as a subject of study. These are linked to our discipline's knowledge base—what we have called, borrowing from Jan H. F. Meyer and Ray Land (2006b, 2006c), the "threshold concepts" of writing studies. Threshold concepts are "concepts critical for continued learning and participation in an area or within a community of practice" (Adler-Kassner and Wardle 2015, 2). Meyer, Land, and Baillie (2010) write that an approach to learning and teaching rooted in threshold concepts "builds on the notion that there are certain concepts, or certain learning experiences, which resemble passing through a portal, from which a new perspective opens up, allowing things formerly not perceived to come into view. This permits a new and previously inaccessible way of thinking about something. It

DOI: 10.7330/9781607328421.c002

represents a transformed way of understanding, or interpreting, or viewing something, without which the learner cannot progress, and results in a reformulation of the learners' frame of meaning" (ix).

Along with a number of colleagues, the two of us participated in a project to identify and define some of these concepts for a book called *Naming What We Know: Threshold Concepts of Writing Studies* (Adler-Kassner and Wardle 2015). To participate in writing about writing courses, students must have opportunity to participate in threshold concepts of the discipline like (but not limited to) the ones named through this project by learning terminology, strategies, practices, and ideas that will enable them to approach the portals represented by threshold concepts. Writing about writing courses that incorporate threshold concepts are built upon research-based ideas intended to lead students to develop research-based ways of approaching and working with writing. For many students, the very idea of approaching writing as a subject of study and through threshold concepts of writing studies is transformative and leads them to new perspectives on what writing is, what it does, and how it does those things (see Bazerman and Prior 2009).

To develop curricula designed to move students toward transformed perspectives on writing, then, it is useful to consider the characteristics associated with approaches to, work with, and passage through threshold concepts that have been identified through empirical research by Meyer and Land, along with the many other faculty researchers who have examined threshold concepts in a range of disciplines. These researchers note that threshold concepts have particular features: "they are *transformative* (occasioning a significant shift in the perception of a subject), *integrative* (exposing the previously hidden inter-relatedness of something) and likely to be, in varying degrees, *irreversible* (unlikely to be forgotten, or unlearned only through considerable effort), and frequently *troublesome*, for a variety of reasons" (Meyer, Land, and Baillie 2010, ix).

It is also important to recognize the difference between threshold concepts and other kinds of concepts or key terms. Threshold concepts are notable for their difficulty as well as the way they transform thinking, seeing, and acting once they are learned. They are different from "core" concepts, which are important but "do not lead to a dramatic shift to a new level of understanding" (Biggs and Tang 2011, 83). Instead, threshold concepts are "superordinate . . . [they] relate previously disparate ideas and . . . give students a broader view of the subject" (84). Clearly, not all learning that happens in any classroom, including writing about writing classrooms, involves threshold concepts. For example, we commonly hear people say that "discourse community" is a threshold concept. It is not; rather, it is a key term related to a number of threshold concepts that underscore the idea of a discourse community and contribute to learners' transformative ways of thinking about the roles that discourse communities play for writers and with writing, such as "Writing speaks to situations and contexts through recognizable forms" (Bazerman 2015), "Writing is linked to identity" (Roozen 2015), or "Disciplinary and professional identities are constructed through writing" (Estrem 2015a).

Next, we will consider what it looks like to encounter and learn threshold concepts in general. Then we will turn our attention specifically to the threshold concepts of our own field and consider how teachers and administrators can support learning those concepts in deep ways without mistaking them for more easily assessable learning outcomes.

HOW DO LEARNERS ENCOUNTER THRESHOLD CONCEPTS?

Threshold concepts theorists have suggested that learners travel through preliminal, liminal, and postliminal states as they grapple with threshold concepts. Initially, learners encounter troublesome knowledge that initiates preliminal engagement with a threshold concept: "The troublesome knowledge inherent within the threshold concept serves . . . as an *instigative* or provocative feature which unsettles prior understanding rendering it fluid, and provoking a state of liminality" (Meyer, Land, and Baille 2010, xi). In order to engage in learning, learners must find a way to integrate new knowledge with previous knowledge or assumptions, which might entail "a letting go or discarding of any earlier conceptual stance" (xi). Learners then make shifts in how they are and know—in other words, in their ontological and epistemological states. At this point, learners can "cross a conceptual boundary into a new conceptual space" and enter "a postliminal state in which both learning and the learner are transformed" (xi). This transformation is usually "irreversible" and can be seen by a change in the way the learner uses discourse.

Such learning is not necessarily linear, nor is it necessarily fast. Meyer et al. (2010) have noted that it involves "recursiveness" and "oscillation" (xi). This is likely because of the troublesome nature of threshold concepts. This "troublesomeness" can occur for a variety of possible reasons: because the commonsense views that threshold concepts call into question are already ritualized or inert; because threshold concepts are conceptually difficult or alien; because learning the concepts "requires adopting an unfamiliar discourse"; or because the learner may not wish to change (x; see also Meyer and Land 2006b, 2006c; Perkins 2006). When learners are left on their own, encounters with troublesomeness can leave them "in a state of 'liminality,' a suspended state of partial understanding, or 'stuck place,' in which understanding approximates to a kind of 'mimicry' or lack of authenticity" (Land et al 2005, x).

While being in a liminal or "stuck" place can be uncomfortable for both learners and teachers, Julie Timmermans (2010) argues that faculty should embrace this troublesomeness directly. Timmermans writes that "some degree of dissonance is often necessary to stimulate development." In fact, "the troublesome . . . nature of threshold concepts may be the very quality that reveals their development potential . . . Their power may be that they trigger dissonance not only at the cognitive and affective levels, but also dissonance at the epistemological level, calling upon learners to 'change their minds' not by supplanting *what* they know, but by transforming *how* they know" (10–11). When introducing students to such difficult concepts, then, faculty should "acknowledge the difficult journey on which we are asking students to embark" and "help them live more comfortably with their discomfort" (11). This discomfort, as a learning process, itself has a number of dimensions: a transformation not just of students' knowledge but of their identities as members of multiple communities and navigators among many new (disciplinary) communities and their threshold concepts (Timmermans 2010; also see Wenger-Trayner and Wenger-Trayner 2015).

WRITING STUDIES AND THRESHOLD CONCEPTS

Because of the role that threshold concepts play in communities of practice (Wenger 1999), it is relatively easy for those of us who study and/or teach writing for a living to understand the importance of a threshold concepts framework for the teaching of writing. Communities of practice are sites where people share common language, values, ideologies, and strategies for learning how to learn. These include religious communities, fan fiction groups, sports teams, and academic disciplines. Within these communities, participation in threshold concepts lead members also to develop a common set of lenses that they use to understand the world and phenomena within it, lenses that often shape what seem to be "common sense."

It's also easy for us to see threshold concepts of writing as central elements in many of the communities of practice in which individuals circulate. Success in these communities depends, in part, on peoples' abilities to participate in threshold concepts; that participation requires embodiment of the concepts through a transformational learning process. In many of these communities, writing (or other forms of composing) is the means by which participation is represented. To write "well" requires writers to understand and use the conventions of genres circulating within contexts or sites of writing (disciplines, community sites, workplaces, and so on) and to demonstrate participation in the epistemologies of those sites in their writing. The more expert one is in a community, the more these epistemologies—the threshold concepts—seem like "common sense," and the "easier" those experts think that representation should be. We writing faculty hear this belief expressed in a frequent lament uttered by colleagues outside of writing: "Why can't students write [this thing in my discipline]? It's common sense!"

Since writing studies focus in part on the study of composed knowledge (aka the study of written products) and the study of knowledge production (aka the study of producing writing), the threshold concepts of our discipline can enable students to learn to understand that: (1) threshold concepts exist and are community/site-specific; (2) expectations for writing are closely related to threshold concepts in different sites/disciplines; and (3) to be successful in any new context requires studying and, ultimately, participating in the threshold concepts (and expectations) of that context. In other words: as they travel across a postsecondary campus, students encounter multiple communities, each of which has its own set of threshold concepts and, related to those concepts, expectations for how participation in them will be represented in composed knowledge, aka writing. (This is true as students travel outside of campuses as well, of course.)

WHAT ARE SOME OF THE THRESHOLD CONCEPTS OF OUR FIELD?

Although writing scholars and others invested in language have been designing curricula focusing on the study of writing for decades, we have been doing so without general agreement or discussion regarding what primary research should be conveyed to students in those courses (see Wardle and Downs 2013). *Naming What We Know*, the book mentioned earlier, represents a modified crowd-sourcing effort to do this very work. Over a period of several months, thirty-one writing scholars and teachers worked together on a wiki to try to identify some of the threshold concepts of writing studies. This work eventually resulted in thirty-six threshold concepts. They begin with the metaconcept "Writing is an activity and a subject of study." Others are grouped within five other major concepts:

> Writing is a social and rhetorical activity.
> Writing speaks to situations through recognizable forms.

Writing enacts and creates identities and ideologies.
All writers have more to learn.
Writing is (also) always a cognitive activity.

In the second part of *Naming What We Know*, authors consider how to use various threshold concepts to design programs, assessments, and professional development projects. A number of these chapters include curricular sites: general education programs, first-year writing courses, writing majors, graduate programs, and writing centers. The chapters describe the threshold concepts underscoring these sites; importantly, though, they are neither exact duplicates of the others nor cookie-cutter in their descriptions of conceptualization and implementation. Each, though, can be seen as addressing "areas [that] present particular challenges," such as those identified by Doug Downs and Liane Robertson (2015) as "addressing misconceptions [about writing] and teaching for transfer" (106). While Downs and Robertson situate these in relation to first-year writing, they can be understood as an example of how threshold concepts of writing studies can be used to meet the challenges, and how faculty can consider appropriate threshold concepts to emphasize for students at different levels. They identify four areas to emphasize for students that can help address common misconceptions about writing that impede knowledge transfer:

Writing as human interaction (rhetoric), with the threshold concept that writing is a rhetorical activity (107).

Textuality, with the threshold concept that meaning is constructed (108).

Epistemology (ways of knowing and the nature of knowledge), with the threshold concept that writing is a means of creating new knowledge (108).

Writing process, with a number of related threshold concepts, including that texts get their meaning from other texts, revision is central to developing writing, writing is not natural, and writing is a technology (109).

Chapters in the book also consider the ways in which engaging threshold concepts as a framework for approaching learning about writing—that is, working from the perspective that successful participation in disciplines (and communities) is in part predicated on embodiment of threshold concepts—contributes to ways of thinking about designing, implementing, and assessing writing curricula. Other texts have also explicitly considered threshold concepts appropriate for teaching at different levels (e.g., Wardle and Downs 2014) or examined the ways in which engaging students in the study of threshold concepts contributes to the development of a perspective on learning across disciplines (e.g., Adler-Kassner, Majewski, and Koshnick 2012). Less explicitly, some texts have laid out readings from the field for upper-level students that inherently describe what are now referred to as threshold concepts (e.g., Peeples 2002) or a methodology for teaching that would result in students gaining a deeper understanding of threshold concepts in various communities of practice (e.g., Kain and Wardle 2005). In outlining the various approaches to teaching threshold concepts in *Naming What We Know* and elsewhere, we hope to illustrate that our field does, in fact, have shared and agreed-upon knowledge about writing upon which writing courses can be built, and that much of this knowledge fits the criteria outlined by Meyer, Land, and other threshold concept theorists.

There is, then, some agreement about both threshold concepts of the field and the usefulness of the study of these concepts in our discipline and as a lens more broadly. At the same time, given what we explained earlier regarding the troublesomeness of learning threshold concepts, we can see why threshold concepts about writing are especially likely to be troublesome if students come with assumptions about their success as writers and/or particular ideas about what writing is and how to do it. This is because, as Chris Anson (2015) explains, "habituated practice can lead to entrenchment" (threshold concept 5.3 from *Naming What We Know*): "When writers' contexts are constrained and they are subjected to repeated practice of the same genres, using the same processes for the same rhetorical purposes and addressing the same audiences, their conceptual framework for writing may become entrenched . . . When this happens, they may try to apply that framework in a new or unfamiliar writing situation, resulting in a mismatch between what they produce and the expectations or norms of their new community" (77; see also Reiff and Bawarshi 2010; Sommers and Saltz 2004). A number of the threshold concepts of writing studies outlined in *Naming What We Know* emphasize both the affective and practice-based elements of writing development, such as "writing is not natural" (Dryer 2015), "writing is performative" (Lunsford 2015), "writers' histories, processes, and identities vary" (Yancey 2015), "disciplinary and professional identities are constructed through writing" (Estrem 2015a), and "reflection is critical for writers' development" (Taczak 2015).

CROSSING CONCEPTUAL BOUNDARIES: PUTTING THRESHOLD CONCEPTS INTO ACTION

At the same time that researchers and teachers must continue to identify threshold concepts of writing studies (and explore whether there is value in the framework and the naming), those who want to use threshold concepts as a basis for teaching must consider some questions associated with operationalizing. Which threshold concepts are important for various groups of students, in what contexts and situations, and at what levels? Where will or might threshold concepts of writing be reemphasized and explored again in the curriculum? We also can begin to explore questions related to student learning of threshold concepts. When can we expect different groups of students to cross the conceptual boundaries associated with threshold concepts? What does it look like for different groups of students to pass through the threshold to transform their understanding and participate in a concept at increasing levels of richness? And how do we know? These questions all concern how threshold concepts are operationalized within curricula.

We do not necessarily have distinct answers to these questions, though we can (and will) point to some illustrative cases. At the same time, we will repeat some admonitions from *Naming What We Know*. First, and perhaps most important, the threshold concepts outlined in that collection are concepts-for-now. They are not a definitive list, nor should they be turned into a checklist for learning, such that they become reduced to items on a rubric or another convenient grading metric that can be ticked off as students appear to achieve them as measured through those rubrics and metrics (Adler-Kassner and Wardle 2015, introduction). Second, faculty and writing program administrators need to recognize that threshold concepts are not outcomes (Estrem 2015b). They are not easily measurable, nor can they be directly taught and then learned in one setting through explanation or reading. Learners encounter them at different times and in different ways, depending on their own experiences and readiness for embracing the liminality that learning such concepts entails. Threshold concepts are learned through experiences across time, and are not necessarily learned once and for all. For example, learners might begin to understand a concept like "writing is not perfectible" in a writing class when they are asked to revise, but not deeply enact what that means for them until they begin writing in a workplace where they must work continually with others to readjust ideas for changing and unpredictable reader needs.

Recognizing, explaining, doing, and then embodying threshold concepts are different things. This process of "learning" is recursive, so it happens at different times (and in different ways), depending on learners and contexts for learning. Consider, for example, a first-year student who might develop the ability to analyze expectations for writing in particular academic disciplines and/or workplaces and recognize differences across these sites. If a first-year student can explain why discourse differs across disciplines and analyze such discourse for a classroom assignment, that certainly seems like an appropriate level of achievement for a first-year course. However, it does not necessarily guarantee that the learner will remember, apply, and enact that concept and employ those analytical skills when she begins writing in her biology major. In other words, it's possible to explain a concept and even apply it in writing without embodying it and enacting it in another setting—a disconnect that transfer researchers have noted repeatedly.

Moreover, the level of conceptual understanding and the ability to enact it grow at each advancing level of engagement with a community of practice. What we would accept from a first-year student as a competent explanation of how discourse conventions vary across disciplines would not be seen as competent if produced by a graduate student. A graduate student would also need to express an understanding of how and why these discourse differences exist, articulating more explicit connections between expectations and ideology or epistemological practices of the discipline or context, in ways that would be beyond the initial understanding of a newer learner. While first-year writing about writing courses do students a service by explaining the notion of threshold concepts and actively presenting some threshold concepts with which students can engage during the term, no one—not teachers, not program administrators, not colleagues in other departments—should expect that any first-year student would "master" a threshold concept during such a limited time.

Given the extended time, experience, reflection, and enactment required for deep learning of threshold concepts, teachers and program administrators might do well to focus on course design, scaffolding of writing courses across time and settings, and advocating for ongoing, structured, and supported programs (like WAC, WID, WEC, CAC, or CEC). But these programs, too, must be intentional. While they do not necessarily need to explicitly use the language of threshold concepts, we must ensure that they immerse students in the study of not just "writing expectations" within other disciplines, but the epistemologies that underscore those expectations. Then, they must also support students as they grapple with engaging those epistemologies, using writing to learn and to represent what has been learned through them.

In the contemporary educational climate, so much comes down to assessment, too often framed in a single and sometimes reductive question: how do we know that what we are doing works? We end, then, by briefly considering how approaching writing curricula through threshold concepts also has implications for assessment. This approach leads us to ask: how can we describe success with threshold concepts? What evidence will we need to examine students' work with them, and what effects might this engagement have on their learning? For example, how will we know that a student can not only *explain* that writing is not perfectible but can also *recognize* this throughout her own drafting process, *use* this knowledge to give herself opportunities for revision and seeking feedback, *feel* a healthy sense of self-worth when her writing is not as successful as she had hoped, and *connect* this idea to other related ideas, such as the idea that discourse conventions and aims vary across communities of practice? The literature on threshold concepts (along with studies such as McCarthy 1987; Sternglass 1997; Beaufort 2007; and Yancey, Robertson, and Taczak 2014) tells us that this level of learning reflects identity-changing embodiment—and that this takes more than a single course or term. Thus, when course-level assessments are designed, they should likely focus on *outcomes* that can be assessed (rather than threshold concepts), outcomes such as demonstrated ability to define and use key terms or to apply key terms to engage in analysis. The approach to and understanding of these terms, the ability to apply them, and so on are associated with the development of knowledge capabilities (Baille, Bowden, and Meyer 2013) intrinsic to the ability to encounter, engage with, and apply threshold concepts. These capabilities, the authors write, "are in fact threshold to professional learning in a defined area of knowledge." To understand the interactions of these capabilities with students' participation in threshold concepts is likely best captured in longitudinal assessments involving multiple data points, such as portfolios, interviews, and observations across time. These seem to be the only ways to determine whether threshold concepts are informing thinking, being, and doing across settings and within particular communities of practice.

REFERENCES

Adler-Kassner, Linda, John Majewski, and Damian Koshnik. 2012. "The Value of Threshold Concepts: Troublesome Knowledge in Writing and History." *Composition Forum* 26 (Fall). http://compositionforum.com/issue/26/troublesome-knowledge-threshold.php.

Adler-Kassner, Linda, and Elizabeth Wardle, eds. 2015. *Naming What We Know: Threshold Concepts of Writing Studies*. Logan: Utah State University Press.

Anson, Chris. 2015. "Habituated Practice Can Lead to Entrenchment." In Adler-Kassner and Wardle 2015, 77–78.

Baille, Caroline, John A. Bowden, and Jan H. F. Meyer. 2013. "Threshold Capabilities: Threshold Concepts and Knowledge Variability Linked through Variation Theory." *Journal of Higher Education and Educational Planning* 65 (2): 227–46.

Bazerman, Charles. 2015. "Writing Speaks to Situations and Contexts through Recognizable Forms." In Adler-Kassner and Wardle 2015, 35–37.

Bazerman, Charles, and Paul Prior. 2009. *What Writing Does and How It Does It*. New York: Routledge.

Beaufort, Anne. 2007. *College Writing and Beyond: A New Framework for University Writing Instruction*. Logan: Utah State University Press.

Biggs, John, and Carolyn Tang. 2011. *Teaching for Quality Learning at University*. 4th ed. London: Open University Press.

Downs, Doug, and Liane Robertson. 2015. "Threshold Concepts in First-Year Composition." In Adler-Kassner and Wardle 2015, 105–21.

Dryer, Dylan. 2015. "Writing Is Not Natural." In Adler-Kassner and Wardle 2015, 27–29.

Estrem, Heidi. 2015a. "Disciplinary and Professional Identities Are Constructed through Writing." In Adler-Kassner and Wardle 2015, 55–56.

Estrem, Heidi. 2015b. "Threshold Concepts and Student Learning Outcomes." In Adler-Kassner and Wardle 2015, 89–104.

Kain, Donna, and Elizabeth Wardle. 2005. "Building Context: Using Activity Theory to Teach about Genre in Multi-Major Professional Communication Courses" *Technical Communication Quarterly* 14 (2): 113–39.

Land, Ray, Glynis Cousin, Jan H. F. Meyer, and Peter Davies. 2005. "Threshold Concepts and Troublesome Knowledge (3): Implications for Course Design and Evaluation." In *Improving Student Learning—Diversity and Inclusivity*, Proceedings of the 12th Improving Student Learning Conference, edited by C. Rust, 53–64. Oxford: Oxford Centre for Staff and Learning Development (OCSLD).

Lunsford, Andrea. 2015. "Writing Is Performative." In Adler-Kassner and Wardle 2015, 43–44.

McCarthy, Lucille. 2007. "A Stranger in Strange Lands." *Research in the Teaching of English* 21:233–65.

Meyer, Jan H. F., and Ray Land, eds. 2006a. *Overcoming Barriers to Student Learning*. New York: Routledge.

Meyer, Jan H. F., and Ray Land. 2006b. "Threshold Concepts and Troublesome Knowledge: An Introduction." In Meyer and Land 2006a, 3–18.

Meyer, Jan H. F., and Ray Land. 2006c. "Threshold Concepts and Troublesome Knowledge: Issues of Liminality." In Meyer and Land 2006a, 19–32.

Meyer, Jan H. F., Ray Land, and Caroline Baillie, eds. 2010. *Threshold Concepts and Transformational Learning*. Boston: Sense.

Peeples, Tim. 2002. *Professional Writing and Rhetoric: Readings from the Field*. New York: Longman.

Perkins, David. 2006. "Constructivism and Troublesome Knowledge." In Meyer and Land 2006a, 33–47.

Reiff, Mary Jo, and Anis Bawarshi. 2010. *Genre: An Introduction to History, Theory, Research, and Pedagogy*. West Lafayette, IN: Parlor /WAC Clearinghouse.

Roozen, Kevin. 2015. "Writing Is Linked to Identity." In Adler-Kassner and Wardle 2015, 50–52.

Sommers, Nancy, and Laura Saltz. 2004. "The Novice as Expert: Writing the Freshman Year." *College Composition and Communication* 56:124–49.

Sternglass, Marilyn. 1997. *Time to Know Them*. Mahwah, NJ: Lawrence Erlbaum.

Taczak, Kara. 2015. "Reflection Is Critical for Writers' Development." In Adler-Kassner and Wardle 2015, 78–79.

Timmermans, Julie. 2010. "Changing Our Minds: The Developmental Potential of Threshold Concepts." In *Threshold Concepts and Transformational Learning*, edited by Jan H. F. Meyer, Ray Land, and Caroline Baillie, 3–20. Boston: Sense, 2010.

Wardle, Elizabeth, and Doug Downs. 2013. "Reflecting Back and Looking Forward: Revisiting 'Teaching about Writing, Righting Misconceptions' Five Years On." *Composition Forum* 27. http://compositionforum.com/issue/27/reflecting-back.php.

Wardle, Elizabeth, and Doug Downs, eds. 2014. *Writing about Writing: A College Reader*. 2nd ed. Boston: Bedford/St. Martin's.

Wenger, Etienne. 1999. *Communities of Practice: Learning, Meaning, and Identity*. Cambridge: Cambridge University Press.
Wenger-Trayner, Etienne, and Beverly Wenger-Trayner. 2015. "Learning in a Landscape of Practice: A Framework." In *Learning in Landscapes of Practice: Boundaries, Identity, and Knowledgeability in Practice-Based Learning*, edited by Etienne Wenger-Trayner, Mark Fenton-O'Creevy, Steven Hutchinson, Chris Kubiak, and Beverly Wenger-Trayner, 13–30. London: Routledge.
Yancey, Kathleen Blake. 2015. "Writers' Histories, Processes, and Identities Vary." In Adler-Kassner and Wardle 2015, 52–53.
Yancey, Kathleen Blake, Tiane Robertson, and Kara Taczak. 2014. *Writing across Contexts: Transfer, Composition, and Sites of Writing*. Logan: Utah State University Press.

3
WRITING ABOUT WRITING IN THE DISCIPLINES IN FIRST-YEAR COMPOSITION

Rebecca Robinson

> INSTITUTION TYPE AND SIZE: Top-ranked public metropolitan research university; 50,000 students enrolled at main campus (Tempe)
> COURSE CONTEXT: Second course in ASU's first-year writing sequence
> STUDY DESIGN/METHODOLOGY: IRB-approved case study included audio-recorded course observations, collection of student process work, final writing projects, and reflective writing, as well as individual follow-up interviews with the instructor and students
> WAW PROGRAM OR NOT: WAW course in non-WAW program
> WAW COURSE OR SINGLE ASSIGNMENT/UNIT: Second-semester FYC course focused on argumentative writing about contemporary social issues; assignment described in this chapter was the third and final project in the writing sequence and the only one with a WAW focus
> INSTRUCTOR TYPE/POSITION: Course taught by tenure-track associate professor
> KEY TERMS: Disciplines; discourse analysis; threshold concepts; first-year writing

ABSTRACT

This chapter argues that a WAW assignment focused on disciplinary discourses helps students both to grasp key threshold concepts of writing studies and to begin engaging with the threshold concepts and rhetorical practices of their own disciplines. This argument is supported by data gathered from an FYC course in which students use discourse analysis tools and expert interviews to surface normally tacit discourse practices within their majors over the course of a single assignment.

INTRODUCTION

Some of the most crucial insights of writing studies are that genres of writing are embedded in communities of practice; that writing is a kind

DOI: 10.7330/9781607328421.c003

of doing, not just of saying; and that the "mutt genres" (Wardle 2009) traditionally taught in FYC bear little resemblance either in purpose or in form to the kinds of writing that students will be expected to produce in their future studies, let alone their careers. Yet writing scholars and teachers still operate within a system where many stakeholders, including our students, still believe it is the job of FYC teachers to help students "fix up" their writing skills in the service of other course work or future employers. Without conceding to the misconception that writing studies is merely a "service discipline" or that writing classes are merely "skills classes," writing about writing pedagogy presents teachers of writing not only with a way to maintain writing studies' disciplinary identity but with a means to address the need to prepare students to learn the kinds of discourse practices that will be expected of them in their future course work and careers. Preparing students to write in such a broad range of contexts does not require us to become experts in the discourses of other disciplines because we can draw on our own disciplinary expertise—the study of writing and its contexts—to help students retheorize writing by engaging with the threshold concepts of writing studies that will prepare them to analyze and adapt to the discourses of their future fields of study.

By using our disciplinary expertise as writing specialists, we can teach students writing studies' content, concepts, and ways of thinking to help them retheorize writing as an object of study, rather than just a skill or activity. We can accomplish this by introducing the concepts of communities of practice and discourse analysis, providing students with some basic discourse analytical tools, and asking them to analyze a community of practice through a selection of the community's written artifacts. In contrast to approaches that ask students to analyze communities they participate in or are familiar with, the assignment outlined in this chapter asks students to embrace an outsider or novice perspective as they analyze discourse practices of the academic communities they are encountering or seeking to major in. In keeping with WAW principles, the assignment's goal is not to teach the content or genres of other disciplines. Rather, it is to help students begin to explore how the academic genres and rhetorical practices they will encounter throughout their college course work are rooted in disciplinary epistemologies, identities, and practices that academic texts enact, facilitate, and represent. This exploration is at the heart of helping students retheorize writing. This chapter will present an overview of the assignment, describe its implementation, and discuss students' written work and detailed follow-up interviews with students about the project.

The assignment asks students to find out what kinds of evidence and arguments experts in their future field would bring to bear in composing knowledge or highly value in assessing it.[1] Students do this by interviewing two experts (typically faculty) in their prospective field of study and analyzing two articles in a peer-reviewed or trade journal to discover and explain key rhetorical features and disciplinary concepts that authorize composed knowledge within the field. In the spring 2015 semester I conducted an IRB-approved study of the assignment as it was taught by Elaine, another member of the ASU Writing Programs faculty. I had originally intended to study my own class, but when I became an assistant director of Writing Programs, the appointment's course release necessitated finding another class to observe. This turned out to be beneficial because it allowed me to see how the assignment worked in the hands of another teacher in the context of another course. I collaborated with Elaine to adapt the assignment to better fit her course, co-taught some class sessions, and observed and recorded each class session during the assignment's unit. My goal for the study was to get a better idea of whether and how students were achieving the assignment's goals.

The second-semester FYC class I observed for this research project did not fully employ a WAW curriculum; it focused on argumentative writing about contemporary social issues. Students were encouraged to select an issue from among the topics in the course textbook and to explore this theme, frame, or open question throughout the course. This necessitated tweaking the WAW assignment in the iteration of the assignment taught by Elaine: students were asked to find out what kinds of evidence and arguments experts in their field would bring to bear or highly value in the context of the student's semester-long open question. For example, Anna's subject was "how students can pick up healthy eating habits throughout their college career to carry on into adulthood" so, as an economics major, she investigated how economists would make predictions about the effects of campus food policies and advertisements.

Using this assignment in a non-WAW course focused on social issues proved to be both a benefit and a challenge. Focusing on a disciplinary approach to a specific social issue rather than disciplinary discourse practices more broadly was a benefit because the concept of disciplinarity itself is new and quite abstract for FYC students; a prior assignment in which students explored their social issue from the perspective of a variety of public stakeholders helped prepare them to grasp why and how scholars in particular fields would approach researching and writing about the issue differently. Focusing on a social issue also helped students narrow their searches for faculty to interview and articles to analyze. However, it also presented a challenge because that very focus tended to draw students' attention away from writing as an object of study and back toward writing as a repository of other content. Elaine often had to remind students to practice discourse analysis rather than merely gather more information about their social issue, but such oscillation should not be surprising since liminality is a key feature of threshold concepts. While I believe that this assignment would be even more successful in a fully WAW-focused curriculum, this study does demonstrate that a single WAW assignment such as this one can teach important writing concepts, adding significant value to non-WAW courses.

To aid students to retheorize writing, the assignment prompts them to engage with three threshold concepts that are key to learning academic writing: the concept of academic disciplines as communities of practice constructed and enacted through writing (Lerner 2015, 40; Estrem 2015, 55); the concept of writing as an object of study (Wardle and Adler-Kassner 2015, 15) as well as an activity and a type of artifact; and the concept of academic writing as an "evidence game," with variations among the kinds of evidence accepted within different disciplinary discourses. Similar goals are shared by many WAW approaches to FYC generally, but in cases where institutional constraints might make a full-scale WAW curriculum impractical, this assignment offers a smaller-scale approach to introducing FYC students to the concept of academic discourse communities.

In the next three sections, I will discuss the assignment's implementation: first, the rationale for and logistics of students' interview of experts in their fields; second, how reading about academic writing helped students prepare for their textual analyses; and third, how students brought their interviews and textual analyses together to draw conclusions about the epistemological values and rhetorical practices of those fields of study.

CONDUCTING EXPERT INTERVIEWS

The purpose of interviewing faculty in addition to analyzing texts is to allow students to engage in dialog with a field's experts about features of the writing they produce and value within their area of expertise. Students' status as novices allows them to identify and interrogate peculiar features of academic writing, but often they need experts to check their interpretations and provide further insight. In turn, the students prompt the experts to reflect on and articulate rhetorical and research practices that, precisely because of their expertise, have become more or less tacit for them.

Students were encouraged to begin requesting interviews with faculty or other experts in their field of study as soon as possible after the assignment was introduced, yet many encountered challenges and delays. Every student within this study who submitted a final reflection cited arranging and conducting these faculty interviews as the most difficult aspect of the class because of both logistical and affective challenges. Logistical issues include locating faculty candidates for interviews, making appropriate requests, negotiating schedules, and follow-up tasks like thank-you messages and transcription. The greater the number of students doing the assignment and the more years it's assigned, the more these problems are multiplied. If many classes are using the assignment, one way to avoid overloading faculty is to make the interview portion of the assignment (or the whole assignment) collaborative, organizing students into groups based on disciplinary similarities.[2] If the assignment is used over a number of years, writing teachers should take care to cultivate good relationships with faculty in other departments who may be asked to be interviewed again and again; this can be a great opportunity to expand the reach of writing programs. While senior graduate students are still somewhat novice themselves, in some ways they can be a good alternative to interviewing tenured faculty, since their disciplinary discourse practices have not yet become entirely tacit, and graduation turnover from one year to the next could mitigate the risk of interview fatigue. Other issues may be alleviated by careful planning of the course schedule and creative problem-solving and negotiation between the FYC teacher and students when problems arise, but some are unpredictable and unavoidable. However, only one of the twelve students in this study was unable to obtain permission to conduct any interviews.

As to the affective challenges of having students conduct faculty interviews, two factors contribute to students' unease at the prospect: social anxiety about meeting with professors and unfamiliarity with conducting interviews. As to the first concern, we have long known that students' interaction with faculty outside of classes is correlated with higher rates of retention, success, and satisfaction; that the assignment gives students a reason to have early contact with faculty within the areas they wish to study is a significant secondary benefit, and despite students' initial misgivings, once the interviews are completed, most cite the experience as enriching. As to the second concern, to prepare for their own interviews, during class time students viewed and discussed example interviews, and practiced interviewing one another about what evidence they would take into consideration before adopting or changing their opinion on an important issue. Students drafted, received feedback on, and refined their interview questions before they met with faculty interviewees.

Because of the logistics involved, some students conducted interviews earlier in the writing process, prior to or concurrent with analyzing their two scholarly texts, while others conducted their interviews near the end of the drafting process. Thus, some students used faculty interviews to shape their reading of the articles they selected, and others used the interviews to refine their initial analyses. Both processes helped students to perceive and inquire into field-specific rhetorical practices. Anna used a particularly noteworthy approach to finding both interviewees and sources. She searched the university website to identify courses relevant to the open question she had been focusing on all semester and requested interviews from faculty who had taught those courses. After Anna shared her strategy with the class, another student, Molly, further evolved it by using faculty CVs posted to their directory profiles to identify a relevant article she could analyze and discuss with one of its coauthors, an approach that proved particularly powerful for her.

READING ABOUT WRITING

To prepare students to analyze scholarly texts, the class read Michael Carter's (2007) "Ways of Knowing, Doing, and Writing in the Disciplines" and Theresa Thonney's (2011) "Teaching the Conventions of Academic Discourse." Carter's article introduces the concept of disciplinarity and provides a framework for thinking about how a particular field of study's ways of exploring phenomena or solving problems are intertwined with the ways that members of the field can acceptably communicate what they have come to know—in other words, by reading Carter students begin to see how *and why* the writing that is expected in some of their classes will be different from what is expected in other classes. Thonney, on the other hand, demonstrates that there are some broadly shared features of academic writing that novice students can take as a starting point. Studying these two articles as a class laid the groundwork for students to analyze discourse features of scholarly texts they identified within their own future disciplines.

Although Elaine was able to assign only these two WAW articles, they did ultimately help students focus on writing about *writing* and not on content. One student, Ralf, initially said in his follow-up interview that he didn't find these two articles useful because he couldn't figure out how to work them explicitly into his final paper; however, later in the interview he did note that they helped him understand important unfamiliar concepts of the assignment. Other students, such as Anna and Molly, explicitly and implicitly referenced key concepts from both Thonney and Carter that transformed their understanding of academic writing. That some students, like Ralf, did not initially recognize the value of this metacognitive work, even when they were able to perform it, points once again to the importance of our drawing students' attention explicitly to the work of reading and writing about writing. It also suggests something interesting about how students may define "usefulness" as it relates to the content of writing classes: for Ralf, anything that he couldn't make visible in his final writing project was initially deemed not valuable. Since we know much of the work of writing is ultimately invisible, this insight is worth attending to in the ways we teach writing.

The metacognitive and metatextual frameworks provided by Carter and Thonney are important because first-year writing students are accustomed to reading texts "for content" rather than focusing on the texts as a way of studying writing itself. Students need a lens, method, or tools to help direct their attention to specific textual features and to consider how those features work to create meaning in specific contexts.

SYNTHESIZING RESEARCH METHODS: USING INTERVIEWS AND GEE'S "TOOLS" TO SEE WHAT TEXTS DO

To further guide students' textual analysis, students were given a handout of seven tools pulled from James Paul Gee's (2011) *How to Do Discourse Analysis: A Toolkit.* Evidence from student essays suggests that three of the seven tools were particularly useful for this project: the "making strange tool," the "why this way and not that way tool," and the "activities building tool." I'll use each of these tools to discuss how they helped students to navigate and synthesize their textual analyses and interviews in their final projects, and to engage with the three threshold concepts at the core of this assignment.

Anna and the Making Strange Tool

Anna, an economics major, was intrigued by a statistical table in one of the articles she analyzed, and she was puzzled by the "z score" column specifically. Rather than perceiving this puzzlement as a deficiency, the making strange tool prompts the analyst to focus on what a text's writer appears to be taking for granted that readers will understand but that an outsider would find "unclear, confusing, worth questioning" (Gee 2011, 195)—thus, it offers a clue to students of something that is likely to be important to the disciplinary community they're studying. When Anna asked one of the experts she interviewed about the z score, she learned not only the purpose of the term in that particular graph but also its importance to the credibility of statistical measurement in economic texts. In other words, she argued that the "z score" is essential to the heavily statistics-based "evidence game" that is standard practice in economics scholarship.

Molly and the Making Strange Tool

As with Anna's experience, noticing something strange led Molly, a business management major, to a key insight about the relationship between one of her texts and the activity systems it participates in. Molly's interest was piqued by a graphic illustrating an evaluative process. At first she attempted to interpret the graphic using her prior knowledge by focusing "on finding synonyms for the words in the ovals and on explaining movement from one oval to the next," a strategy she came to see as being "like a student completing a homework assignment." Molly describes how her interview of one of the text's coauthors transformed not only her understanding of the graphic in question but also of the purpose of writing within her field: "Professor West's interpretation of the graphic shows her 'contribut[ing] to the conversation' in business management. [She] is not only interpreting the graphic through the use of scenarios . . . she is dramatizing the value of the model—and the piece of scholarship in which it appeared—to the field of business management."

Molly's experience illustrates the power of combining text analysis and expert interviews. The conversation Molly had with this professor deepened her understanding not only of the text and concept in question but also of the values and activities of the community of practice she was preparing to join. Additionally, the experience powerfully illustrated for her an essential concept of academic writing generally: successful academic writers "contribute to the conversation" (Thonney 2011, 349). While achieving such insights does not depend on students speaking to the authors of the texts they analyze, similar arrangements may render that outcome more likely.

Students' status as novices makes the making strange tool one of the easiest to grasp and apply to academic texts, but perceiving outsider status as a tool they can use, rather than merely a deficiency of understanding, also better enables them to approach unfamiliar and challenging texts with agency. Thus, the outsider status of FYC teachers and students relative to the broad range of majors our students pursue, rather than being a limitation, can actually position them to surface and scrutinize discourse practices often taken for granted by those who have already crossed disciplinary thresholds, *if* they are prompted to view their novice status as an asset rather than a liability.

Ralf and the Why This Way and Not That Way Tool
Ralf's exploration of how technical jargon is deployed and defined strategically in the articles he analyzed provides a good example of a student using the why this way and not that way tool, which prompts the analyst to consider other ways authors might have said what they wanted to say, and what reasons they had for making the specific rhetorical choices they made (Gee 2011, 197). Ralf, a business law student, began his analysis by creating a word cloud to identify "the most prevalent words" in each of his articles and then asking, "What's the difference between how I first thought to define and use the term . . . versus the particular ways these authors use these term in their own field-style?" In other words, Ralf was asking why these scholarly authors were using technical terms rather than more commonplace ones, or why they were using familiar words in specialized ways.

One such word was *intervention*, which he initially understood to mean "to step in and prevent," but his analysis revealed to him that the authors "connect the concept to other systems—whether marketing, law or business. . . . Intervention . . . went from meaning stepping in to meaning a policy." Ultimately, Ralf concluded that "rather than only seeing these specialized words (like 'mutagenicity' and 'intervention') as scary, I've learned I can use these differences to my advantage . . . Later in my career as a college student, I can continue to keep an eye and ear out for when specialists use language in their specialized form and I can look for patterns as to what make those forms valuable to other readers and the specialists themselves." Here we see that Ralf is learning to recognize technical language not as merely stylistic but as constructing particular relationships among people and activities. Like the making strange tool, the why this way and not that way tool focused Ralf's attention on specific textual features in order to explore how those rhetorical choices functioned within a larger system, and helped him to see how he could employ similar rhetorical moves in his own writing.

Anna and the Activities Building Tool

We've already seen how their textual analyses led both Ralf and Molly to engage with the threshold concept that academic writing is always also a kind of doing, that texts do things by existing as texts and by facilitating related activities, and that understanding a text requires understanding the activity systems of which it is a part. Gee's (2011) activities building tool renders this concept more explicit. For Anna, this tool came to the foreground through her interviews, in which she learned that "a core value within the field of economics is impact . . . the influence that an authority has on moving economic theory and practice forward" by writing successful grant proposals and publishing cutting-edge research. Her interviewees helped her to see how each of the texts she analyzed contributed to the authors' impact.

Although Anna is able to define "impact" in its scholarly context and repeat examples and illustrations provided by her interviewees and texts, it clearly remains a liminal concept for her. She uses the opportunity to interview experts as a way of testing the value of a research idea she's been developing through the first two writing assignments, and attempts to use her newfound understanding of "impact" as an important concept in economics research to explain the feedback she got: "Grebitus made a strong *impact* on how most students are not aware of what they are eating . . . When analyzing the material from these experts, I agree that consumer trends are absolutely *impacted* by students who may not be aware of how many calories they are consuming . . . With this information, I strongly believe that marketing healthier foods and making an effort to educate students on calorie intake would have a largely positive *impact* on consumer food choices on college campuses" (emphasis added). In these three passages, which occur within just one page of text, we can see Anna moving conceptually from a more commonplace definition of "impact" toward a definition specific to a scholarly community of practice; she's not quite there yet, but she's closer to seeing how research and writing together enact and construct disciplines and scholarly identities.

By encouraging students to focus on key rhetorical features and to inquire into their significance, each of these discourse analytical tools helped students to engage with the threshold concept that writing is an object of study as well as an activity and a means of conveying ideas. And while the students in my study remain novices, they are beginning to see that what counts as "evidence" and "good writing" differs across disciplines, and that those differences both represent and facilitate the activities of their communities of practice.

NEXT STEPS

The assignment was developed and implemented outside of a writing about writing course, yet clearly shares many of the same curricular content and pedagogy that underlie a threshold concepts–based WAW course. It is likely that a WAW curriculum that took threshold concepts as its starting point would significantly increase student success with this assignment.

The goal of this assignment is to help students retheorize writing through encountering and exploring the ways in which, and the reasons why, academic writing differs from one field to another, to see that writing both shapes and is shaped by the values and practices of various fields of study. Students' final projects vary in the ways they engaged with these concepts, and a longitudinal study would be required to investigate whether, and in what ways, they are able to transfer either these concepts of writing studies or the other discipline-specific concepts and rhetorical strategies they identified. This learning across time is to be expected; as Adler-Kassner and Wardle (2015a) explain, "Threshold concepts are liminal, and learning them happens over time at varied levels of understanding. They often cannot be taught directly by explication but must be experienced and enacted over time with others before they are fully understood" (8). Yet students' projects demonstrate that this assignment succeeds in its goal of prompting students to retheorize academic writing.

NOTES

1. My colleague Stephanie Schatz created the original version of this assignment in 2008, and she and I collaboratively developed and taught it for two years. I continued to teach a slightly modified version of this assignment for my own use at a different institution. Beginning in spring 2012, when I first taught the assignment at my current institution, Arizona State University, I added the text analysis component. Since then, I have further revised the assignment to more specifically focus on discourse communities and writing about writing. In spring 2015, in consultation with Elaine, I adapted the assignment to fit within her course design for the purposes of the study described in this chapter. Though this assignment differs from Ms. Schatz's earlier version and though she did not participate in the curriculum development or IRB study at ASU, I want to acknowledge her creation of an early version of this assignment.
2. Some groups will inevitably be semi-heterogeneous; Michael Carter's (2007) "Ways of Knowing, Doing, and Writing in the Disciplines" suggests ways of organizing majors into metadisciplinary categories, which I have found helpful in creating student teams in previous iterations of this project.

REFERENCES

Adler-Kassner, Linda, and Elizabeth Wardle. 2015a. "Naming What We Know: The Project of This Book." In Adler-Kassner and Wardle 2015b, 1–11.

Adler-Kassner, Linda, and Elizabeth Wardle, eds. 2015b. *Naming What We Know: Threshold Concepts of Writing Studies.* Logan: Utah State University Press.

Carter, Michael. 2007. "Ways of Knowing, Doing, and Writing in the Disciplines." *College Composition and Communication* 58:385–418.

Estrem, Heidi. 2015. "Disciplinarity and Professional Identities Are Constructed through Writing." In Adler-Kassner and Wardle 2015b, 55–56.

Gee, James Paul. 2011. *How to Do Discourse Analysis: A Toolkit.* New York: Routledge.

Lerner, Neal. 2015. "Writing Is a Way of Enacting Disciplinarity." In Adler-Kassner and Wardle 2015b, 40–41.

Thonney, Theresa. 2011. "Teaching the Conventions of Academic Discourse." *Teaching English in the Two-Year College* 38:347–62.

Wardle, Elizabeth. 2009. "'Mutt Genres' and the Goal of FYC: Can We Help Students Write the Genres of the University?" *College Composition and Communication* 60:765–89.

Wardle, Elizabeth, and Linda Adler-Kassner, eds. 2015. "Metaconcept: Writing Is an Activity and a Subject of Study." In Adler-Kassner and Wardle 2015b, 15–16.

4
Student Voice

REFLECTIONS ON OUR FRESHMAN WRITING COURSE

Emma Gaier and Megan Wallace

> INSTITUTION TYPE AND SIZE: 1,800 students; private liberal arts college
> COURSE CONTEXT: 100-level freshman writing course, required for students who do not pass the college's first-year writing requirement
> STUDY DESIGN/METHODOLOGY: Reflective narrative
> WAW PROGRAM OR NOT: No WAW program, stand-alone course as one section of the freshman writing course, Expository Writing
> WAW COURSE OR SINGLE ASSIGNMENT/UNIT: WAW Course
> INSTRUCTOR TYPE/POSITION: Students, now graduates
> KEY TERMS: Writing process; writing concepts; transfer; dual-enrollment

INTRODUCTION

In the fall of 2012, as high school seniors, we took a writing about writing course at Taylor University. The principles we learned, the discussions we had, the articles we read, and the responses we wrote influenced our understanding of writing and how to write. Our experiences in this class did not seem out of the ordinary, and we would have assumed this WAW course to be the typical freshman course for the college level; we did not realize until later on that this was a WAW course. Furthermore, we did not realize either the benefit or the implications of this course until asked to reflect on it for this chapter. In the meantime, we have taken this learning on to college—Megan to Taylor University and Emma to Purdue University—and have applied it in various fields of study as we continue to grow in our writing ability and application. This chapter outlines our reflections as we sift through and articulate the impact this WAW course had on our writing.

We enrolled in the class during our senior year of high school as a dual enrollment course, taking it with approximately twenty Taylor University first-years. As high school students, we benefited from this class in many ways. The profound skills we developed, not just in our writing but in our ability to think critically in peer discussions, encouraged us to own the skills and knowledge we gained despite our comparatively younger age. Taking this course as high school students opened up an opportunity for academic growth. It also fostered in us the confidence to better articulate our thoughts and communicate them through the written word. Most of our other senior friends were taking an advanced placement (AP) English course at the high school, which provided different assignments than we encountered in the WAW course. There, we were asked to discuss and write about writing, not the symbolism and themes in works of literature. We were asked to find the importance of writing heuristics and pedagogies and how they applied to becoming better communicators through both the spoken and written word. We found that these WAW assignments enabled us to more easily see the value of different written works because we were taught to appreciate not only imagery but also the style in which the imagery was expressed. Such lessons challenged us to engage in academic conversations with more eloquence and concise knowledge, and have since helped us in other classes during our experiences at Taylor and Purdue.

The principles learned in a WAW course are the necessary bones to form the skeleton for a writer—they help to guide his or her future writing in order to produce a more holistic work. As demonstrated by our individual experiences, these principles are not bound to one institution or even one discipline, but can and should be applied across a broad spectrum of paths. While Megan is engaged in a variety of communities at Taylor University, a small, rural, Christian liberal arts university, Emma is engaged in the history community, among others, at Purdue University—a large, secular school in a midsize town.

Emma's learning in the WAW course helped mentally prepare her for the kind of writing she would face in her higher-level history courses. The ability to see her history writing as a process in which she engages in the conversations of her field, the conversations to which her writing would be a response, allowed the typical activities of discussion, research, and peer evaluation to be natural, logical, and enjoyable steps in the writing process. The ability to view writing in this way can wholly transform a student's engagement with a writing assignment, providing the excitement of analysis through conversation and the treasure of research through inquiry and questioning.

Megan's experience differs from Emma's. Not only is the Taylor community smaller and classes of a more intimate size, but the mission statement of the university's academic curriculum is "the integration of faith and learning." As a small Christian university with its academic foundation in liberal arts, not only is Taylor's community different from Purdue's, so are the conversations within it.

In this chapter, we reflect on the varying impacts of our WAW course on our later college learning first by describing some aspects of the course itself. We use Megan's research project in the course as an example of how our work integrated writing concepts such as *exigence*, the principle Megan found most valuable and memorable. After some description of the course, our discussion divides. Megan offers her perspective on bridging from her learning about exigence into understanding her later work in psychology, political science, and public health as *joining conversations* in contrasting discourse communities. Emma writes about readings and concepts from the WAW course that she has identified as recurring in her studies at Purdue as a history major, such as James Reither's emphasis on writing process and written product, and Patricia Bizzell's ideas on academic discourse communities. Our voices rejoin in the conclusion to the chapter.

TAKING WAW AS DUAL-ENROLLMENT STUDENTS

In general expository writing classes, the topics studied can be anything the student wants to write or read about—a narrow approach confined to material interesting to the writer or reader, but not necessarily the best material for stretching students in their writing abilities. Our WAW expository writing class covered material about writing as a conversation, persuasion in writing, inquiry in writing, and affect in texts. The WAW approach enabled us to more effectively analyze readings and works assigned in other classes, and it allowed us to consider a greater range of perspectives when establishing an understanding of the topic at hand. For example, WAW enabled Megan to learn both how to become a better writer based on our professor's instruction and how to appreciate the power behind the art of writing and engage this appreciation through the way she interacts with other classes' reading and writing assignments at Taylor.

Midway through the semester in our WAW class, we were assigned a research paper in which we were to demonstrate the use of writing knowledge we had learned in the course. We had been given assignments throughout the semester that followed readings about writing pedagogy or about writing with certain techniques, such as the use of exigence—a gap in or an opening into a conversation where a person can share and incorporate creative thinking to input something new and original. We learned that to engage in our writing and reading assignments is to act as if joining into a larger conversation, not merely to read black print on white pieces of paper.

For example, Megan—whose paper "The Meteorologist in Us" was about the March 2011 tsunami in Japan—chose to apply concepts of audience, persuasion, creative thinking, and particularly exigence in her research process to produce a project reflective of her newly mastered WAW concepts. After submitting our research papers, we were required to write a reflection on them that reported to our professor how we were able to engage the lessons we learned from our WAW course in various kinds of subjects. Megan's employment of exigence enabled her not only to *talk* about what she had learned and its application in writing her paper, but to *use* it in a way that opened up the audience to the larger conversation about the Japanese tsunami. Her paper addressed meteorologists as the intended audience because of their crucial role in weather tracking and predicting. She explored how exigence, tracking conversation patterns, and knowing how and when to input knowledge each functioned in meteorologists' work.

She was thus able to apply this concept of exigence to a topic very dear to her heart—weather. Given her passion for watching swollen, churning storm clouds, observing the distant black skies roll in as the temperature suddenly drops in preparation for rain, and then enjoying the hard rain and rattling thunder, Megan wanted to use these WAW concepts to relate two seemingly separate subjects, writing and meteorology. She wanted to be passionate about what she was writing about so that writing about writing would become just as engaging as writing about the actual subject material.

Later in the class, we were encouraged to refer back to the long list of concepts developed throughout the semester, exigence being one, and reflect on how we were to incorporate them into our research papers, which did not specifically need to be about writing. We had learned how to discuss writing concepts and had portrayed such knowledge in the form of a written paper, but we had yet to master the use of these concepts within a genre outside of the classroom. This challenge encouraged our minds to stretch beyond the confines of our classroom studies and apply these concepts to other subjects as we sought to apply what we had learned in class. To reflect on how we've carried our learning into new, very different scenes of writing, we will now individually discuss what we have discovered since our shared WAW course.

MEGAN: ENTERING INTO CONVERSATION

My knowledge of exigence as an important WAW concept has since been applied to many different fields, challenging me to relate them. The fields of psychology (my major), political science, and public health (my concentration) have given me significantly different communities in which I've been able to enter into engaging conversations. Additionally, the liberal arts requirement for all students to take a wide range of classes has enabled me to find many similarities among a variety of topics and conversations. I've therefore learned how to engage in conversations of different kinds, many concerning topics in which I am not well experienced or educated. I've developed a greater passion for entering into subjects and topics not just as someone needing to write about the topic but as someone eagerly joining a larger conversation in which many different backgrounds, cultures, and beliefs around the world are engaged. What can I bring to the conversation that is insightful and original, making the conversation even richer and spurring on greater learning? These appreciations, concepts, and principles have some of their roots in our WAW course, especially in understanding conversations and writing.

I am challenged every semester with different genres of information and writing styles. On one hand, for example, I might be required to write about a psychological study in which I join a large, scientifically minded conversation, demonstrating awareness of exigence, while on the other hand, I might be required to write about my views of controversial topics such as abortion, same-sex marriage, or euthanasia, and what emotions arise from the topics and my stances on them. In my political science classes, I am asked to write papers about my views of capitalism and its relevance today, and some days my assignment is to write about justice and what stirs my heart.

When I have wondered why I had to take an art history class as a psychology major, or why I had to study chemical equations and formulas, I have realized the rich knowledge to be gained from variety. Would one rather be treated by a doctor with solely medical schooling and training, or by a doctor who is also educated in people skills, communication skills, and an appreciation for art and music? Variety in coursework has enabled me to practice the skills I learned from my WAW class in many different areas and forms—so I have grown a lot in my knowledge and experience of writing and reading.

One constant throughout my two years at Taylor, therefore, has been that what I learned in my WAW class about *joining conversations* has proven to be knowledge extremely valuable to my college experience.

When I apply myself in this way to any subject, I walk away with a greater understanding of what it means to be inspired for an academic work as well as a greater appreciation of the subject I am writing about.

EMMA: LEARNING AND APPLYING THE WRITING PROCESS

In my experience as a history major, I can see how knowledge introduced in our WAW course reappeared in my history courses. The WAW course has shown me how to approach writing and communicating well, preparing me for further work in college and beyond.

In the middle of my junior year at Purdue, I reread James A. Reither's (1985) article "Writing and Knowing: Toward Redefining the Writing Process" to prepare for this paper, evaluating how my experiences with different writing classes and teaching methods shaped my writing over the years, and how that teaching had progressed. Reither essentially advocates that students should be taught that a "process not product" is the end goal, emphasizing that the process by which writing works is more important, in some ways, than the paper itself (620).

In my junior year of high school, I took an AP United States history course in which the teacher taught us a method, or structure, for how to write our history papers. Explaining to us that writing for history was different than writing for English, she encouraged us to answer the questions posed to us by evaluating the historical evidence provided and then using it to defend our position through a thesis developed into three points. Although that is somewhat of a "product" way of teaching, she had begun to introduce us to parts of the process that Reither (1985) advocates—reading/inquiry and response (624–26). This continued in our WAW course at Taylor. Although I did not realize it at the time, the articles we read and the discussion we partook in pushed us to learn about writing and how it works, seeing the other pixels of the picture that surrounded the one pixel that had been our paper, or product, for so many years. In that freshman WAW class, I wrote in response to Reither's article: "I guess I never realized how much goes into and affects our writing, not only the quality but what we write about and how effective or relevant it is or is not to those around us." Though I did not fully understand what Reither was pushing for, I had begun to understand the importance and reality of writing within a community. I realized, as Reither advocates, that my writing was a voice in a community, and that I was responsible for adding to the conversation of that community.

What I had not yet come to understand was who and what that community consisted of and how I was supposed to interact with it in a meaningful way. Toward the end of his article, Reither encourages teachers to explain the importance of writing in a community to their students and to help them learn how to do so (1985, 623–26). As I look back on my two years of college experience, I can see how my professors were beginning to ease us into this type of writing and study. At first, my freshmen history courses operated much like my AP United States history course—I would listen to lectures, participate in discussion, and then respond to writing prompts, backing up my position with the primary source documents or monographs I had read as evidence. But in the years that followed, my higher-level courses involved much more reading and discussion with minimal composition work. In light of Reither's article, I have concluded that my professors have begun to introduce us to "real writing," the kind that Reither spoke of that demands interaction with a community and inquiry into questions that produce, through this process, a paper in response, not a paper as a product. Two courses in particular come to mind: one was a discussion-based course about how memory affects the telling and remembrance of historical events, and the other was my junior research seminar, which combined lecture and discussion with peer review and primary source research to help us, as history students, understand the process of historical writing.

The memory course allowed my classmates and me to read "the literature of [our] 'scholarly field'" (Reither 1985, 625), thus introducing us to that scholarly field, or community. Our professor acted as the leading voice in our discussions, and at first we tended to address her when we spoke, but soon we began to discuss the readings before class while our professor was absent—we had begun to develop our own version of what Patricia Bizzell calls "the academic discourse community" (1982, 81), an important part of the writing process, as Reither explains.

Bizzell's notion of an academic discourse community was also apparent in my junior research seminar as we answered and occasionally discussed the professor's questions. This professor pushed our understanding of the writing process further when she gave us parameters for our class papers and then told us to develop our own topic. For example, we would have to write a paper on race relations between the years 1600 and 1860, and we could research whatever race-related topic we wanted so long as it fell between those years. This allowed us to take the academic discourse community we had experienced in class and apply it to our inquiry in order to come up with a research question we would answer through writing, and then submit that writing to classmates for peer review. We had finally reached something similar to a process of writing that resembled what Reither (1985) had advocated, working itself out throughout the entire semester-long class, and *it made sense.*

The further I went in my college career, the more my understanding of writing deepened as I talked with my professors about what they were researching and planning to write about. As I helped one of my professors with research, I saw the long and sometimes tedious process of inquiry that comes before writing. Before I finished assisting her with research, we *talked* over and *discussed* the results I had found—I had engaged in an academic discourse community with her that continued to develop how I understand writing.

So, if I truly understood the significance of placing first-years in a WAW course, I should now ask myself what prompted me to write this piece, and has it added to the discussion of how to teach writing? Initially, I was encouraged to write this piece by a professor, but as I began inquiring, through reading, as to what I would write, I began to see that this essay was a response not simply to a professor's request, nor to James Reither's article, but to the past four to five years of my writing development—this is a summary of how my writing has developed and how I have come to learn about the writing process, part of which was influenced by the WAW course.

SUMMING IT UP (MEGAN AND EMMA)

So, has this piece of writing added to the conversation? That is partially for the reader to answer, but in our eyes, this essay, written in response to the context of the past two to three years, serves as confirmation of how a WAW course can teach a student the process of writing and the necessity of achieving that process, not just a paper. Although that realization may not come completely clear to a student during the WAW course, the implications of the teaching will eventually hit home in subtle ways in the student's future experiences.

Emma saw this very clearly over the last few months of her college career as she wrapped up and submitted an undergraduate honors thesis. Throughout the research and writing process for the thesis, she needed to sift through various materials and bring them together into a cohesive and conclusive whole. This could not have been accomplished without a process, without organization. Research and writing take time, and even though Emma had a glimpse of this in her WAW course, it really solidified with the thesis project. Both the WAW course and the AP United States history course had cultivated in her the need for analysis, understanding, and poignant thought in writing—skills and requirements that have carried on into the rest of college study and that were especially crucial over the last few months during the most important project of her academic career. For Emma, the most valuable result of her experience in a WAW course was the opportunity it afforded her to write analytically and discuss among peers the conclusions and opinions of other writers—which later on shaped her thinking and writing in vital ways. WAW was part of Emma's training ground for later writing, giving her an advantage in understanding and executing good writing.

Megan's experience in the WAW course equipped her to understand the process and importance of academic dialog, engaging in complex and complicated discussions on the pressing social issues around her and in the classroom. The background of peer discussion groups in the WAW course laid the groundwork for later conversations she will encounter within the scope of her plans for future work in disaster relief around the world. Without the background of the WAW course, Megan may not have fully understood the importance of these cross-culturally relevant discussions and how an academic should enter into and operate within them.

Examples like Emma's demonstrate how WAW was a part of our training ground for later writing, giving us a leg up in understanding and executing good writing, while experiences like Megan's exemplify how WAW was a starting point for a heightened appreciation for and understanding of peer discussion.

REFERENCES

Bizzell, Patricia. 1992. "Cognition, Convention, and Certainty: What We Need to Know about Writing." In *Academic Discourse and Critical Consciousness*, edited by Patricia Bizzell, 75–104. Pittsburgh: University of Pittsburgh Press.

Reither, James A. 1985. "Writing and Knowing: Toward Redefining the Writing Process." *College English* 47:620–28.

5
(DIS)POSITIONING WRITING CONFIDENCE, REFLECTING ON WRITER IDENTITY
A Writing about Writing Curriculum Aimed at Knowledge Transfer

Lisa Tremain

> INSTITUTION TYPE AND SIZE: 1,500 students; private liberal arts college
> COURSE CONTEXT: 200-level intermediate writing course, required for students who do not pass the college's first-year writing requirement
> STUDY DESIGN/METHODOLOGY: Curriculum design after IRB-approved ethnographic study (interview transcript analysis and case study methods; one-on-one interviews with participants across the secondary to postsecondary transition)
> WAW PROGRAM OR NOT: Stand-alone WAW course in writing and rhetoric department
> WAW COURSE OR SINGLE ASSIGNMENT/UNIT: Sequence of WAW assignments in a WAW course
> INSTRUCTOR TYPE/POSITION: Non-tenure track assistant professor
> KEY TERMS: Self-efficacy; confidence; writer identity; writing transfer; threshold concepts

ABSTRACT

This chapter argues that the thinking and practices involved in WAW should include explorations of self-efficacy and writer identity. The chapter briefly summarizes findings from an ethnographic study that investigated the relationship between self-efficacy and writing knowledge transfer for seven students as they navigated the high school to college transition. It then describes features of a WAW curriculum that responds to the study's findings and seeks to promote writing transfer across contexts. This curriculum enables students to examine and construct their writer identities by engaging with and understanding their self-efficacy as well as essential concepts of writing development in and

DOI: 10.7330/9781607328421.c005

across specific contexts for writing. It aims to serve as a framework for transfer, one through which students can recognize their evolving writing knowledge and writer identities.

INTRODUCTION

An understanding of how individuals conceptualize and transfer prior writing knowledge into new contexts has been an important data point in writing studies research. But prior knowledge—that is, the knowledge that is brought into new contexts for writing, for better or for worse—is made up of more than just cognitive information. Prior knowledge also includes our understandings of ourselves-as-writers, such as our degree of confidence in writing and in our capabilities to develop as writers when tackling new or challenging writing tasks. Confidence (or self-efficacy) in writing is a crucial disposition that impacts writing knowledge development, including the transfer of prior knowledge across contexts; it functions as a belief-construct about our personal competence in organizing and executing performances of learning (Pajares 1996). As writers, we use our self-efficacy to orient to new tasks and new knowledge, and we use it to access, evaluate, and apply our prior writing knowledge in new contexts. In essence, our writing development is informed by our degree of writing confidence.

This chapter discusses the connections between confidence and writing development—and how these are tied to our writer identities. First, I briefly describe a research study where I found that self-efficacy is inseparable from how individuals perceive their writing knowledge and writer identities. In responding to these findings, I designed—and share here—features of a WAW curriculum that support students' investigations into their writing knowledge and identities through the framework of threshold concepts. In the recent collection *Naming What We Know*, editors Linda Adler-Kassner and Elizabeth Wardle (2015) argue that there are threshold concepts of writing that are critical for epistemological participation in the discipline of writing studies. By connecting threshold concepts of writing to self-efficacy, I suggest that students' epistemological participation in their writing development is both more conscious and more robust. The curriculum described here includes assignments and activities through which students can better understand their developing writing knowledge, confidence, and selves-as-writers in academic settings—and beyond them.

Formative experiences with writing in part help to construct our initial writer identities. Andrea Lunsford's (2015) threshold concept "writing is informed by prior experience," for example, references a pattern noticed over years of research, where reported negative formative experiences with writing (such as left-handers being forced to write as right-handers, and children punished by having to write repeated sentences such as "I will not _____") constructed individuals' beliefs about writing (54). School-based writing practices create beliefs about writing, too, such as five-paragraph essay expectations or timed on-demand writing. Such literacy experiences are, as Lunsford argues, linked to "possibilities for selfhood" and can be formative in how we think about ourselves as writers (54). As Lunsford suggests, some of these experiences can damage our construct of writing as an enjoyable or even useful activity. However, "prior experiences [with writing] can be mitigated or changed, and that often happens as writers become more confident or encounter more positive experiences with writing" (54). It is this possibility of change that I seek to explore in my research and WAW curriculum.

THE STUDY

In a recent interview-based ethnographic study I followed seven student writers across the high school to college transition. The seven participants in the study went to the same urban public high school in twelfth grade, then went on to attend different postsecondary institutions. The study examined the prior writing knowledge that participants accessed and used when attempting to transfer knowledge from secondary to postsecondary contexts for writing, and found that self-efficacy was essential in how these learners engaged transfer opportunities. Their self-efficacy was also evident in how they perceived themselves as writers; in fact, findings revealed that they oriented to writing tasks and knowledge *through* their writing confidence and their beliefs about their capabilities as writers, for better or for worse.

I recorded and transcribed monthly interviews with individual participants during the spring of their twelfth-grade year and into March of their first year of college. Interviews focused on upcoming, ongoing, or completed writing assignments for school. I also repeated questions across interviews that explored participants' prior writing knowledge and affective orientations toward writing, including their sense of self-efficacy. Through transcript coding and analysis, I gained many insights about these learners' writing knowledge and their perceptions of writing and themselves as writers. When reporting self-efficacy, for example, participants regularly described their enjoyment of writing as an activity (e.g., "I like to write" or "I don't like my writing"). When I asked them to talk more specifically about *what* they liked—or didn't—about writing, trends of their writing knowledge emerged, such as "coming up with an argument," "writing an introduction," or "writing a draft." In order to code for, categorize, and understand their writing knowledge, I adopted Anne Beaufort's (2007) five domains of writing development: *discourse community knowledge, genre knowledge, rhetorical knowledge, writing process knowledge,* and *subject matter knowledge.* Through coding with these terms, findings revealed that while writing confidence varied across the participant group, as a whole, students' writing knowledge was limited as they entered college. That is, participants predominantly described using *writing process knowledge* and *genre knowledge* when transferring writing knowledge into postsecondary writing contexts, but *rhetorical, subject matter,* and *discourse community* types of knowledge were minimally reported or not reported at all.

As the study participants encountered the transition from high school to college writing, those who described writing confidence before college were more able to access and evaluate their prior writing knowledge, including how (or whether) to transfer it. Meanwhile, participants with low writing self-efficacy described a lack of confidence in their writing abilities and struggled to access and apply prior writing knowledge when writing college assignments. Such evidence illuminates the important connection between self-efficacy and writing transfer, but the lack of reporting across Beaufort's domains problematizes this connection. As they entered college, all seven participants had gaps in their writing knowledge. In thinking about these findings and my approaches to the teaching of writing, some questions emerged. Since comprehensive writing knowledge and high self-efficacy are both essential for writing development and transfer, how might a curriculum be designed to address limited writing knowledge *and* low self-efficacy? How might writing pedagogy tap into and sustain high self-efficacy *and* fill the gaps in students' writing knowledge? The second half of the chapter describes how my current writing about writing curriculum responds to these questions.

THE CURRICULAR MODEL

I use this writing about writing curriculum in a second-year writing course at the liberal arts college where I teach, but it could easily apply to first-year writing or any lower-division writing studies–oriented course. Because there is no entrance-level writing assessment at my institution and all students are required to take the same first-year writing sequence, this course is required for those who don't meet writing benchmarks in the first year. I tend to see many gloomy faces on the first day of class. Low writing self-efficacy and negative perspectives of themselves as writers are common for students in this class. In response to this teaching context—and to my research findings—this curriculum has three specific goals: (1) to facilitate students' meta-awareness of their degree of confidence in writing, (2) to explore writing through writing about writing activities that apply four specific threshold concepts of writing aimed at developing students' knowledge, and (3) to enable students to explore how writing knowledge and writing confidence inform writer identities, which develop over time. What is described in the remainder of the chapter is not representative of the entire curriculum for the course, but instead highlights activities and assignments around threshold concepts in the course related to these goals.

Threshold Concepts

On the first day of class, I present students with the course's threshold concepts (TCs):

> All writers have more to learn.
> Writing enacts and creates identities and ideologies.
> Writing speaks to situations through recognizable forms.
> Writing is a social and rhetorical activity.

The ordering of the course's TCs is purposeful; we study them separately but also recursively, beginning with a deep exploration into TCs 1 and 2. The language of these TCs comes from the recent publication *Naming What We Know* (Adler-Kassner and Wardle 2015). Over the past few years, while I have used the idea of "course concepts" to guide students through the curriculum, upon the publication of *Naming What We Know* (*NWWK*), I began to explicitly use the term "threshold concept" and specific phrasing from the book to articulate course concepts. Most of the assigned readings in the course come from the text *Writing about Writing* (Wardle and Downs 2014) and I share the authors' chart in appendix 11.A that describes all activities, assignments, and readings associated with each TC.

We begin with TC 1, "All writers have more to learn." In the first few class meetings we read from *NWWK* and I ask students to make personal connections to this concept. I assign works such as "The Composing Processes of Unskilled College Writers" (Perl 1979), "Shitty First Drafts" (Lamott 1994), "Hidden Intellectualism" (Graff 2001), and *This Is Water* (Wallace 2009). I ask them to explore questions such as "What does it mean to learn to write?" and "How does literacy learning take place?" These texts help to illuminate writing (and learning) as a developmental, messy, and imperfect process. As we transition to TC 2, "Writing enacts and creates identities and ideologies," students draw connections between TCs 1 and 2 and their personal experiences; they reflect on how they learned to read and write, their beliefs about writing, and their writing confidence. We ground these reflections in research and theories of literacy, such as "What No Bedtime Story Means: Narrative Skills at Home and at School" (Heath 1982), "How to Tame a Wild Tongue" (Anzaldúa 1990), "Keeping Close to Home: Class and Education" (hooks 1993), and "Sponsors of Literacy" (Brandt 1998). As we investigate TCs 1 and 2, discussions, class activities, and readings reveal how different literacy identities are constructed through experience.

One of the most valuable class activities is the short in-class "freewrite" response. Freewrites are an important tool in fostering students' investigation into and eventual embodiment of the TCs into their understandings of themselves as writers. In class, after students have read assigned texts for homework, we begin our meeting with individual freewrites where I ask them to draw connections between the text, their own experiences or knowledge, and the TC. I push them to write without stopping and without overthinking or pausing to edit. Students discuss their reactions and connections in pairs or small groups before I open the discussion up to the class. This scaffolded process gives them time to think and ask questions. The larger group discussions following freewrites reveal valuable insights about each threshold concept and serve as formative assessments of writing knowledge and confidence.

In a recent discussion, Andrew, for example, initially felt disappointed in himself for failing the first-year writing requirement and was convinced that he was a "bad" writer. During class activities that explored TC 1, however, he shared that he could learn from this failure and was pleased that he was getting a new opportunity to develop as a writer. This example notes the potential for a shift in Andrew's writing confidence. Using the freewrite as a framework for exploring each TC, students reflect on the ways that their own thinking about writing has inhibited their writing development; they describe experiences as second-language learners or first-generation college students that have affected their writing confidence. Through freewrites that explore the TCs, students begin to look "inward"—exploring who they are as writers and how they feel about writing in and for school—and "backward"—examining where their self-perceptions about writing and writing identity come from (Yancey, Roberston, and Taczak 2014).

Auto-ethnography of Literate Practices
Reading, freewriting about, and discussing TCs 1 and 2 lead to two formal assignments that more deeply explore writing development and writer identity: the auto-ethnography of literate practices and the literacy narrative. In investigating TCs 1 and 2, students become increasingly aware of their epistemological beliefs and literate practices, and how these are linked to their writing confidence and writer identities. This awareness becomes more explicit when I assign the auto-ethnography, where students simultaneously gather data on their *own* reading and writing practices as they complete course tasks.

The first step of this assignment is to understand auto-ethnography. To introduce the purposes and practices of such self-study, we review models of different methods for recording auto-ethnographic notes and I ask students to choose a method by which they will document what they do, as objectively as possible, while reading and then writing a response to an assigned text. First, I ask students to document what they do as readers: how do they attempt to understand the text? What are their processes for reading? What happens before, during, and immediately after reading? How long does it take?

In the next class meeting, we review their auto-ethnographic notes about reading practices and process, sharing and comparing methods and notes. I then ask them to write a summary of the text, which creates a bridge to TCs 3 and 4 and Beaufort's domains of *genre* and *rhetorical knowledge*. The purpose in assigning "summary" is for students to consider how genre constraints may impact thinking and writing processes. Before they write, we discuss the genre conventions of summary and its rhetorical purpose. We discuss the extent to which we think the writer's identity "shows up" in the genre of summary versus other genres. Students write their summaries as homework, and simultaneously record a second set of auto-ethnographic notes of their writing practices and processes.

Through this activity, students collect data on themselves during at least two sessions of literate practice. For some, this means using the clock, noting the time it takes to complete the tasks and distractions away from it. Others create long memos-to-self, where they reflect on what they thought about as they completed these tasks. Some students use audio or video recordings to collect data and then write transcripts. In class, we examine the data and notice patterns and/or rich points across their notes. I ask them to identify the types of practices that are "typical" of reading and writing, as well as what factors facilitate or inhibit these practices. Next, they formally react to and interpret their findings in a one-page reflection. Some questions they consider are: What surprised me in completing this self-study? When or where is it most difficult to read or write? What types of writing or reading processes do I use and/or avoid? What emotions come up for me during each of these practices and/or afterward? Through examining and writing about their data, students begin to see ways that they orient themselves toward particular tasks and witness their writing identities in action. The auto-ethnography deepens their understandings of how they read and write *and* how they feel while doing it. It shows them what they believe about writing and themselves as writers.

This inward-looking assignment contributes to students' deepening understandings of course TCs 1 ("All writers have more to learn") and 2 ("Writing enacts and creates identities and ideologies"). It is ultimately aimed at supporting writing transfer beyond the course. In completing the sequence of auto-ethnographic activities, students begin to understand that their literacy practices, writing knowledge, and writing confidence *can* and *do shift*. They begin to articulate their strengths and gaps in their reading and writing knowledge and develop goals to create change. This metaknowledge is often something they have never fully explored before—and it elicits an increased self-awareness that, once revealed, they take with them.

The Literacy Narrative: Examinations of Literate Identity

The auto-ethnography, then, is an important activity that leads up to the literacy narrative. This assignment asks students to write an account of their literacy experience(s), to explore their literacy histories, and to reflect on their writer confidence. Before assigning the literacy narrative, I introduce, through explicit teaching, Beaufort's (2007) five domains of writing development and we unpack TCs 3, "Writing speaks to situations through recognizable forms," and 4, "Writing is a social and rhetorical activity." Students read, freewrite about, and discuss theories of discourse, such as "Literacy, Discourse, and Linguistics: Introduction" (Gee 1989), "The Concept of a Discourse Community" (Swales 1990), and "Speech Acts, Genres, and Activity Systems: How Texts Organize Activity and People" (Bazerman 2004). Students begin to recognize the power of language by looking at how beliefs and ideologies of discourse are enacted through texts in terms of genre, lexicon, and rhetorical approach. They develop definitions for these terms and I ask them to use them as frames through which they might examine their literacy histories and writer identities in the literacy narrative.

Ultimately, the literacy narrative is a textual space for students to explore their writer (and reader) identities. In their narratives, students describe how their own experiences exemplify, extend, or even contradict the concepts or theories we've been studying in course readings, Beaufort's domains, and TCs. Students reflect on their self-efficacy, locating it in their educational (and other) experiences. Some write about feeling "disconnected" from writing; others explore their love of creative writing; some students consider institutional or school policies that have impacted their writing, such as No Child Left Behind. Ultimately, students write about the impact of their personal histories on their writing identity and begin to understand and investigate their particular subject positions in the postsecondary institution as writers. The literacy narrative, then, is a powerful tool for facilitating transfer and revealing an evolving writer identity; it illuminates constructions of self that, once understood, can be shifted, more deeply studied, compared, and capitalized on as they transfer their writing knowledge and continue to develop as writers in and beyond the academy.

Self-Assessment and Reflection

This metaknowledge of a literate self—students' ways of learning and knowing how to read and write—becomes a welcome outcome of this curriculum. It allows them to understand that this literate self has and will continue to move across contexts for writing. Having students consistently self-assess and reflect on their writing is another way to support the development of writer identity and transfer beyond the course. When we finish any major assignment, students complete short self-assessments and longer written reflections that make the development of their writing knowledge, writing confidence, and writer identities explicit to them during the course. We frame self-assessment through Beaufort's domains, and students evaluate their understandings of particular types of writing knowledge. I ask them to evaluate their response to the assignment, including how well they think that they met discourse, genre, and rhetorical constraints and their writing processes in completing it. I also ask them to self-assess their current understandings of the TCs, framing these questions through self-efficacy, asking, for example: "How confident are you in explaining the concept of discourse community to a colleague?" or "In which TC(s) do you feel most confident in your understanding?" I ask them to justify their self-evaluations and to identify one or two "next steps." In this way, students see themselves of agents of their writing development as they refine their writing goals and recognize their strengths and gaps.

I also ask them to write open-ended reflections, about two pages or so, where they can more freely explore their evolving writer identities. I ask them to consider questions such as "Who are you as a writer today?" "How are you changing as a writer?" and/or "What are the most useful things you've learned about writing and writing development?" Here, I employ a reiterative approach aimed at transfer, where constant "reflective practice provide[s] a unique set of resources for students to call upon when they encounter new writing tasks" (Yancey, Roberston, and Taczak 2014, 5). I tell them that their insights may change across reflections or that they might see patterns across them.

We close the course with a reflective essay, which serves as the introductory text to their final writing portfolio. In these reflections, students articulate their understandings of their current writing selves, including their personal theories of writing and literacy development, and their thoughts about course assignments and TCs. I also ask them predict how they might take their writing knowledge "forward" and "outward" (Yancey, Roberston, and Taczak 2014). Students often point to the literacy narrative as a moment where a spotlight illuminated an aspect of a writer-self they had never fully considered before; they report that this new knowledge helps them think differently about their attitudes toward writing and their writing development in college. They describe new ways that they view and understand texts that they read and write, particularly how they function in relationship to academic discourses. They articulate the extent to which their evolving writer identities fit into these discourses and how they feel empowered as agents of their writing development as they move forward in college. They report feeling more confident as writers.

IN CLOSING

This is a fairly new curriculum for me, and there are many kinks to work out in it. One of my more recent adjustments was to reduce the number of readings in the course, to choose a more limited number of distinctive and powerful texts that I hope clarify or extend students' understanding and engagement of course TCs. The texts cited here, then, are a list to choose from rather than required reading. Still, in purposefully designing a course aimed at illuminating connections between literate identity, self-efficacy, writing development, and transfer, I believe these activities and assignments have been largely successful, especially insofar as they have attempted to respond to my research findings.

The writing about writing activities I have described here are meant to create spaces where students can analyze and reflect on their writing practices in relationship to institutional and disciplinary expectations. In being offered room to explore, students are able to key into the ways that they affectively orient to important concepts of writing, such as genre awareness, rhetorical purpose, and the participatory nature of discourse. All of the activities described here are meant to underscore students' agency in facilitating their writing development, which includes its connections to self-efficacy. In reflecting on my research and this curriculum, I suggest that self-efficacy and writer identity are inextricable from how writing transfer is successfully enacted. When students have examined their own literacy development in terms similar to those shared here as TCs and Beaufort's domains, they have a more explicit understanding of how their writing knowledge has transferred (and can transfer) across contexts. In order to promote writing transfer, then, teachers of writing must conceptualize "writing" as more than a knowledge-based phenomenon. In fact, we must acknowledge that it includes students' belief constructs about writing and themselves as writers, including the self-efficacy that they use throughout any writing transfer opportunity in order to engage in it. In having a more explicit awareness of *how* writing knowledge develops, students can more confidently engage opportunities for writing in the future contexts they will encounter in the institution—and beyond it.

REFERENCES

Adler-Kassner, Linda, and Elizabeth Wardle, eds. 2015. *Naming What We Know: Threshold Concepts of Writing Studies.* Logan: Utah State University Press.

Anzaldúa, Gloria. 1987. "How to Tame a Wild Tongue." In *Borderlands: La Frondera: The New Mestiza*, 1st ed., 203–12. San Francisco: Spinsters/Aunt Lute.

Bazerman, Charles. 2004. "Speech Acts, Genres, and Activity Systems: How Texts Organize Activity and People." In *What Writing Does and How It Does It: An Introduction to Analyzing Texts and Textual Practices*, edited by Charles Bazerman and Paul Prior, 309–39. Mahwah, NJ: Lawrence Erlbaum Associates.

Beaufort, Anne. 2007. *College Writing and Beyond: A New Framework for University Writing Instruction.* Logan: Utah State University Press.

Brandt, Deborah. 1998. "Sponsors of Literacy." *College Composition and Communication* 49 (2):165–85.

Gee, James Paul. 1989. "Literacy, Discourse, and Linguistics: Introduction." *Journal of Education* 171:5–17.

Graff, Gerald. 2001. "Hidden Intellectualism." *Pedagogy* 1:21–36.

Heath, Shirley Brice. 1982. "What No Bedtime Story Means: Narrative Skills at Home and School." *Language in Society* 11:49–76.

hooks, bell. 1993. "Keeping Close to Home: Class and Education." In *Working-Class Women in the Academy*, edited by M. Tokarczyk and E. Fay, 99–111. Amherst: University of Massachusetts Press.

Lamott, Anne. 1994. "Shitty First Drafts." In *Bird by Bird: Some Instructions on Writing and Life*, 1st ed., 21–26. New York: Pantheon Books.

Lunsford, Andrea. 2015. "Writing Is Informed by Prior Experience." In Adler-Kassner and Wardle 2015, 54–55.
Pajares, Frank. 1996. "Self-Efficacy Beliefs in Academic Settings." *Review of Educational Research* 66:543–78.
Perl, Sondra. 1979. "The Composing Processes of Unskilled College Writers." *Research in the Teaching of English* 13:317–36.
Swales, John. 1990. *Genre Analysis: English in Academic and Research Settings*. Boston: Cambridge University Press.
Wallace, David Foster. 2009. *This Is Water: Some Thoughts, Delivered on a Significant Occasion, about Living a Compassionate Life*. New York: Little, Brown.
Wardle, Elizabeth, and Doug Downs. 2014. *Writing about Writing: A College Reader*. 2nd ed. Boston: Bedford/St. Martin's.
Yancey, Kathleen Blake, Liane Robertson, and Kara Taczak. 2014. *Writing across Contexts: Transfer, Composition, and Sites of Writing*. Boulder: University Press of Colorado.

6
Student Voice

WRITING ABOUT WRITING
Leading to New Perspectives

Hiroki Sugimoto

> INSTITUTION TYPE AND SIZE: Private university best known for its degrees in aviation, with campuses in Daytona Beach, Florida, and Prescott, Arizona
>
> COURSE CONTEXT: ESL-designated sections of the only required 100-level FYC course, which focuses on secondary research-based academic argument
>
> STUDY DESIGN/METHODOLOGY: Reflective narrative
>
> WAW PROGRAM OR NOT: Stand-alone WAW course in first-year writing program
>
> WAW COURSE OR SINGLE ASSIGNMENT/UNIT: Sequence of WAW assignments in a WAW course
>
> WRITER: Undergraduate student
>
> KEY TERMS: International; cultural; rhetorical; discourse community

In this essay, I am going to explore some learning outcomes of COM 122 NNS: Composition for Non-Native Speakers of English, focusing on writing about writing (WAW). This was the second writing class in college for me, following a more basic communication class. At the beginning of COM 122 NNS, Dr. Ives introduced thinking about writing as a way to communicate in a discourse community by having the students read an Ann M. Johns (1997) work about it. Following that, we read, discussed, and wrote about writing in different cultures, the process of learning a new language, and how people communicate through writing. For me, an international student in an English learning process, the class turned out to be quite inspirational and educational because it was not just about the language itself but the discourse communities within which different communication styles take place.

DOI: 10.7330/9781607328421.c006

We read several articles and wrote an analytical essay for each. I was especially impressed by Carolyn Boiarsky's (1995) work on cultural and rhetorical conventions. Through her analysis of different writing styles, formats, and tones, I learned that people, not knowing the cultural conventions, will sometimes fail to convey or interpret the right ideas even though their language skill is sufficient to communicate the information. This was exemplified in my school life with people from different backgrounds. One day my friend's family offered me a fruit cup. I turned down the offer despite my true feeling: I craved the multicolored, fresh fruit cup on a hot day in Florida. My refusal was a polite fiction meant to spare my hosts bother. Similarly, I refused a Christmas gift from them, but this time, they explained to me that to them my refusals meant that I was not being sincere. Rather, they found it more pleasing if I accepted such gifts because their offers were expressions of caring about me. My saying no, which I intended to be nice to them, was actually distressing to them. My recognition of such small frictions in daily communication, combined with the WAW approach to learning English in an academic context, helped me to adjust my writing to American academic writing styles, since I saw similar frictions when writing papers in English. Reading an article by Lucille P. McCarthy (1987) about a student learning to write in different communities helped me to connect the class to my real-life experiences.

I learned by reading the Boiarsky article that direct, clear expressions, for instance, are preferred in the American writing community, while in Japanese culture more complicated, poetic expressions are usually used in such contexts. By thinking about those differences in written communication styles from culture to culture, I slowly shaped my understanding of my own culture, which I had not considered before.

This awareness brought me to the realization that if different cultures have formed different rhetorical conventions, why not different discourse communities within one culture, such as the medical field or engineers? There is a preferred style of communication in every discourse community.

This thought process led me to the subject of my final essay assignment: the cultural impact of communication among pilots. In the aviation world, English is the lingua franca, but the pilots' communication styles vary from person to person depending upon their backgrounds, even though they are all speaking English, and that can lead to plane crashes. Depending on their cultural conventions, some first officers may attempt to mitigate rather than speak up about possible risks, or some captains may be too bossy rather than cooperative (Gladwell

2008). What I learned in this analytical essay can be applied to my future job. When I join a certain discourse community and start working as a member of the group, I will communicate with other members through multiple genres, and there will likely be some unfamiliar cultural and rhetorical conventions that I have to consider in order to communicate effectively.

COM 122 NNS was a valuable class as it gave me insight into cultural influence on rhetorical convention and communication. What I learned in the class and what I thought throughout the semester have formed my base for successful writing in college and communication in my future workplace. As it was for me, the WAW method will be quite helpful to international students who are learning new communication styles or to domestic students who are eager to join a new community in the future.

REFERENCES

Boiarsky, Carolyn. 1995. "The Relationship between Cultural and Rhetorical Conventions: Engaging in International Communication." *Technical Communication Quarterly* 4 (3): 245–59.

Gladwell, Malcolm. 2008. *Outliers: The Story of Success.* New York: Hachette Book Group.

Johns, Ann M. 1997. *Text, Role and Context: Developing Academic Literacies.* Cambridge Applied Linguistics. Cambridge: Cambridge University Press.

McCarthy, Lucille Parkinson. 1987. "A Stranger in Strange Lands: A College Student Writing across the Curriculum." *Research in the Teaching of English* 21:233–65.

7
Vignette

WAW-PROFESSIONAL WRITING FOR STEM CO-OP STUDENTS

Joy Arbor

> INSTITUTION TYPE AND SIZE: 2,000-student predominantly engineering STEM university
> COURSE CONTEXT: First course in a required general education sequence
> STUDY DESIGN/METHODOLOGY: Reflection
> WAW PROGRAM OR NOT: Stand-alone WAW course
> WAW COURSE OR SINGLE ASSIGNMENT/UNIT: WAW approach
> INSTRUCTOR TYPE/POSITION: Tenured assistant professor
> KEY TERMS: Professional writing; WAW; WAW-PW; co-op; STEM

From the first day of COMM 101, a first-year professional writing and speaking course at my co-op–intensive STEM institution, my work-focused engineering and applied science students and I discuss transfer. Transferring rhetorical knowledge is crucial because students alternate three-month academic and co-op/work terms, a schedule that in theory allows students to integrate academic and work-related learning. In practice, however, many co-op placements are paid work assignments not structured as learning experiences, so when co-op employers complain that students "can't write professionally," both co-op employers and the university see it as communication instructors' responsibility to teach students immediately transferable professional writing skills. Because students encounter diverse writing assignments at their different workplaces, I find, as Scott Warnock does, that it's necessary to teach "transferable writing knowledge that they can take with them to help work through any writing/communication assignment" (quoted in Downs and Wardle 2012, 15). I am not alone in finding writing about writing pedagogy, with its focus on transferable writing/rhetorical knowledge, useful for teaching professional writing; Sarah Read and Michael

J. Michaud recently argued in *College Composition and Communication* that "WAW-PW is a coherent and viable approach to teaching generalizable rhetorical knowledge that can be transformed across contexts, and workplace contexts, in particular" (2015, 429). In order to help students develop generalizable rhetorical knowledge that can help them teach themselves to write in new situations at their co-op placements, I have structured my professional writing course so that each project requires reflection on developing transferable principles in writer's memos that are then collected and deepened in final portfolios. I also include a specific WAW-PW–inspired assignment investigating professional communication in a particular field in a short report.

DEVELOPING TRANSFERABLE PRINCIPLES IN WRITER'S MEMOS AND THE FINAL PORTFOLIO

Because the course goal is to develop knowledge to apply to new situations, I explain to students, we need to reflect on and develop principles and knowledge that can be transferred. On the syllabus I include that research has found that in order for transfer to occur, "students need to explicitly *create general principles* based on their own experience and learning; *be self-reflective*, so that they keep track of what they are thinking and learning as they do it; and *be mindful*, that is, alert to their surroundings and what they are doing rather than just doing things automatically and unconsciously" (Wardle and Downs 2011, vi). The research-based emphasis on creating general principles as well as being mindful and self-reflective helps my mostly resistant and science-focused students understand and buy into an approach that demands reflection on each project in writer's memos. These memos, a variation of the more familiar author's notes, must discuss process; rhetorical crafting for purpose, audience, and genre; any specific project goals; and their learning. Writing about process and rhetorical crafting encourages students to become mindful and reflective about these activities, inquiring into their practices' efficacy and applicability to future writing situations. Articulating their learning helps students to develop principles that they can transfer to future writing situations; these principles may be general rhetorical knowledge about professional writing, such as that purpose statements inform busy readers about a document's scope, or more focused on strategies, such as that peer response can be very helpful for feedback about audience. Students write writer's memos for all projects, whether technical descriptions, short reports, proposals, or presentations (when we call them rhetor's memos). These memos help me to understand the process and rhetorical challenges my students have faced in a particular project so that I can address their strategies as well as the product; more important, the memos give students a way to record and inquire into patterns and challenges in their process, rhetorical crafting, and learning. My feedback on their projects includes specific prompting to transform project-specific learning into transferable principles for future use.

At the end of the term, students construct a traditional learning final portfolio with a reflective introduction that collects their principles and learning from the class. Students include the learning, principles, and generalizable knowledge they've articulated in their writer's memos as well as the patterns they've identified from examining their various projects and memos next to one another. While I've experimented with a number of end-of-term projects, I've found a traditional learning portfolio that reflects and articulates what they've learned and principles they can use in the future (for example, professional writing values succinctness, so concise writing is worth revising for) the most beneficial because it highlights the transferable principles students are likely to use at their co-op placement, to which they'll return at that point in the term in a few weeks. Students often note in their final portfolios their surprise that reflecting consciously on their writing helps them pay attention to what to improve and how, a process they can apply to teach themselves how to write in new writing situations at their co-op.

INVESTIGATING AND REPORTING ON PROFESSIONAL COMMUNICATION IN A SHORT REPORT

A particular WAW-PW assignment I've found useful is a professional short report on communication within a specific profession, inspired by Michaud's project (Read and Michaud 2015, 449). In my course, students must find a professional to interview, develop questions that address rhetorical concepts without using specialized vocabulary, set up and execute an informational interview, and write up their results in a professional short report. While the usefulness and level of detail of the communication information gathered from the interviewee often depends on the vocabulary that professional has for writing and communicating (a good lesson in itself for students who must learn to communicate with others who do not share their technical expertise), students learn not only how to report information clearly and concisely in a flexible professional genre, but how important communication is for their future professions. Students often return from these interviews with material asserting the vital importance of writing and communication skills, along with more detailed information about specific genres to learn and skills to develop. These experiences help students to understand not only that writing and communication are important to their lives as professional engineers and scientists, but that being mindful and reflective about their communication leads directly to success in their professional goals.

While my institution is unique, it's my hope that these reflections on my use of WAW argue implicitly for the expanded range and flexibility of WAW and WAW-PW pedagogy, especially in co-op–intensive environments, and illuminate how WAW-PW might prove useful to others teaching professional and technical writing.

REFERENCES

Downs, Doug, and Elizabeth Wardle. 2012. "Re-imagining the Nature of FYC: Trends in Writing about-Writing Pedagogies." In *Exploring Composition Studies: Sites, Issues, and Perspectives*, edited by Kelly Ritter and Paul Kei Matsuda, 123–44. Logan: Utah State University Press.

Read, Sarah, and Michael J. Michaud. 2015. "Writing about Writing and the Multimajor Professional Writing Course." *College Composition and Communication* 66:427–57.

Wardle, Elizabeth, and Doug Downs, eds. 2011. *Writing about Writing: A College Reader*. Boston: Bedford/St Martin's.

8
"I AM SEEN; I AM MY CULTURE; AND I CAN WRITE"
How WAW Returns Multilingual Learners to Voice, Building Self-Efficacy and Rhetorical Flexibility

Christina Grant

> INSTITUTION TYPE AND SIZE: 40,000-student research university (one of top 5, Canada)
> COURSE CONTEXT: 3-credit first-year college composition course
> STUDY DESIGN/METHODOLOGY: Case-based reflection
> WAW PROGRAM OR NOT: Stand-alone course
> WAW COURSE OR SINGLE ASSIGNMENT/UNIT: Whole-course WAW
> INSTRUCTOR TYPE/POSITION: Contract instructor
> KEY TERMS: Multilingual, second-language acquisition, voice, self-efficacy

ABSTRACT

Compared to native English speakers, multilingual writing students need more support to survive the often painful sociocultural role transitions and rhetorical adaptations necessary for thriving in their university life in English. It is every writing teacher's responsibility to draw on research from the fields of second language acquisition (SLA) and second language (L2) writing to assist students in forging new writerly identities. I cite researchers from both fields as well as students of Writing Studies 101: Exploring Writing to show how a WAW design helps multilingual students reestablish their voices and roles, integrate their mother tongue rhetorical traditions, and start on the road to becoming confident, multidimensional, linguistically hybrid thinkers and writers.

INTRODUCTION

> *I feel writing is near to me now. I think I am a writer now.*
> —Huarui Ji

Most first-year university students undergo crises of identity as they adapt to the realities of more personal responsibility and higher intellectual expectations within a new and often intimidating discourse community. The stakes also rise dramatically; how a student "does" in the first year or two of postsecondary education can affect the trajectory of his or her life. For multilingual students, achieving a balanced and healthy sense of self—which is always "multiple, conflictual, negotiated, and evolving" (Canagarahah 2004, 267)—in an English-speaking university environment is especially challenging. Often they are far from home, bewildered by a new culture, and unable to easily talk with classmates and teachers. Ure Bronfenbrenner (1979) calls this an "ecological transition" (6): different climates, different foods, different people, different lifestyles, different rules, and—perhaps most significant—different worldviews.

In our increasingly global world, more English-language learners enter our writing classrooms each year, and many undergo life-altering "transitions in identity" fraught with "considerable agony" (Hirvela and Belcher 2001, 88).[1] In these classrooms, every writing instructor is both a language teacher *and* a role-transitioning guide, helping his or her students struggle to be seen and heard in their new ecological environment.[2] A carefully structured WAW course is one way we can help multilingual students find—or perhaps more accurately, reposition—themselves in their new contexts and develop the multiple, confident discursive voices they will need to succeed.

In teaching Writing Studies 101: Exploring Writing, a first-year, contract- and portfolio-graded workshop course at the University of Alberta, I have witnessed striking changes in English-language learners, both in sections restricted to Bridging Program (BP) students and in sections open to the wider university community.[3] Importantly, BP students can choose which section to take, but most opt for BP WRS 101 due to its smaller class size (sixteen instead of twenty-five) and dedicated in- and out-of-class tutor trained by the university's Centre for Writers. I will focus on the BP sections since that is where I have seen the biggest evolutions.

The deep WAW roots and design of WRS 101, I believe, account for its extraordinary impact. The course was created in 2007 out of the pioneering "subject is writing" approaches of Bishop and Strickland (1993) and Elbow and Belanoff (1999).[4] It emphasizes both declarative and procedural writing knowledge; students not only read and write about what makes writing work, but they also try out multiple generative, composing, feedback, and revision strategies across a range of genres. In WAW tradition, the course offers students ideas and methods they can use to continue to teach themselves to write well in any rhetorical situation throughout the university and beyond. Over the course of the term, students complete two major writing assignments: an interview paper in which they investigate someone else's writing processes, and a multiple-source research paper on some aspect of writing.

I use the WAW textbook *Conversations about Writing: Eavesdropping, Inkshedding, and Joining In* by M. Elizabeth Sargent and Cornelia Pareskevas (2005) for its accessibility to multilingual learners and its range of strategies and genres. Students read and inkshed about "Revision Strategies of Student Writers and Experienced Adult Writers" by Nancy Sommers, "Internal Revision: A Process of Discovery" by Donald Murray, "The Study of Error" by David Bartholomae, and "Ranking, Evaluating and Liking: Sorting out Three Forms of Judgment" by Peter Elbow, gaining declarative writing knowledge and discovering a field of study most have never heard about.[5] In encountering the process writing of published writers such as Gail Godwin ("Watcher at the Gates") and Natalie Goldberg ("Writing Down the Bones"), students realize that experts also grapple with how to write and deem it worthy of reflection. And by engaging with literacy narratives such as "Saved" by Malcolm X and "Lost in Translation: A Life in a New Language" by English learner Eva Hoffman as well as supplemental English learner–oriented texts such as Shanti Bruce's (2009) "Listening to and Learning from ESL Writers," students legitimize and work through, at least to some degree, their personal trials and gain insights into the power of oral and written language to shape lives—including their own. Also, students study Anne Beaufort's (2007) five knowledge domains that expert writers draw on: discourse community knowledge, subject matter knowledge, rhetorical knowledge, genre knowledge, and writing process knowledge (19). This helps them grasp how complex, messy, and recursive writing is and why it takes most people a lifetime to gain any degree of mastery. As students compare and contrast what *they* do with what *expert* writers do, they gain valuable personal insights and see how they can strengthen their writing processes—and ultimately their writing.

In the rest of this chapter, I will show how specific elements of BP WRS 101 help multilingual students reclaim their voices and build new roles in a foreign context. Further, I will suggest that in doing so they learn to appreciate and even integrate their mother tongue rhetorical traditions and begin to believe that they will—over time—become strong, multidimensional, linguistically hybrid thinkers and writers.

"I AM SEEN": HOW WAW RETURNS MULTILINGUAL STUDENTS TO VOICE

> *Before, I never found my voice. I just wrote an essay, agreed or disagree with this or that. WRS 101 teaches me how to express my own voice. I found my voice.*
>
> —Le Pu

Writerly voice can be conceived in myriad ways, but when a writer somehow disappears behind his or her words, most of us find those words less informative, engaging, and persuasive. Writing needs voice—along with a relevant message—to have power in the world and thus to empower its writer. If students cannot "do voice" in the "right" ways—that is, reflecting Western values of "*clear, overt, expressive,* and even *assertive* and *demonstrative*" prose (Ramanathan and Kaplan 1996, 48)—instructors often declare their papers inferior, weak, or just plain wrong.[6] The issue of voice in the sense of being fully heard and valued, then, is urgent for multilingual students. As they work on their syntax, grammar, and spelling, they also badly need to hang onto "the person behind the written words" (Hirvela and Belcher 2001, 85) to maintain their senses of identity and feel like they belong in their new place. In **WRS 101**, I work to help them reestablish whatever oral and written voices they've lost in their transition; to see voice as multiple, not singular; to acknowledge that they already have a voice in their first language; and to believe that they can learn new discoursal voices appropriate for Western contexts. Before arriving in my class, You Li had failed a pre-university English course twice. In an inkshed—a form of public freewriting—he confided: "I always wrote something made others confused. So I did not like to write and share it to others, let alone read it aloud for others. Also, the weakness of writing make me lack of confidence. As a result, I even felt fear to talk to others and tried to avoid the eye contact of others."[7] Underseen and underheard, You Li stopped wanting to communicate. He had begun pressing himself into the background; in class, he gazed at the floor, swallowed his words, and wrote as little as possible.

For homework after the first day, You Li, his classmates, the class tutor, and I wrote informal introductory letters to each other about our cultural and linguistic backgrounds and why writing well matters to us. And—reflecting the WAW tenet of writing as dialog—everyone read and commented on (not corrected) everyone else's letter. Marginalia such as "Tell me more!" and "Yes—lots of writing in Business," welcomed students' current voices and encouraged more. For You Li and his classmates, this activity was radically unfamiliar. It gave them their first taste of "writing as communication and connecting rather than performing for a judgment" (Elbow and Belanoff 2000, 521). The experience presaged a sea change in You Li's conceptions of writing.

I have discovered that if students free their physical voices, their writing voices follow, gaining in both volume and substance. Therefore, in my classes, students share their ideas by talking as well as writing. Like the others, You Li spoke quietly at first—and only because he had to. Then, as he learned to trust in my positive reactions, he gradually spoke more often and with more authority, a trajectory I saw paralleled in his writing. By the time he joined me and another student for an hour-long conference on his final paper (a letter urging a friend to embrace writing as a tool for thinking and communicating), You Li was meeting my gaze and speaking with breath and vigor. Though his paper still needed work, his warm, inquisitive, and gently persuasive voice bubbled clearly and pleasingly beneath his words. Recalling this evolution in an inkshed, You Li wrote: "To be honest, the WRS 101 course not only help me to improve my writing strategies, but also help me to be more confident and allow me to stand front others to express my feeling and thinking. In the paper conference, we are required to read our paper out loud. I was really enjoy it, and I could not image it before."

Besides reclaiming their physical voices, WRS 101 students encounter declarative knowledge on voice, identity, and language through carefully selected and scaffolded readings. Diverse authors model a range of voices that students can examine and mimic—trying them on for size in their own writings. Students encounter such ideas as all writers "have *more* than one" authentic voice, "a sense of voice in writing is crucial," and "something important is lost . . . when the sound of a human voice is absent or ignored in a piece of writing" (Sargent and Pareskevas 2005, 14). They measure these claims against how they respond to and learn from—among others—the authoritative and logical voice of David Bartholomae ("Writing with Teachers: A Conversation with Peter Elbow"), the effusive and persuasive voice of Natalie Goldberg ("Be an Animal"), and the poignant and poetic voice of Kim Stafford ("My Father's Place").

Through such engagement, students begin to view their own writing in new ways. You Li's classmate Yutong Chen admitted that before WRS 101 he dismissed writing as a "dull" time-wasting enterprise with little relevance to his future job as an economist. If he had to write, he said, he left it to the last minute and wrote "like a robot, without any emotions" according to the strict, five-paragraph scheme he understood as good academic writing. Through listening in and joining multiple conversations about writing, Yutong Chen slowly shed his mechanical writing voice and began injecting himself into his work, concluding that "writing is a human's root," fundamental to how we are seen and understood in the world.

Another way WRS 101 students rediscover their preexisting voices and create alternative ones is through low-stakes generative writing strategies. While many writing courses include freewriting, WRS 101 makes especially purposeful use of multiple forms, including inkshedding, Perl Guidelines writing, and loop writing.[8] Copious writing without worrying about correct form builds students' procedural writing process knowledge (discovering writing-to-learn), increases their fluency, helps them engage with and understand challenging texts (experiencing writing as cognition), and enables their rediscovery of old or discovery of new discursive voices (writers and readers construct meaning together).

Besides its essential role in the course in integrating declarative and procedural writing knowledge, inkshedding has almost magical abilities to reconstitute and invigorate the voices of English-language learners. Writing twenty or more of these ungraded responses in a summarize-respond-reflect (SRR) format on shared readings shows students that they *do* have ideas and that they *can* write a lot on any topic—even under time pressure.[9] By commenting on the content of each other's inksheds (never correcting spelling, grammar, or punctuation), students start to think more critically and realize that others *value* their ideas. Frequent inkshedding and giving and getting feedback to and from authentic readers—their classmates and instructor—helps students tap their voices and make them flow. Reflecting on inkshedding in an inkshed, Xinmiao Fu wrote: "Before I really afraid to write, because I think I do not have enough information to write. Inkshedding is one strategy help us to come up new ideas. When we get a topic, I can write down everything that connect with this topic, nothing is wrong from my writing. I can write more than 500 words in 20 mins. I never need worried about I do not have enough thing to write, and worried about the grammar mistakes and spelling things. I also start write diary, before I never write that. They make me like to write." You Li, too, found that inkshedding broke his unproductive habit of endlessly stopping to think: "Inkshedding made me relax and feel free to writing something." He knew that after spilling his words onto the page, he could later return to pick out the best ones to develop into a finished piece.

Such low-stakes WAW WRS 101 strategies helped convince You Li and his classmates that as young adults fully literate in speaking and writing in their native languages they were "not voiceless or devoid of a writerly identity" on arrival but had "already learned how to establish relationships with the texts they create and the readers they address" (Hirvela and Belcher 2001, 84, 83). Their struggles in revoicing themselves were not signs of deficiency but a natural stage as they transitioned from one set of writing identities to another. You Li commented on his progress: "This course taught me that writing is not just used for assignments, but can help me open my mind to express my ideas and thoughts. I used to think writers had to be experienced, highly educated and published a lot of books. Now, my critical thinking always pushes me to think more deeply. Somehow, I found that everyone can be a writer as long as he or she considers writing as a way to thinking." WRS 101's WAW design helped You Li and his classmates acknowledge, build on, and more fully tap their pool of voices to emerge from the background and join their new discursive and social communities.

"I AM MY CULTURE": HOW RECLAIMED VOICE LEADS TO RHETORICAL FLEXIBILITY

> *If I was in normal English course I feel I need to get rid of all my culture, all my own voice, all my Chinese ways to write. I need to get rid of all of that. But in WRS 101 I feel I can connect both of them.*
>
> —Le Pu

Revoiced by WRS 101's WAW generative writing and feedback immersion strategies, multilingual students learn about and practice ways to enact their newly emerging selves that do not deny their pre-English-university identities. Swearingen and Mao (2009) argue that "for too long" North American instructors have "looked at Chinese and other non-Western rhetorical traditions 'Under Western Eyes'" (831); they urge us to avoid comparing and contrasting and instead celebrate and harness the differences.[10] From WRS 101 students' initial shared letter assignment, they begin to wrestle with the important concept of the rhetorical situation. They gradually learn to shape their words at the point of utterance for specific audiences. Textbook readings exhort students to ask of each writing task: "What is the context? Who or what is making me do this writing . . . Who will decide if it 'works' or not?" (Sargent and Pareskevas 2005, 13). Engaging with "Entering the Conversation: The Rhetorical Situation" (Glenn 2004) convinces them that such situations "are everywhere—as pervasive as the air we breathe"(2)—and that it is their job to effectively (and ethically) respond to them using whatever rhetorical resources they have.

WRS 101's WAW design helps students negotiate this challenge by facilitating transparent conversations about power relations in language (who gets to speak and why) and about how diverse peoples discuss, persuade, and argue. Students find themselves surprised and intensely engaged by discussions about Elbow's (2012) claim that a person's natural-born language strongly contributes to his or her thinking and writing in subsequent languages. They write passionate, thoughtful, and lengthy inksheds about his call for writing teachers to make room for students' native tongues in the spirit of democracy, and in BP WRS 101 they experience that room (and that linguistic respect). I encourage them to "harness for writing"—that is to think and to inkshed in— "whatever language comes quickest and easiest to mind and mouth" and to view their original languages as "storehouse[s] of linguistic and cognitive riches" (Elbow 2012, 6). Through these measures, students come to believe that their native rhetorical traditions are equal, not inferior, to Western ones, and that "good" writing means different things in different places. Most important, they discover that their voices can remain vibrant and strong in any language. The sense of control they gain over their writing is transformative.

In a conversation, former BP WRS 101 student Le Pu—now a third-year psychology major—recalled chafing at the restrictions imposed on her writing by her first-year university English instructors. She had been considered a strong writer in China, but here she was labeled weak. In writing her first papers, she attempted to use some Chinese metaphorical and figurative rhetorical devices. "In China," she explained, "you don't need to write something directly; you let people fill it in." In her mind, such rhetorical moves were natural, artful, and respectful of the reader's readiness to actively co-create meaning. However, her teachers' negative responses ("it's not clear, it's not direct, it's off topic") and low grades convinced her that "there was only one way to write . . . only their way, the five paragraphs way." Thereafter, she toed the Western rhetorical line. She got through her English courses, but because she was unable to put any of her (former) writing voice into *any* of her writing in English, and because nobody helped her to understand that she can and should examine the needs of each audience and choose which rhetorical moves to make, she rapidly lost interest and confidence. She reasoned, "My voice developed under my culture . . . and in order to express my voice, my culture must be involved in my writing."

To Le Pu's relief, she discovered rhetorical breathing space in BP WRS 101. She and her classmates read about, discussed, and practiced diverse rhetorical styles, and I encouraged her to interanimate her texts—to find ways to blend traditions that called on *all* her rhetorical resources. Le Pu's final paper, "The Importance of Voice in Writing," blended personal anecdotes, expert sources, and Confucius philosophy in a circuitous yet cohesive letter advising multilingual students to quash their fears and take risks in their writing: "If we are taking a risk," she declared, "we have a chance to do something new. Maybe we can even write in our unique voice."

"I CAN WRITE": HOW RECLAIMED VOICE BUILDS SELF-EFFICACY

> *Through this course I understand now that writers might don't know what they are going to write and they don't come up with a perfect first draft . . . I think I am a writer and myself is the biggest fan!*
>
> —Ge Li

Few multilingual students arrive in my classes feeling that they know how to master writing in English; they've already had too much evidence against it and the learning curves seem impossibly steep. By reestablishing and empowering multilingual students' voices, BP WRS 101 bolsters their "perceived self-efficacy" (Bandura 1982, 122), giving them the sense that they *can* succeed. While it may seem minor, strong perceived self-efficacy has been unequivocally linked to better writing (McCarthy, Meier, and Rinderer 1985, 465; Kormos 2012, 399). For ecologically transitioning English-language learners who feel unsure about almost everything, a sense of "I can" about their writing is especially important; without it, they will lose heart and stamina for the long and difficult task ahead. Recalling the course as a whole but especially inkshedding, Le Pu said, "It guided me to think more, to think fast, to think bravely. Having more words in my mind gives me confidence."

As Wardle and Downs (2013) observe, "Teaching our field's research-based conceptions of writing can radically change what people do and think about as writers." Le Pu added:

> I think this course changed my view of writing. It made me become a real thinker and writer. Before, the only thing I cared about in writing in English was grammar grammar and grammar (although this concern never helped me out). Maybe because I had never found a right way to learn English, or because I lacked a guide. WRS 101 was my guide . . . The course changed my understanding about writing in English. It made me know that as a learner, my critical thinking, my understanding towards the current topic, and my useful ideas are far more important than just focusing on the grammar.

Le Pu now speaks with authority about seeing herself as "a real thinker and writer" rather than as a learner dabbling on the surfaces of things. In making these metacognitive claims she reveals her metamorphosis from a timid victim of English to an emerging master of her own thinking and writing capacities. Because I have repeatedly witnessed, to greater or lesser degrees, this end-of-course student takeaway with hundreds of multilingual students, I continue to use and promote the writing about writing approach for this unique population.

FINAL THOUGHTS

While second language writing (SLW) and second language acquisition (SLA) experts continue to debate about how to best teach writing to multilingual learners, most agree, as Raimes (1985) says, that compared to native English-speaking students "they need more of everything" (670) to adapt to an English university environment.[11] Plunged by their educational life choices into a complex and often traumatic ecological transition, they deserve empathetic and purposeful guidance and support to recognize, reflect upon, and ultimately change their attitudes and behaviors to ones that will help them succeed.[12]

BP WRS 101 helps lift students out of their linguistic dispossession. Through its WAW design they become active, participatory learners and experts on their own writing processes who feel they have important contributions to make to ongoing conversations about writing and much else. Clearly seen and heard—often for the first time as English-language writers—students reconstitute and reshape their discoursal voices for new contexts while appreciating and occasionally finding ways to integrate their enculturated rhetorical traditions. Fueled by increasing levels of perceived self-efficacy, they practice and retain tangible writing acumen—attack strategies—that they can and do transfer to the rest of their lives. BP WRS 101 works because it embodies the understanding that writing is "part of a much larger and more basic activity: the development and negotiation of individual identity in a complex social environment" (Brooke 1991, 5). As You Li admits with happy surprise, "Not only has my writing competence increased significantly through WRS 101, but also it has changed me into a more sunny and confident person." While the course never helps all of the students all of the time, overwhelmingly it converts fearful, timid students who "hate . . . really hate" (Doan Trung Duong) writing to those who believe they can do it and even come to "love" it (Yu Li, Hanqi Zhang, Yutong Chen, Yiqin Li, Le Pu).

NOTES

1. For an important discussion about the new global writing classroom, see Matsuda 2006, "The Myth of Linguistic Homogeneity in U.S. College Composition."
2. For a salient discussion about the effects of students' self-perceptions, see Carroll 2002, *Rehearsing New Roles: How College Students Develop as Writers*.
3. The Bridging Program is a language-learning program that helps students increase their English-language skills while taking some courses for credit before they enter full-time programs of study.
4. A twenty-member university-wide Writing Task Force designed WRS 101 based on its research into high- and low-road knowledge transfer; members were convinced that a writing course focused on writing as content would better support high-road transfer—would better help students transfer what they had learned to subsequent courses and rhetorical situations. For details on the WRS 101 original design, see "Exploring Writing (EW) Courses" on the University of Alberta website.
5. Inkshedding is a focused, shared form of freewriting designed to generate ideas, develop critical thinking, foster communities of writers, and position writing as a dialogic activity. See Hunt 2005, "What Is Inkshedding?"
6. For a helpful discussion on how multilingual writing differs from that of native English speakers and how to respond to those differences, see Matsuda and Cox 2004.
7. In WRS 101, students learn to separate generative writing (aimed at creating and developing ideas) from editing (aimed at correcting errors in grammar, punctuation, spelling, etc.). Most quotations in this chapter are from students' original, unedited inksheds; therefore, language inconsistencies are evident. Students are taught that in high-stakes formal writing such as final essays, good ideas must be supported by correct language, and they learn to achieve it by mini-lessons in grammar based on their actual errors as well as by such means as getting feedback from native English speakers and using *SpellCheckPlus* (an online software program particularly useful in helping English-language learners edit their writing) on their close-to-final drafts.
8. Perl Guidelines writing is a private, generative writing exercise drawing on Gendlin's "felt sense" that leads the writer, through a series of prompts, successively deeper into a topic. See Elbow and Belanoff (2000). Loop writing is an exploratory writing exercise that prompts students to consider their topic from diverse perspectives, helping them get to what they want to say while spurring original thinking and creativity.
9. SRR was inspired by writing scholar Kathleen Blake Yancey (1998).
10. On this point, also see Mao 2013.
11. For a cogent argument about how and why writing instructors should keep up on developments in both second language writing and SLA/TESL to provide the best possible supports *before* multilingual students start struggling, see Moussu 2013. Also see the Conference on College Composition and Communication 2009.
12. For a seminal discussion on how we must treat multilingual writers differently in order to be fair, see Silva 1997.

REFERENCES

Bandura, Albert. 1982. "Self-Efficacy Mechanism in Human Agency." *American Psychologist* 37:122–47.

Bartholomae, David. 1980."From 'The Study of Error.'" In Sargent and Pareskevas 2005, 419–29.

Bartholomae, David. 1995. "Writing with Teachers: A Conversation with Peter Elbow." In Sargent and Pareskevas 2005, 186–94.

Beaufort, Anne. 2007. *College Writing and Beyond: A New Framework for University Writing Instruction*. Logan: Utah State University Press.

Bishop, Wendy, and James Strickland, eds. 1993. *The Subject Is Writing: Essays by Teachers and Students*. Portsmouth, NH: Boynton/Cook.

Bronfenbrenner, Ure. 1979. *The Ecology of Human Development: Experiments by Nature and Design*. Cambridge, MA: Harvard University Press.

Brooke, Robert E. 1991. *Writing and Sense of Self: Identity Negotiation in Writing Workshops*. Urbana, IL: National Council of Teachers of English.

Bruce, Shanti. 2009. "Listening to and Learning from ESL Writers." In *ESL Writers: A Guide for Writing Centre Tutors*, 2nd ed., edited by Shanti Bruce and Ben Rafoth, 217–29. Portsmouth, NH: Boynton/Cook.

Canagarahah, Suresh A. 2004. "Multilingual Writers and the Struggle for Voice in Academic Discourse." In *Negotiation of Identities in Multilingual Contexts*, edited by Aneta Pavlenko and Adrian Blackledge, 266–89. Clevedon, UK: Multilingual Matters.

Carroll, Lee Ann. 2002. *Rehearsing New Roles: How College Students Develop as Writers*. Carbondale: Southern Illinois University Press.

Conference on College Composition and Communication. 2009. "Statement on Second Language Writing and Writers." CCCC. http://www.ncte.org/cccc/resources/positions/secondlangwriting.

Elbow, Peter. 1993. "From 'Ranking, Evaluating and Liking: Sorting out Three Forms of Judgment.'" In Sargent and Pareskevas 2005, 351–61.

Elbow, Peter. 2012. *Vernacular Eloquence: What Speech Can Bring to Writing*. New York: Oxford University Press.

Elbow, Peter, and Pat Belanoff. 1999. *A Community of Writers: A Workshop Course in Writing*. 3rd ed. Boston: McGraw Hill.

Glenn, Cheryl. 2004. *The Harbrace Guide to Writing*, 2nd ed. New York: Cengage Learning.

Godwin, Gail. 1997. "Watcher at the Gates." In Sargent and Pareskevas 2005, 88–90.

Goldberg, Natalie. 1986a. "Be an Animal." In Sargent and Pareskevas 2005, 576–77.

Goldberg, Natalie. 1986b. "Writing Down the Bones." In Sargent and Pareskevas 2005, 88–90.

Hirvela, Alan, and Diane Belcher. 2001. "Coming Back to Voice; The Multiple Voices and Identities of Mature Multilingual Writers." *Journal of Second Language Writing* 10:83–106.

Hoffman, Eva. 1989. "Lost in Translation: A Life in a New Language." In Sargent and Pareskevas 2005, 39–46.

Hunt, Russell. 2005. "What Is Inkshedding?" In Sargent and Pareskevas 2005, 134–41.

Kormos, Judit. 2012. "The Role of Individual Differences in L2 Writing." *Journal of Second Language Writing* 21:390–403.

Malcolm X. 1964. "From 'Saved.'" In Sargent and Pareskevas 2005, 31–34.

Mao, LuMing. 2013. "Beyond Bias, Binary, and Border: Mapping out the Future of Comparative Rhetorics." *Rhetoric Society Quarterly* 43:209–25.

Matsuda, Paul Kei. 2006. "The Myth of Linguistic Homogeneity in U.S. College Composition." *College English* 68:637–51.

Matsuda, Paul Kei, and Michelle Cox, M. 2004. "Reading an ESL Writer's Text." In *ESL Writers: A Guide for Writing Center Tutors*, edited by Shanti Bruce and Bruce Rafoth, 39–47. Portsmouth, NH: Boynton/Cook.

McCarthy, Patricia, Scott Meier, and Regina Rinderer. 1985. "Self-Efficacy and Writing: A Different View of Self-Evaluation." *College Composition and Communication* 36:465–71.

Moussu, Lucie. 2013. "Let's Talk! ESL Students' Needs and Writing Centre Philosophy." *TESL Canada* 30:55–68.

Murray, Donald. 2005. "Internal Revision: A Process of Discovery." In Sargent and Pareskevas 2005, 394–409.

Raimes, Ann. 1985. "What Unskilled Writers Do as They Write: A Classroom Study of Composing." *TESOL Quarterly* 19:229–58.

Ramanathan, V., and Dwight Atkinson. 1999. "Individualism, Academic Writing, and ESL Writers." *Journal of Second Language Writing* 8:45–75.

Sargent, M. Elizabeth, and Cornelia C. Pareskevas, eds. 2005. *Conversations about Writing: Eavesdropping, Inkshedding, and Joining In.* Toronto: Nelson.

Silva, Tony. 1997. "On the Ethical Treatment of ESL Writers." *TESOL Quarterly* 31:359–63.

Sommers, Nancy. 2005. "Revision Strategies of Student Writers and Experienced Adult Writers." In Sargent and Pareskevas 2005, 414–18.

Stafford, Kim. 2002. "My Father's Place." In Sargent and Pareskevas 2005, 99–101.

Swearingen, C. Jan, and LuMing Mao. 2009. "Introduction: Double Trouble: Seeing Chinese Rhetoric through Its Own Lens; Comparative Rhetorical Studies in the New Contact Zone: Chinese Rhetoric Reimagined." *CCC Symposium* 60 (June): W32–121.

Wardle, Elizabeth, and Doug Downs. 2013. "Reflecting Back and Looking Forward: Revisiting Teaching about Writing, Righting Misconceptions' Five Years On." *Composition Forum* 27. http://compositionforum.com/issue/27/reflecting-back.php.

Yancey, Kathleen Blake,. 1998. *Reflection in the Writing Classroom.* Logan: Utah State University Press.

9
Vignette

EL ENSAYO
Latinxs Writing about Writing

Nancy Wilson, Rebecca Jackson, and Valerie Vera

> INSTITUTION TYPE AND SIZE: Public Hispanic-serving institution (at least 25 percent of the total enrollment is Hispanic); 38,000 students
>
> COURSE CONTEXT: Basic writing course required of students who score below 363/4 on the Texas Success Initiative (TSI)
>
> STUDY DESIGN/METHODOLOGY: IRB-exempt; focus groups
>
> WAW PROGRAM OR NOT: Non-WAW program
>
> WAW COURSE OR SINGLE ASSIGNMENT/UNIT: A sequence of WAW assignments in a non-WAW course
>
> INSTRUCTOR TYPE/POSITION: Tenure-track assistant professor, now associate; tenured professor; undergraduate student, now graduated
>
> KEY TERMS: Latinx; basic writing; Hispanic-serving institution; identity; liminality

It's late afternoon, and five Latinx writing center clients are participating in a focus group study about how Texas State University–San Marcos, a Central Texas "Hispanic-serving university" (HSI), might help Latinx students build upon the writing proficiencies they already possess.[1] In listening to our Latinx students, we were hoping to develop changes in the writing center space itself, its programming, and its tutor training.

Initially, the five emphasize that their needs are no different from any other students' and that the university is doing a good job of supporting them. Indeed, when asked if they might find it helpful to have access to tutors fluent in Spanish, they not only see no point, they argue that being able to use Spanish during the writing process would weaken their English.

In response to what she perceives as the students' deficit thinking about their bilingualism, Valerie, our focus group facilitator, shares how

Gloria Anzaldúa code-switches throughout *Borderlands/La Frontera* and feels unabashed pride in the fact that she is fluent in eight language varieties, including Standard English as well as Chicano Spanish and Pachuco. "You know, sometimes it's great to throw your Spanish in there," Valerie tells them, "even in your academic essays. Just saying."

In essence, Valerie launched a WAW lesson, asking these students to reconsider negative attitudes about bilingualism by sharing *scholarship* about why these negative attitudes exist (e.g., such attitudes reflect linguistic imperialism and linguistic racism). Valerie's extemporaneous lesson seems to have had an impact. Admittedly, our participants never acknowledged the viability of code-switching in academic work and in this we are reminded of Kells's (2004) observation that using Tex Mex requires trust, but they do code-switch with one another, almost joyously, concerning academic issues (see their discussion of *ganas* below), as though not only their two languages but also their two identities have finally been given permission to merge. Anna even notes that "maybe the writing center could serve hot chocolate, like my *abuela* always had for us when we visited her in Mexico," revealing a burgeoning awareness of how the Latinx culture and language are marginalized by the academy. Certainly, by the end of the session, no one is claiming that her cultural and linguistic identity does not matter.

Buoyed by this focus group's responses to WAW and mindful of recent calls for reform of basic writing pedagogy, we decided to integrate WAW assignments into coauthor Nancy Wilson's upcoming developmental writing class taught at Texas State. The result?—a basic writing course titled *Escribir Sobre la Escritura*. Importantly, we also decided that the course would not be founded on the "assimilationist set of assumptions" that Kells, Balester, and Villanueva (2004) warn against. Instead, our WAW reading and writing assignments would encourage students to become aware of the "interconnections between their academic identity and language experiences" and to use such interconnections as "resilient strategies to negotiate language difference in the academy." In terms that speak directly to our context, we would focus on the *value* of linguistic diversity, of *la familia*, and of liminality (aka *Nepantla*) and thereby answer Jaime Mejía's call to develop rhetoric and composition pedagogies that "incorporate our students' ethnic identities and cultures" and "advance the critical literacy skills of Mexican-American students" (2004, 51).

This WAW with a Latin twist approach is not entirely new. In "Discovering a 'Proper Pedagogy,'" Dora Ramírez-Dhoore and Rebecca Jones (2007) employ a similar pedagogy: in a composition pedagogy class, Jones assigns readings from Kells, Balester, and Villanueva's *Latina/o Discourses: On Language, Identity, and Literacy Education* (2004), and in a 4000-level course Ramírez-Dhoore assigns Kells's and Balester's *Attending to the Margins*, as well as Anzaldúa's *Borderlands* (2012) and Américo Paredes's *George Washington Gómez*. Speaking to the benefit of this approach, Ramírez-Dhoore comments that "for the first time, some students find their voices (or sense that they are part of the linguistic terrorism for others and for themselves) amidst the dominant language of the area—whether it is English or Spanish" (Ramírez-Dhoore and Jones 2007, 69). But these were not basic writing courses. Conversely, although McCracken and Ortiz (2013) do discuss teaching WAW in basic writing classes at an HSI, they do not explicitly comment on including specific texts designed to address Latinx-specific writing issues, and while Colin Charlton (2009/2010) assigns Deborah Brandt's "Remembering Reading, Remembering Writing," he does so in a developmental reading course.

On the first day of her developmental writing class, Nancy prepared the foundation for ongoing conversations on language, power, and cultural identity by asking students to share their thoughts about being placed in a non-credit-bearing course. Because the course was small (twelve students) and because it had a varied ethnic makeup (eight Latinx students, three African American students, and one white student), we knew this opening conversation would be essential in helping students understand that the critical literacy of the course would unite them, even if the title of the course was *Escribir Sobre la Escritura*. All eight Latinx students wrote that they were excited to learn to write better (e.g., "write less simple," "get ready for English 1310"), thus corroborating Ramírez-Dhoore and Jones's (2007) finding that their Spanish-speaking students often "understood 'success' as being tied to their language skills" and a belief that "speaking English well would lead to 'better things'" (70). Responding to her students' goals, Nancy emphasized that having only twelve students in the class would allow for intensive and individualized writing instruction that would no doubt help them improve their writing skills. However, she also emphasized the importance of interrogating the monolithic notion of writing as "skill," and substituting in its place culturally specific "ways with words" that might encourage linguistic pluralism.

For the first class activity, the students took turns reading aloud excerpts from Gloria Anzaldúa's (2012) "How to Tame a Wild Tongue" in which she recalls "being caught speaking Spanish at recess" and receiving "three licks on the knuckles with a sharp ruler" as punishment

(75). Students then read aloud an interview with Geneva Smitherman (Sellers 2014), who discusses how language researchers had to counter the labeling of black speech as "baby-talk," "lazy lips," and "jungle tongues." Despite these personal struggles, both authors tout the rhetorical and psychological value of code-switching, a perspective Nancy hoped would resonate with her own students.

For homework, in keeping with the WAW premise that we should ask our students to read, discuss, and write about issues with which students have firsthand experience, Nancy assigned a short essay in which the students were to discuss how their home languages have affected them, positively and/or negatively. By way of example, Nancy shared that she grew up speaking so-called white trash English, saying, for instance, "ain't got no" and "tumped," so that when she went to college, she struggled to learn academic writing. She felt that to be successful, she had to distance herself from her home language, to shed an important aspect of her identity. Several students responded with similar stories. For example, Gabriela Soto-Lopéz said, "Learning English actually brought a lot of problems into my life since according to my family I'm trying to lose the part that made me unique, which was being Latina."

For the second class, Nancy asked students to draft a thesis statement about language and/or writing and to support their statements with personal experiences. She selected two of these thesis statements to model an effective approach to academic writing tasks: "Everybody is evaluated based on the way they sound. People who only use slang are worth less than people who know how to code-switch and talk depending on their location and audience" and "Having many dialects and languages isn't something to be ashamed about. It's actually an asset." Working collaboratively, students combed through the excerpts of their classmates' work to select those experiences that best supported one of the two theses. One group chose the following comment to support thesis 1: "Growing up on the east side of Austin is extremely different than growing up in the rest of Austin. One may grow up with peers just trying to get through school and pass while the other grows up with very smart people around her. The difference between their dialects will mean one has an easier time in school than the other." They argued that this person's story would help to explain, as they phrased it, "why everyone don't just naturally speak proper."

Nancy also shared excerpts from published scholarship that mirrored the students' observations in their homework essays. Paired with thesis 1, for example, was this excerpt from "Ain't So/Is Not: Academic Writing Doesn't Always Mean Setting Aside Your Own Voice" by Graff and

Birkenstein (2014): "Ultimately, your judgments about the appropriate language for the situation should always take into account your likely audience and your purpose in writing" (127–28). The goal of this closing activity was to help the students recognize the knowledge they bring to the classroom. This was certainly the case with Jabari, who remarked that he had a new thesis he wanted to try out: "It really isn't about the language at all. It's about the people who use the language." Everyone nodded in agreement. Jabari had realized *and* articulated a linguistic theory informed by critical race theory.

Although WAW assignments facilitate important discussions about language, identity, and power, students also needed help with their self-efficacy—confidence that they could succeed as writers—especially because they had been placed in a "remedial" English class. With that goal in mind, Nancy shared with her class an excerpt from Easley, Bianco, and Leech's (2012) "*Ganas*: A Qualitative Study Examining Mexican Heritage Students' Motivation to Succeed in Higher Education." The authors write that "*ganas*, a deeply held desire to achieve academically fueled by parental struggle and sacrifice," was evident in 46 percent of their 103 immigrant and first-generation Mexican heritage students' autobiographies (169). Nancy paired this reading with data from the earlier writing center focus group about Easley, Bianco, and Leech's findings:

> ANNA: I immediately thought of my family: When they call they're just like, "How are you doing? Okay, fine whatever. *Echale ganas a la escuela. Y echale.*" So whenever I have an exam, I'll be like [*whispers*], "*Echale ganas.*"
>
> AMARILIS: We're from the Dominican Republic, and they would say more like, "*tener ganas*"—really wanting it, like you're gonna go for it. "*Tener las ganas para hacer algo.*"
>
> VALERIE: Oh, I'm gonna say that. I'm gonna steal it!

During class discussion, the non-Spanish speakers asked for a translation of *ganas*, and the Spanish speakers in class earnestly set about explaining the term: "It means working hard because people are depending on you" and "It means doing your best to make your family proud." When asked if they had personally experienced this sort of helpful push from their family, Gabriela replied,

> Just like Anna's and Amarilis' parents said to them, I can relate a lot to both girls because we are working hard in college to become something better and actually show the people that look down on Hispanics or on any other culture. "*Que si se puede.*" I have always had a parent that would tell me, "*Te tienes que mejorar, no por mi si no para ti misma, no quieres vivir*

como vives ahorita, verdad? Así que echale ganas"—do better for myself; do not live the way I am living, but live better, so I have to try my best.

All of these Latinas' comments are particularly noteworthy in light of Méndez-Newman's argument that "the HSI student will always simultaneously exist in two cultures: the culture of home and family and the culture of the academy, with the culture of family almost always trumping the culture of the academy" (2007, 22). Yet what these students had done was successfully marry cultural values, drawing support from their families in order to succeed in the academy. They had not only joined the conversation but also built upon it.

As the semester wound down and we contemplated ways to bring full circle the conversations and WAW activities with which students had been engaged all semester, we decided to share a draft of this article with them. For one, we wanted them to understand how their experience and knowledge had shaped us (as teachers and researchers). We also wanted them to extend the insights they'd been developing all along by weighing in on the value of reading about other people's—including their classmates'—writing struggles and triumphs. Reading their final essays, we found that even those students who had heretofore remained reticent about their own writing challenges appeared buoyed by reading about their classmates' experiences. Yesenia, for example, wrote,

> Growing up as a bilingual student was difficult for me because I would have to switch from speaking and writing in Spanish to English. For example, I would only speak Spanish at home and English at school. As I got older, I slowly started speaking more English and less Spanish. My dad would get mad at me because I was evolving into the American culture and he didn't want me to lose my Hispanic heritage. Like Gabriela stated, "Learning English actually brought a lot of problems into my life since according to my family I'm trying to lose the part that made me unique, which was being Latina." I can relate to what she said because I struggled to learn academic writing and felt I had to give up part of my home language to become a respected writer.

Even the one Anglo student in the class found value in hearing about others' struggles with writing. Mary wrote, "As a student, feeling alone in struggle isn't easy. You can start to feel less than or irrelevant in your academics, but when you read that other students have these same challenges of not wanting to lose their voice in writing or whatever the struggle may be it becomes comforting and reassuring that you and your peers can overcome these writing issues together."

Other students focused on what they'd gotten from the scholarship they read. As Jabari wrote, "A woman named Geneva Smitherman uses code switching in her academic papers about speech, and she says it's better to add different ways of speaking like 'slang' and 'proper English' while writing your paper to get that diversity they are looking for. So when my dad told me, 'I'm gone stop talkin slang around tha house for now on, and ima start using good, propa English' I said, 'it's o.k. You just have to switch it out whenever you are talking to different people.'" We hear in Jabari's comment a keen understanding of the power of linguistic liminality, of deliberately weaving in and out of identity and language without sacrificing multiple identities and languages. Too, in Jabari's comment to his dad that "you just have to switch [language use] out," we hear the whispers of a more radical linguistic stance: permission not only to code-switch but, perhaps, to code-mesh.

Although we want to be careful about drawing conclusions from just one class, we have no doubt that continuing to incorporate WAW into our basic writing classes, and specifically assigning texts that focus on minority writers, is the best choice for our program. WAW allows us to foreground what is generally ignored in our composition handbooks and in our classrooms: the problematic nature of a one-size-fits-all "standard" of writing and of English. The fact that the students who have faced discrimination—linguistic and otherwise—already recognize the inequities of the system makes avoiding this conversation a glaring oversight.

Too, given the opportunity to read and write about scholarship that is relevant to their own writing lives, students begin to think about themselves *as* writers. They begin to think strategically about what they can *do* with writing. This makes sense, of course: as Stephen Krashen's (1982) theory of the Affective Filter posits, as individuals' self-confidence and motivation increase and their writing anxiety decreases, they are better able to acquire a "second language" (31), which is an apt description of "Standard English" for basic writers in general and English-language learners in particular. Contributing to this increase in the students' self-efficacy is the fact that in the context of this class, their bi- and multi-lingualism and bi- and multiculturalism helped them to understand the readings.

But if teachers are already reluctant to adopt WAW pedagogy for fear that students cannot handle the complexity of the content and/or will be bored by our scholarship, they will perhaps see our WAW approach focusing on a specific group such as Latinx students as yet another step too far. When Nancy specifically asked for her students' perspective on why teachers tend not to incorporate writing scholarship in their classes, Nicholas observed, "I feel that English teachers don't do this method as often because it may not relate to the topic that is being taught and will be considered 'irrelevant' considering that they have to follow a certain criteria given to them. However, it may not be a bad idea for teachers to at least consider it and give it a try, and the instructor may see another side of the students and get to know them just a little bit more and not just stand in front of them as a whole and teach a class." Indeed. Nicholas aptly captures both the problem and the solution. Writing *can be* the topic; writing *can be* the content; writing *can be* the curriculum.

NOTE

1. For a university to be a Hispanic-serving institution, 25 percent of the total enrollment must be Hispanic.

REFERENCES

Anzaldúa, Gloria. 2012. "How to Tame a Wild Tongue." *Borderlands/La Frontera: The New Mestiza*, 4th ed., 75–86. San Francisco: Aunt Lute.

Charlton, Colin. 2009/2010. "Forgetting Developmental English: Re-reading College Reading Curricula." *BWe: Basic Writing e-Journal* 1 (2010). orgs.tamu—commerce.edu/BWe/Issue_8.1.html.

Easley, Nate, Jr., Margarita Bianco, and Nancy Leech. 2012. "*Ganas*: A Qualitative Study Examining Mexican Heritage Students' Motivation to Succeed in Higher Education." *Journal of Hispanic Higher Education* 11:164–78.

Graff, Gerald, and Cathy Birkenstein. 2014. "'Ain't So/Is Not': Academic Writing Doesn't Always Mean Setting Aside Your Own Voice." In *They Say/I Say*, edited by Gerald Graff and Cathy Birkenstein, 121–28. New York: Norton.

Kells, Michelle Hall. "Understanding the Rhetorical Value of Tejano Codeswitching." In Kells, Balester, and Villanueva 2004, 24–39.

Kells, Michelle Hall, and Valerie Balester, eds. 1999. *Attending to the Margins: Writing, Researching, and Teaching on the Front Lines*. Portsmouth, NH: Heinemann.

Kells, Michelle Hall, Valerie Balester, and Victor Villanueva, eds. 2004. *Latino/a Discourses: On Language, Identity, and Literacy Education*. Portsmouth, NH: Heinemann-Boynton/Cook.

Kirklighter, Cristina, Diana Cárdenas, and Susan Wolff Murphy, eds. 2007. *Teaching Writing with Latino/a Students: Lessons Learned at Hispanic-Serving Institutions*. Albany: State University of New York Press.

Krashen, Stephen D. 1982. *Principles and Practice in Second Language Acquisition*. New York: Pergamon.

McCracken, I. Moriah, and Valerie A. Ortiz. 2013. "Latino/a Student (Efficacy) Expectations: Reacting and Adjusting to a Writing-about-Writing Curriculum Change at an Hispanic-Serving Institution." *Composition Forum* 27. http://compositionforum.com/issue/27/student-expectations.php.

Mejía, Jaime. 2004. "Bridging Rhetoric and Composition Studies." In Kells, Balester, and Villanueva 2004, 40–56.

Méndez-Newman, Beatrice. 2007. "Teaching Writing at Hispanic-Serving Institutions." In Kirklighter, Cárdenas, and Murphy 2007, 17–35.

Paredes, Américo. 1990. *George Washington Gómez: A Mexicotexan Novel*. Houston, TX: Arte Publico.

Ramírez-Dhoore, Dora, and Rebecca Jones. 2007. "Discovering a 'Proper Pedagogy.'" In Kirklighter, Cárdenas, and Murphy 2007, 63–86.

Sellers, Frances Stead. 2014. "Q&A: Geneva Smitherman, Michigan State Professor Emerita of English, on the Study of African American English." *Washington Post*, July 10. https://www.washingtonpost.com/news/arts-and-entertainment/wp/2014/07/10/qa-geneva-smitherman-michigan-state-professor-emerita-of-english-on-the-study-of-african-american-english.

10
Vignette

"WRITING IS LIKE SHAPING A BONSAI TREE"
Writing about Writing and Culture in a Developmental Composition Course

Gwen Hart

> INSTITUTION TYPE AND SIZE: 900-student private, 4-year, comprehensive university
>
> COURSE CONTEXT: Developmental writing course, required for students who test below English 100 level
>
> STUDY DESIGN/METHODOLOGY: Assignment description
>
> WAW PROGRAM OR NOT: Non-WAW First-Year Writing Program
>
> WAW COURSE OR SINGLE ASSIGNMENT/UNIT: Sequence of WAW assignments in one unit of a developmental writing course
>
> INSTRUCTOR TYPE/POSITION: Assistant professor; now associate professor
>
> KEY TERMS: Developmental composition; ESL; metaphors for writing

I teach a diverse college student population in northwestern Iowa. The local high school is over 70 percent "minority" students, and *USA Today* has called the county I teach in part of the "changing face of America" (Toppo and Overberg 2014). The small university where I teach is drawing more and more from this local but diverse population, including multilingual students originally from El Salvador, Thailand, and Sudan who finished high school in the U.S. In the preceding chapter, Wilson, Jackson, and Vera discuss developing a specific WAW curriculum for multilingual students, including Latinx students. Here, I present a starter assignment for educators who are working with multilingual students but who may not have the pedagogical background or institutional support to tackle a large-scale WAW project with their multilingual students.

In my developmental writing course, which serves ESL students and native English speakers, I begin with a WAW assignment that asks students to think about how they understand writing by comparing it to another familiar activity. The goal is to get students to start thinking about their writing processes in a nonthreatening way so that they can examine the strengths and weaknesses of their current approaches to writing. This assignment allows students who are feeling uncertain about their writing skills to draw on their other areas of expertise, which often arise from their home cultures. It also harnesses the power of metaphor to help students do three important things: articulate (Armstrong 2008), discuss, and potentially revise their ideas about writing as the semester progresses (Hart 2015). As Lad Tobin (1989) points out, students may not have the vocabulary to describe their writing process in the same language writing experts would use, but "these same students can describe writing in terms of concrete experiences for which they have technical vocabulary and expertise, such as hitting a baseball or making a phone call to a friend" (446). Beginning with this assignment puts the focus of the class on the writing process right away while also engaging apprehensive or reluctant writers by allowing them to talk about and share their triumphs in other areas of their lives.

On the first day of the semester, students read Georgia Heard's (1995) brief essay "Writing is Like Making Tortillas." We discuss Heard's comparison, noting the parallels she draws between these two disparate subjects: both require lots of practice, can be frustrating at times, can be considered art forms, and so on. Students then write their own metaphors for writing by completing the sentence stem "Writing is like . . . because . . ." They share and discuss these metaphors for writing, learning how other students in the class view writing and how other people respond to their metaphors.

Over the next few classes, students revise and expand their metaphors. We read excerpts from Anne Lamott's (1995) *Bird by Bird*, such as "Shitty First Drafts" and "Perfectionism," and I ask students to include in their expanded metaphors a description of the writing problems they have encountered and potential solutions to those problems. Students compare these problems and solutions to other difficulties they have worked through in other arenas, such as playing soccer, mastering the guitar, or making dumplings. Thus, students create their own framework for working through writing problems instead of giving up in despair when they hit a stumbling block. I encourage students to create metaphors that reflect their unique experiences, and I find that they are usually eager to tell their stories. For example, a South Korean student shared a humorous story about her initial attempts to make her own kimchi rather than relying on store-bought jars of the staple food. She stressed the importance of trying different recipes (or approaches to writing) and learning from negative feedback from taste-testers (or peer reviewers). She concluded that cooking and writing, while difficult, were important means for preserving her cultural heritage. Students wrap up their papers with their writing goals for the semester.

At the end of the semester, students reevaluate their metaphors for writing to see if their ideas about writing have changed, discuss how well they've met their goals, and set new goals for the next semester. These short essays the students write are valuable because they allow diverse students to share their ideas about writing and some aspect of their culture. For example, a Chinese student wrote "Writing is like shaping a bonsai tree" and educated the class about selecting, trimming, and caring for a bonsai tree by sharing photos of his own bonsai creations. A Salvadoran student wrote "Writing is like making pupusas" and described learning to make pupusas from her mother. No one in the class (including me) knew what a pupusa was, so the student expanded her description of how to craft the thick corn tortillas and what choices one makes when preparing the filling—whether to include pork, beans, or cheese, which spices to use, and so on. She compared these selections to the choices one makes while writing an essay—which details to include and which to leave out. She even added a recipe for pupusas at the end of her essay. A Thai student wrote "Writing is like wrestling" and compared the rules of different types of wrestling he had practiced in Thailand and the U.S. (e.g., Greco-Roman, freestyle, and folkstyle) to different genres of writing. Using the sport he has practiced in two cultures, he was able to discuss the different expectations for school writing across cultures and to describe his own understanding of college-level writing expectations in the U.S.

This assignment helps my developmental composition students begin to see themselves as writers and to become a community of learners. By sharing ideas about writing and aspects of their home cultures, students become more comfortable with the writing class and with each other. Students who complete these activities report feeling less alone in their struggles with writing and more hopeful about writing classes (Hart 2015, 275–76).

REFERENCES

Armstrong, Sonja L. 2008. "Using Metaphor Analysis to Uncover Learners' Conceptualizations of Academic Literacies in Postsecondary Developmental Contexts." *International Journal of Learning and Development* 15 (9): 211–18.

Hart, Gwen. 2015. "Beyond 'Elicit and Run' Metaphor Research: Why Conversations among Participants Matter." In *Elicited Metaphor Analysis in Educational Discourse*, edited by Graham Low and Wan Wan, 265–88. Amsterdam: John Benjamins.

Heard, Georgia. 1995. "Writing Is Like Making Tortillas." In *Writing toward Home: Tales and Lessons to Find Your Way*, 22–23. Portsmouth, NH: Heinemann.

Lamott, Anne. 1995. *Bird by Bird: Some Instructions on Writing and Life*. New York: Anchor.

Tobin, Lad. 1989. "Bridging Gaps: Analyzing Our Students' Metaphors for Composing." *College Composition and Communication* 40 (4): 444–58.

Toppo, Greg, and Paul Overberg. 2014. "Second Immigration Wave Lifts Diversity to a Record High." *USA Today*, October 21.

11
WHY I KEEP TEACHING WRITING ABOUT WRITING IN QATAR
Expanding Literacies, Developing Metacognition, and Learning for Transfer

Mysti Rudd

> INSTITUTION TYPE AND SIZE: 550 engineering students at the international branch campus of Texas A&M at Qatar (TAMUQ), which offers bachelors of science degrees in one of four majors: chemical engineering, mechanical engineering, electrical and computer engineering, and petroleum engineering
>
> COURSE CONTEXT: All TAMUQ students are required to enroll in a single semester of FYW; the only other required writing course is technical writing, which students generally take in either their sophomore or junior years
>
> STUDY DESIGN/METHODOLOGY: Teacher action research based on classroom discussion, students' course reflections, and textbook satisfaction survey (IRB reviewed / exempt)
>
> WAW PROGRAM OR NOT: Only instructor out of eight to use WAW approach in FYW
>
> WAW COURSE OR SINGLE ASSIGNMENT/UNIT: WAW course; assignments from first edition of WAW textbook
>
> INSTRUCTOR TYPE/POSITION: Visiting assistant professor now on tenure track
>
> KEY TERMS: FYW; international branch campus; Qatar; transnational; transfer

ABSTRACT

This article considers six semesters (2012–2015) of FYW students' responses to the first edition of *Writing about Writing* (Wardle and Downs 2011) in a specific transnational context: Texas A&M at Qatar, a small international branch campus that offers undergraduate degrees in engineering. The use of teacher action research allowed the gathering of data via classroom discussions, student reflections, and textbook satisfaction surveys to gauge students' perspectives on the usefulness and appropriateness of the reading and writing assignments in the textbook. Based on this data, the instructor was convinced to continue adopting the text as it benefited engineering students by expanding their rhetorical reading skills and developing their metacognitive awareness, thus increasing the likelihood of transferring what they have learned about writing to future writing.

INTRODUCTION

While tens of thousands of college students have been taught FYW as an introduction to writing studies in the U.S., what happens when Wardle and Downs's first edition of *Writing about Writing* (*WAW* 2011) is adopted by a compositionist teaching FYW in a particular kind of transnational space: Texas A&M in Qatar (TAMUQ), an engineering international branch campus (IBC) of an American university situated in the Middle East? In this chapter, I attempt to answer this question as I explore the challenges as well as the benefits of adopting *WAW* to teach FYW to international engineering majors, half of whom are Qatari, half hailing from various countries in the Middle East–North Africa region, and all of whom are English as an additional language (EAL) students, their first language most often being Arabic or Urdu, and their second language either English or French.

Because I was concerned about the effect that EAL student reading levels might have on student engagement with the readings in *WAW*, I conducted textbook satisfaction surveys (see appendix 11.A) at the end of each semester. Having adopted the first edition of *WAW* for six semesters over the course of three years (2012–2015), I have now collected responses to *WAW* concepts introduced in FYW from more than a hundred students. These responses have been solicited not only through surveys but also through classroom discussions and end-of-course reflections. By gathering student responses to *WAW*, I hoped to prove to both myself and my department that our EAL students could not only rise to the task of understanding the difficult articles anthologized in *WAW*, but they could also benefit from the content of these articles introducing them to the field of writing studies. I was very willing to let go of the adoption of this textbook and the WAW approach to teaching FYW in subsequent semesters if a majority of students made this recommendation via end-of-semester surveys.

To my surprise, however, an overwhelming majority (85–95 percent) of my students each semester has recommended that I continue to adopt *WAW* to teach FYW at TAMUQ. As one EAL student noted in her textbook satisfaction survey, "I strongly recommend [*WAW*] for every student in this life, not only TAMUQ students, because it changes a lot in the person when it comes to writing!" Another student described *WAW* as "a powerful tool to improve students' reading and writing abilities," while a third student gushed, "I have never read a book that is more effective than *WAW*." So what happened to turn these students' initial perceptions of *WAW* from a "hard, boring, difficult, uninteresting, fat, and colorless" text into an experience that one student fondly called a "hobby"? To explore answers to this question, this chapter considers engineering students' responses, reflections, and reactions to the adoption of *WAW* for their FYW course in Qatar.

THE BEGINNINGS OF THE GRAND EXPERIMENT

They'll never be able to keep up with the readings.
—Senior instructor of ESL at TAMUQ

A veteran English teacher at the IBC where I was about to begin teaching uttered the statement above as I announced my decision to adopt *WAW* for my two sections of FYW for the fall 2012 semester. I had arrived in Qatar just three weeks before classes were to start, and I knew I was taking a gamble adopting a new textbook for an unknown population to teach FYW in a brand-new way—a gamble not just for my students but also for me.

When I accepted this visiting professorship at TAMUQ, I strongly suspected that my former assignments in FYW would not work in this new transnational context as they had been created with a critical pedagogy mindset and were focused on interrogating American perspectives regarding work, literacy, and the role of education in pursuing the so-called American Dream. I had read about the WAW movement in *College Communication and Composition* (Wardle and Downs 2007) and was convinced of its efficacy by conference presentations given individually by first Downs and then Wardle, and so I was curious about its application to the FYW classroom in general, but particularly in a transnational context. Would the students be able to relate to the readings culturally? Would the reading levels of the anthologized journal articles be too difficult for EAL students? Would engineering majors find articles written in the discipline of composition to be useful to their future careers as engineers?

I had no idea how my students would respond to *WAW* when I was hired to teach College Composition and Technical Writing—the only required English courses for engineering majors at TAMUQ. Since

TAMUQ'S entire student body is composed of EAL students, class sizes for all English writing courses are limited to fifteen students. Although College Composition had historically been taught as an argument-based course at TAMUQ, my curiosity about using the innovative WAW approach in a transnational context, plus my belief that students rise to the expectations we have for them, led me to experiment in teaching FYW by adopting *WAW* that first semester.

A ROCKY START

> *But why would you want to leave the U.S. to*
> *come here to teach writing to us?*
> —FYW student during class discussion, fall 2012

In my first semester at TAMUQ, I taught two sections of College Composition. Students in the afternoon section exhibited more resistance to the WAW approach, asking why they couldn't write arguments, research papers, and literary analyses as they had in high school. If this had been the only section of College Composition that I taught that semester, I would have concluded that the experiment of teaching *WAW* in Qatar was an abysmal failure and that I should either change direction (adopt a different text and approach) or abandon ship (go back to teaching in the U.S.).

The students in the morning section, however, showed a greater willingness to compose multiple drafts of the writing assignments in *WAW* and to reread difficult passages in the articles assigned. Their final presentations displayed the arcs of their respective learning curves over the semester, often revealing the pride they felt in their accomplishments—sometimes measured by these engineering majors as the total number of words written, displayed by one student in large, bold font on his final presentation slide: "16, 253!"

In observing students who rose to the challenge of the difficult assignments, I began to suspect that the rigor required to understand the articles in *WAW* was an excellent match for EAL learners who, in order to succeed in the university, needed to learn how to read difficult academic texts more carefully and critically as well as more quickly. In short, these first-year students benefited from the relentless practice in reading, writing, and critical thinking that this rigorous text provided for them. Meeting the challenge of revising both their understanding of the readings plus their responses to the written assignments contributed to their "academic self-efficacy" (Bandura 2005), preparing them for further success in the academy. Because I witnessed tremendous growth in both the reading and the writing abilities of many of these EAL students, as evidenced in their written responses to the assigned readings plus the changes they made to their drafts along with their reflections on why they made these changes, I decided to gather data for at least one more semester on the usefulness of using *WAW* to teach College Composition at TAMUQ.

THE USEFULNESS OF DIFFICULT READINGS FOR EAL STUDENTS IN FYW

> *At the beginning of this course I thought that the book is all about writing. But I didn't know it was about reading.*
> —Survey respondent, fall 2013

Confirming my observations about the usefulness of *WAW* in providing significant reading practice for EAL students, over 30 percent of the end-of-semester textbook satisfaction surveys included positive comments on this issue. Many students claimed that the difficulty of the vocabulary and the use of "elevated language" were useful for "people who have English as their second language." The length of the articles anthologized in *WAW* and their original target audience of writing scholars also required sustained focus from student readers, as one survey respondent remarked, "I felt the hard words and complexity of it made me a better reader. Sitting for two hours reading through a complicated text had to do something to my reading abilities!"

From classroom discussions, I have learned that most of our engineering majors at TAMUQ prefer to write for an hour—whether in Arabic or English—rather than read for an hour. I have also been informed by some of my TAMUQ students that reading is not a large part of their home cultures—that parents don't read to their children before they go to bed because, as one student proclaimed in his literacy narrative, "It is not the Arab way!"

From informal class surveys that I conduct every semester, I have discovered that nearly half of my FYW students, on average, have never read an entire book cover to cover. Therefore, I have great respect for the tenacity exhibited by these EAL students as they struggle to make meaning from difficult readings, and I rejoice with them when they succeed in doing so; as one *WAW* textbook satisfaction survey respondent stated, "It [felt] amazing that I studied a 'college book' by which I mean a black and white book with too many words and so little images." But it is not simply the challenging reading level and article length that make the readings anthologized in *WAW* so beneficial for EAL students;

rather, it is *WAW*'s promotion of rhetorical reading, which teaches students to read critically and efficiently. One survey respondent noted that assignments that took him eight hours to read at the beginning of the semester could now be completed in two hours—not just because his English vocabulary had improved but because he had a new approach to reading thanks to the content of the articles assigned. This led me to wonder which readings in particular that students found most useful of those anthologized in *WAW.*

THE APPROPRIATENESS OF SPECIFIC READINGS AT AN ENGINEERING IBC IN THE MIDDLE EAST

> *Gravity is a fact, not a claim. There is no disputing that, and so Margaret Kantz is dead wrong.*
> —Mechanical engineering major, class discussion, spring 2015

When canvassed about particular readings in *WAW* assigned throughout the semester, I was not surprised by the top three articles that students deemed too difficult: Margaret Kantz's "Helping Students Use Textual Sources Persuasively," Keith Grant-Davie's "Rhetorical Situations and Their Constituents," and James Porter's "Intertextuality and the Discourse Community." Interestingly, while being named by students as the articles they found most difficult, these articles also topped the list of readings that students found most useful. This reinforces a tenet of my teaching philosophy: that students benefit from being challenged, and in this case, from grappling with texts labeled even by themselves as too difficult to understand.

Kantz's (2011) article elicited the most negative responses during class discussions as it challenged my students' beliefs that "a fact was a fact," and many refused to consider Kantz's position that "a *fact* is a claim that an audience will accept as being true without proof" (76). Some of my students found Kantz's description of *fact* to be quite disturbing and even reckless, as the epigraph that begins this section attests. I consider my students' difficulties with Kantz's definitions and terms to be connected to the positivistic stance of the hard sciences, including engineering.

Besides the difficulty of adjusting between ways of knowing as reinforced by different academic disciplines (thinking like an engineer versus thinking like a compositionist), many of my FYW students also experienced a cultural difficulty in trying both to understand and to apply Kantz's notion of *rhetorical reading*. Kantz elevates the questioning of texts over the passive acceptance of the written word, and this was a novel concept to many of my students. In her summary and response to Kantz's article, one student wrote that questioning texts in the way that Kantz suggests could even "cause her to question her religion," following that with the understatement, "This is something that I do not wish to do." Indeed, questioning the validity of a text—or even the textbook that the teacher chose for a course, for that matter—did not come naturally to any of my students, and so reading critically and unpacking rhetorical situations required almost daily practice.

In classroom discussions, students also displayed cross-cultural difficulties with the article by James Porter (2011), which introduced the term *intertextuality*. Trying to teach my students this concept may have muddied the waters of plagiarism for them as many were already struggling to understand American requirements for the correct citation of sources in several systems of documentation (MLA, APA, IEEE, etc.). The rules for crediting sources may seem simple to American English majors, but they don't make logical sense to many of the engineering students at this IBC—and so some used Porter's notion of intertextuality (88) as a slippery slope to defend their lack of citations, asking during class, "Since we can't cite *all* of the textual borrowings we use, why should we have to cite *any*?" Another student quipped, "Must I cite a phrase used in my video game? How about a player who utters something while we are playing? When will all this citing of stuff end?!" One survey respondent named intertextuality as the concept that he would remember long after the course had ended, stating, "We don't really write purely as we write influenced by other people. We don't really own our words; we usually borrow and steal to write our words."

As an instructor who is expected to prepare EAL students for the Western citation practices expected of them in their other liberal arts courses at this IBC, I wondered if Porter's article served as justification for them to ignore these practices. In subsequent semesters I substituted James Purdy's "Calling Off the Hounds: Technology and the Visibility of Plagiarism" (2005) for Porter's article to avoid wading into the confusing transnational waters of intertextuality with my FYW students at TAMUQ.

Since TAMUQ's engineering majors must complete dozens of labs plus conduct and design their own research projects in order to graduate, perhaps the most relevant *WAW* article for their majors is John Swales's "Creating a Research Space" (2011, 6–8). When prompted, my FYW students were able to recognize the commonalities between the IMRAD format of many of the research articles anthologized in *WAW* and the required structure of their lab reports. Some of my

FYW students seemed particularly interested in the *WAW* studies that included empirical data presented in the form of tables and graphs, and they were eager to critically evaluate the solutions offered by these studies. The IMRAD heuristic and the thinking behind the designing of the various studies anthologized and assigned in *WAW* provide useful models for future engineers as they learn to practice research both logically and rhetorically.

To this end, the metacognition promoted by the many "Meta Moment" prompts in *WAW* encourages students to become aware of the rhetorical choices they make rather than unquestioningly responding to an assignment or blindly following a template—even the IMRAD template. The application of critical inquiry, then, is required in figuring out how to succinctly frame a problem, how to determine which research design is the most logical, and how to plan for the most efficient and/or rewarding ways of gathering, presenting, and analyzing rich data. The development of these rhetorical research skills can be transferred by engineering students to new situations and genres, including responding to requests for proposals (RFPs), whether from the academy (in upper-level courses in their majors and in graduate school) or from industry (where RFPs are a common genre that engineers both write in and respond to). The emphasis that *WAW* places on reading, writing, responding to, and reflecting upon research studies and proposals effectively prepares my students to transfer these skills to the engineering profession, and this potential for transferring learning is a major contributor to my decision to keep teaching *WAW* in Qatar.

LEARNING FOR TRANSFER

> *At the end of this course, when I had read most of the book's articles, I had really important concepts that influenced my writing.*
> —Survey respondent, spring 2014

Currently in my sixth semester of adopting *WAW* to teach FYW at TAMUQ, I am still adjusting my syllabus and learning to listen to my students' needs—those recorded in end-of-semester surveys and on teacher evaluations as well as those communicated via class discussions, student reflections, and one-to-one conferencing. Students know that if they put the work into my WAW courses (lots of reading, lots of drafting, lots of revising, lots of thinking, and lots of conferencing), they will most likely make a pretty good grade, but more importantly, they will emerge from the course stronger writers as well as better readers. They sense, especially as EAL learners, that they need this practice, and they have learned from upperclassmen that *WAW* will turn out to be more than "that big, fat, blue, boring book" they initially perceive it to be. They will come to realize that the metacognition and mindfulness at play in their informal research journals can go a long way toward helping them succeed in other courses, and that writing by hand can help them figure out what it is they really want—or need—to say (Goldberg 1990, 73).

By working through the readings and assignments in *WAW* throughout the semester, FYW students will have explored their identities as writers and reflected upon the usefulness of the premises they previously held about academic writing and reading. And they will carry ideas from *WAW* with them as they move not only through the academy but also into the rest of their writing, reading, and thinking lives. When cued by the textbook satisfaction survey to comment on the concepts from *WAW* that they will remember long after our course has ended, students had plenty to say. Many commented on how the concept of a rhetorical situation can be applied to more than just television commercials, with one respondent declaring, "I now see life as a rhetorical situation." Another respondent wrote, "The concept of the rhetorical triangle and its components will forever influence my writing," while another stated, "I will remember how to analyze what I read or write *before* doing it."

RECOMMENDATIONS FOR FUTURE USE OF WAW

Yes, I recommend future adoption of WAW, *but . . .*
—15 percent of surveyed FYW students

At the end of each semester after grades have been distributed and I tear open the sealed envelopes for each of my FYW section's textbook satisfaction surveys, I am no longer surprised that 85–95 percent of my former students recommend that I adopt *WAW* for the next semester. But I also pay attention to the responses of the 15–20 percent of my former FYW students who write a qualified "Yes, but . . ." because these students often make astute suggestions for subsequent semesters. For example, one student asked for an "an explicit introduction of the book and what it contains," and so I have learned to spend more time introducing the WAW movement to my FYW students before we even open the textbook.

Although I am still the only instructor in my department—and perhaps in all of Qatar—currently using *WAW* to teach FYW, I am convinced by my students' numerous testimonials of the effectiveness of this approach in expanding their literacies (e.g., improving their academic reading in L2, designing IMRAD research projects, applying digital tools to multimodal composing). The questions included in the "Applying and Exploring Ideas" section at the end of each article and the periodic "Meta Moment" prompts have aided my students in developing and practicing metacognition. Through their testimonials, I have been informed by some of my former students that their increased awareness of how writing works plus their newly gained ability to talk about rhetorical concepts with an expanded vocabulary of key terms have allowed them to enact the kind of transfer "of knowledge and practice" described in *Writing across Contexts* (Yancey et al. 2014, 37–59).

To conclude, not only are the EAL students at this engineering IBC capable of rising to the challenge of the critical reading and writing assignments in *WAW*, but their future success as engineers depends upon their abilities to read rhetorically, to reflect on their learning, and to transfer this rhetorical knowledge to "read" new situations in order to solve "real-world" problems. Therefore, *WAW* is a great textbook to adopt for the FYW courses at TAMUQ as it prepares our students for the rhetorical situations and problem solving associated with engineering. Since the rigor and the content of *WAW* have made its adoption a respectable choice in the judgment of 85–90 percent of the EAL engineering students at this IBC in the Middle East who have tried it, their responses have convinced me, a student-centered teacher, to continue to use *Writing about Writing* to teach College Composition to engineering undergraduates in Qatar.

APPENDIX 11.A

Textbook Satisfaction Survey Questions

- What was your impression of the textbook (*WAW*) at the beginning of the course?
- Were there specific articles or assignments that you found useful? If so, please describe.
- Were there specific articles or assignments that were too difficult to do or understand? If so, please explain.
- Without looking back at the textbook, what concepts from the text do you think you will remember long after this course has ended?
- In what ways did your impression of the textbook change by the end of the course?
- Do you recommend that this textbook be adopted for future ENGL-104 courses at TAMUQ? Please explain your answer.

REFERENCES

Bandura, Albert. 2005. "Self-Efficacy." In *Encyclopedia of Mental Health*, edited by Howard Friedman. San Diego: Academic.
Downs, Doug, and Elizabeth Wardle. 2007. "Teaching about Writing, Righting Misconceptions: (Re)Envisioning 'First-Year Composition' as 'Introduction to Writing Studies.'" *College Composition and Communication* 58 (4): 552–84.
Goldberg, Natalie. 1990. *Wild Mind: Living the Writer's Life*. New York: Bantam Books.
Grant-Davie, Keith. 2011. "Rhetorical Situations and Their Constituents." Wardle and Downs 2011, 104–18.
Kantz, Margaret. 2011. "Helping Students Use Textual Sources Persuasively." In Wardle and Downs 2011, 68–84.
Porter, James E. 2011. "Intertextuality and the Discourse Community." In Wardle and Downs 2011, 87–99.
Purdy, James P. 2005. "Calling off the Hounds: Technology and the Visibility of Plagiarism." *Pedagogy* 5 (2): 275–96.
Swales, John. 2011. "Creating a Research Space." In Wardle and Downs 2011, 6–8.
Wardle, Elizabeth, and Doug Downs, eds. 2011. *Writing about Writing: A College Reader*. Boston: Bedford/St. Martin's.
Yancey, Kathleen Blake, Robertson, Liane, and Kara Taczak. 2014. *Writing across Contexts: Transfer, Composition, and Sites of Writing*. Logan: Utah State University Press.

12
NEXT STEPS, OR RATHER, ONE STEP AT A TIME
A How-To Guide for Implementing Writing about Writing

Kristen di Gennaro

> INSTITUTION TYPE AND SIZE: Private, midsized urban university
> COURSE CONTEXT: Final course in a three-course sequence; required
> STUDY DESIGN/METHODOLOGY: Case-based reflection
> WAW PROGRAM OR NOT: Stand-alone version of WAW
> WAW COURSE OR SINGLE ASSIGNMENT/UNIT: WAW course
> INSTRUCTOR TYPE/POSITION: Tenure-track assistant professor, now associate professor
> KEY TERMS: Applied linguistics; defining writing courses; metacognitive awareness; multilingual and monolingual writers

ABSTRACT

This chapter describes a WAW course based upon research in both composition and applied linguistics. While the course was initially created for multilingual writers, it has since been implemented successfully with monolingual English students. Intended for readers unfamiliar with WAW or those seeking guidance on how to implement such a course, this chapter includes suggestions and descriptions of potential course readings and assignments. For readers familiar with WAW, the chapter offers suggestions for articulating the approach to those less familiar. The chapter concludes with a discussion of advantages and other observations accompanying my experience using WAW.

INTRODUCTION AND OVERVIEW

Major changes have been taking place in college writing courses, greatly altering how English composition course are envisioned and taught. This "quiet academic revolution" (White 2015) arguably began

DOI: 10.7330/9781607328421.c012

decades ago when graduate programs in composition and rhetoric began offering graduate students an alternative to the study of literature. Previously "mocked and pitied," according to White, those who chose to specialize in writing and the pedagogy of writing were actually at the forefront of this revolution, as they influenced writing faculty to reconsider what constitutes a writing course. Scholars such as Hairston (1992) and Lindemann (1993), who challenged composition faculty to defend or abandon writing courses that borrowed heavily from other disciplines such as literature and cultural studies, encouraged, if not forced, writing faculty to identify course content unique to writing courses.

Around the same time, scholars in applied linguistics specializing in instruction for multilingual learners observed that people tend to focus attention on one language dimension at a time (Skehan 1989) with a preference for interpreting meaning over form (VanPatten 1990). Course content that diverts students' attention from language toward theme- or literature-based content can disadvantage the development of students' language ability. These findings hold significance for writing courses as well, as they suggest that requiring students to think critically about writing (as opposed to about ideas expressed through writing) is an effective pedagogical approach. Merging composition pedagogy with research from applied linguistics, the writing about writing (WAW) pedagogy offers a solution to the problem of content in a writing course and focuses students' attention on the subject of writing.

This chapter describes a WAW course based upon research in both composition and applied linguistics. While the course was initially created for multilingual writers, it has since been implemented successfully with monolingual English students. Intended for readers unfamiliar with WAW or those seeking guidance on how to implement such a course, this chapter includes suggestions and descriptions of potential course readings and assignments. For readers familiar with WAW, the chapter offers some suggestions for articulating the approach to those less conversant with, or even skeptical of, the pedagogy's appeal. The chapter concludes with a discussion of advantages and other observations accompanying my experience using WAW.

COURSE DESCRIPTION

Just as many models exist for what constitutes a writing course, there are many possibilities for how to interpret a WAW approach. In fact, the approach described here grew out of a suggestion from an applied linguistics article (Casanave 2003), and I taught the course several times before seeing the name WAW applied to it.

In the interpretation I have adopted, the first "writing" in WAW is read as a noun (i.e., published research), and could also be plural, as in *writings* about writing. The second "writing" is the object of this research, that is, the features of written texts and how these serve as reflections of writers' adherence, or not, to certain discourse conventions, preferences, and expectations. By this definition, the growing body of research on written discourse provides the course content in the same way that historical documents provide content for a history course or that literary texts and analyses provide content for a literature course. A sample course description would include a focus on explorations of various genres and "rules" for writing, such that students are led to observe the conventions, preferences, and expectations of their own disciplines in order to gain confidence as writers in different academic settings. Figure 12.1 provides a possible course description and list of potential outcomes.

COURSE CONTENT

In attempting to describe my implementation of WAW to composition faculty who come from other disciplines, I've noticed that, while many have little difficulty envisioning students engaging in writing about their own writing experiences, they struggle to grasp the idea of a course organized around scholarly research on writing, probably because scholars outside rhetoric, composition, and applied linguistics are unaware of this large and growing body of research. For faculty familiar with the research, the challenge is less about grasping the WAW concept and more about finding content that is relevant and accessible to students. Indeed, it is difficult to intentionally search for and find content that meets both the relevance and accessibility criteria. Most of the content I've used in this course, aside from the articles recommended by Casanave (2003), I found while reading or browsing composition and writing journals for my own research. Below, I briefly describe several of the sources I've used successfully with students. I then summarize the course in terms of topics, which can serve as search terms to find additional sources. At the end of this chapter, I provide a separate list of the articles used as course content (appendix 12.A) as well as a list of the journals I regularly consult for additional content (appendix 12.B).

As a subscriber to *Teaching English in the Two-Year College*, I find that journal to be one of the best sources of accessible content. I usually have students read an article by Teresa Thonney (2011) on the conventions

> What is academic writing? How does academic writing compare to other types of writing? Are there different types of academic writing? Are there special "rules" for academic writing? In this course, we explore these questions and other related topics. The course readings, class discussions, and writing assignments will allow you to explore the conventions, preferences, and expectations of your own discipline as you gain more confidence as a writer in academic settings.
>
> <u>Student Learning Outcomes</u>
> In this course, you will ...
> ✓ Examine how language varies across contexts
> ✓ Develop an awareness of various features of academic writing
> ✓ Engage in both introspective and empirical methods of data collection
> ✓ Produce writing in a variety of academic genres
> ✓ Assess your own and your peers' writing
> ✓ Discover your writing strengths and weaknesses
> ✓ Develop strategies for improving your writing

Figure 12.1.

of academic discourse as an introduction to the course. The article not only outlines the common features Thonney has found in academic writing across various disciplines, it also provides a very readable account of Thonney's research questions, method, materials, and findings. The literature review is relatively short, so readers unfamiliar with the works cited are less likely to feel like complete outsiders to the discourse community, and the information provided in the summary is of immediate value for students as they complete writing assignments in composition and other courses.

Another journal that has provided several sources is *ELT* (*English Language Teaching*). Focusing on the teaching of English to speakers of other languages, articles from this journal are especially relevant for multilingual writers but many apply to monolingual writers as well. The relative brevity of articles is especially appealing to students. Most articles also include empirical research, allowing them to serve as models for students' own research. Articles I have drawn from this journal include Crewe's study of students' (mis)use of logical connectives (1990), Ken Hyland's examination of personal pronouns in academic writing (2002), and Colin Sowden's and Dilin Liu's point-counterpoint articles on the relationship between plagiarism and students' cultural backgrounds (2005).

Scanning the contents of the *Journal of English for Academic Purposes* reveals a wealth of relevant articles, such as Karen Bennett's (2009) survey of English academic style manuals, but in my experience, students need some scaffolding to work through them. For example, when reviewing Bennett's article in class, I found it helpful to divide the article into sections (very easy to do with the article's subheadings) and have groups of students work together to reread and summarize individual sections that they then explain to the rest of the class.

Some difficult articles are worth the struggle and extra class time spent on them for the discoveries they allow students to make. Robert Kaplan's classic article in *Language Learning* on cultural thought patterns in writing is one such. While Kaplan's work is certainly dated and his findings are somewhat reductive, his observation that preferences in organizational patterns vary across cultures remains valid. International students in particular find this article eye-opening, as it helps explain feedback they may have received on their writing. Monolingual English writers also benefit from the understanding that what determines good writing varies across cultures and contexts.

Another challenging article, and one that I almost always include on my syllabus, is Thomas Huckin and Linda Pesante's (1988) extremely detailed empirical analysis of the use of existential *there* in writing, from *Written Communication*. The authors' approach to challenging a common writing rule and then investigating the application of the rule by real writers also helps students to discover that rules vary across contexts. More specifically for the course, I draw on this article to encourage students to identify rules that may or may not apply to the genres they produce in their own disciplines and to then search for evidence supporting or refuting their initial observations.

Since one main objective of the course is to develop students' awareness of important yet often tacit conventions, preferences, and expectations of academic writing, several articles I've used address less obvious features of academic writing, such as writers' use of metadiscourse markers. Research on metadiscourse has exploded since Vande Kopple (1985) drew attention to its relevance in writing, providing a wealth of articles to draw from. While many studies in this area have been conducted by corpus linguists and consequently are less readable for undergraduate students, some are both accessible and suitable for students from a variety of disciplines. Two examples I've used are Hyland's (1998) article on the use of hedges and boosters in academic writing and Jennifer Wishnoff's (2000) article on second-language writers' use of pragmatic devices in academic writing and email.

Another method for finding potential course content (other than browsing these and other journals) is to search journals and databases using the course topics as key words. In general, the course focuses on academic writing conventions and how these vary across discourse communities. Breaking this into topics produces searchable terms such as *defining academic writing, organizational patterns in academic writing, genre analysis, logical connectors and transitions, use of personal pronouns, tone, metadiscourse markers* (i.e., *hedges, boosters*), *plagiarism,* and *citation styles.*

In sum, course readings require students to engage in the subject of writing on both theoretical and practical levels. Rather than read texts whose main purpose is to entertain the reader, discuss current events, or support positions on social issues, students read research about writing that can provide them with information they can apply in their own writing and with tools they can use to make additional discoveries relevant to their specific disciplines.

COURSE ASSIGNMENTS AND ASSESSMENTS

For the course to be coherent beyond the selection and organization of reading material, assignments and assessments need to be aligned with course readings and objectives as well. While this may seem obvious, I have observed cases where writing instructors adopt a WAW course description but then use readings almost exclusively from the literary canon or assign tasks designed to convey the writer's opinion. The primary objective of this WAW course, in addition to overall improvement in students' writing ability, is the development of explicit awareness of writing features that are typically implicitly learned, if learned at all, regarding writing in their disciplines. While some course assignments are based on course readings, the main focus remains on students' observations and their writing, not their reading comprehension or their support or opposition to a particular statement.

A useful first assignment is an autobiography of writing, where students reflect upon and write about their experiences with writing. Students' responses invariably lead to lively class discussions and reveal many questions they have about writing "rules." A subsequent assignment could include a summary of one of the readings. Eliciting and elaborating on the summary content as a group allows students to place attention on the genre of the summary (rather than on the content of the article) and focus on its writer's choice of organization, vocabulary, verb forms, and other written discourse features. Assignments easily build upon one another, with students writing a critique of the same article they summarized, and later writing an annotated bibliography including their course readings along with additional articles related to their course projects. For each assignment, students' attention is drawn to features of the writing task, such as preferred word choice, sentence structure, and organization. Paying attention to these details further encourages students to observe similarities and differences across disciplines and genres.

To complement the readings and writing tasks, a presentation assignment allows students to work in pairs to prepare mini-lessons on common writing issues. In their presentations, which they give to the class throughout the semester, students share information they have collected about the writing issue they have chosen (usually from sources such as the Purdue OWL), provide examples, and offer writing strategies for their classmates. An alternative presentation task is to have students lead discussions of the course readings. Students' presentations easily lead to discussions regarding students' observations of the writing practices in their individual disciplines, which further raises their awareness about how writing works in different contexts. Topics for students' mini-lessons have included the choice between active or passive verb forms, the use of hedges and boosters, the use of personal pronouns in academic writing, and distinctions between paraphrase and plagiarism.

Continuing to build upon previous assignments, for the final project, students work in pairs on an empirical research project involving both secondary and primary data on a writing feature or issue. For example, students might examine the use of hedges in two different academic disciplines and then count and compare the number of hedges they find in samples of writing from those disciplines. Students might conduct surveys or interviews with other students to gauge their awareness of various prescriptive rules or preferences for certain features (such as the rule to avoid the passive construction). Through these projects, students conduct their own empirical studies similar to those they read in the published literature. For this assignment, thus, students create their own "writings about writing." Scaffolding for this assignment might include a prescribed structure similar to that of the published research students read throughout the course. Specifically, students can be guided to include an introduction to the topic and why it matters, a brief review of published literature, a description of the data collection method they used, details of their findings, and a discussion of the difficulties and limitations they encountered. It might be useful to return to a few of the readings to examine how the authors introduce and describe tables and charts summarizing their data and use these as models for students' projects. At the end of the course, students share their findings with their peers during class presentations.

In addition to graded writing assignments, students can complete several informal tasks, such as defining academic writing (both at the beginning and end of the course), engaging in peer reviews, and completing self-assessments. These reflective assignments not only draw students' attention to writing but also help them focus on their own relationships with writing, and in the process potentially reduce their anxiety and raise their self-confidence when it comes to writing.

BENEFITS OF WAW

I have taught a version of this course for the past several years and have noticed several benefits, some expected and some surprising. As already noted, designing a course with a WAW model solves the problem as to what constitutes a composition course (David, Gordon, and Pollard 1995; Downs and Wardle 2007) and offers the added benefit of distinguishing the field of composition from literary studies. Unlike other models of composition pedagogy, such as process-based, literature-based, and expressivist approaches, which can privilege monolingual middle-class students (Hyland 2003), a WAW approach potentially minimizes differences in student performance due to socioeconomic and linguistic diversity in that it values and explores the multiple literacies that students have already acquired as well as the literacies valued by their academic disciplines.

Since students study writing as both an object and a means of expression, WAW helps raise their metacognitive awareness. Such an approach is supported by research in applied linguistics showing that reducing the cognitive load can help learners focus better on the writing task compared to when they are required to read and discuss topics unrelated to the practice of writing (Skehan 1989). In other words, when writing constitutes both the content and practice of a writing course, there is less competition for a learner's attentional resources, as both declarative and procedural knowledge converge to support one another. Courses focusing on developing students' metacognitive awareness are also said to promote deep learning, which has been linked to greater student retention (Bain 2004) and may lead to knowledge transfer beyond the composition course (Wardle and Downs 2013).

The WAW model described in this chapter is inherently interdisciplinary, since students read about and explore how writing works in a variety of contexts, including across disciplines. WAW not only provides students with a clear purpose for reading about and practicing writing, it also encourages students to identify with a community of students and faculty within their disciplines, another practice closely linked to student retention (Bain 2004).

OBSERVATIONS

I have found students' reactions to the WAW model overwhelmingly positive. Since few multilingual students major in literature, they often express relief upon learning that the course is not based on literature or "hot topics." I sense that students find the course material difficult at first but also refreshing, as it differs greatly from their previous experiences (positive and negative) in other composition courses. Students seem to particularly appreciate the course once they recognize its applications to all types of writing, beyond the requirements of an individual course.

I have found the approach equally effective with monolingual and multilingual students. As composition classrooms become increasingly heterogeneous in terms of students' linguistic backgrounds (di Gennaro 2012), such flexible pedagogies will become increasingly critical.

An unexpected benefit I have observed is that WAW assignments, especially those focusing on primary research methods and students' observations, encourage academic integrity, as I have yet to encounter a problem with plagiarism since implementing WAW.

Finally, by requiring students to think critically about writing (as opposed to ideas expressed through writing), WAW both enables and empowers students, as they are not simply novices pretending to be experts (Bartholomae 1986), "mushfaking" their way through writing assignments (Gee 1989), but observers, collecting and analyzing writing for their own uses and contexts. In sum, I find WAW an effective pedagogical approach for all types of learners, since it allows students to develop their writing in ways that are meaningful to them, as they gain greater awareness of the norms, preferences, and expectations of their own discourse communities.

REMAINING CHALLENGES

The greatest challenge I have faced in my attempts to provide guidance to others wishing to adopt a WAW approach is the lack of a short and simple answer to the question "What is writing about writing?" In fact, on several occasions, I have witnessed enthusiasm from faculty who misunderstood WAW as an extension of the expressivist model of composition, where students write primarily about their own experiences with writing. While WAW writing tasks might draw on students' observations and reflections, WAW, as envisioned here, is not writing about *my* writing. Despite the growing appeal and implementation of WAW approaches, there remain many writing instructors whose training did not include research in the field of composition, leaving many unaware of the existence of this research and without an interest in teaching it. As WAW becomes more widespread, and more writing teachers emerge from doctoral programs in composition, rhetoric, and applied linguistics, answering this question will become less of a challenge. In the meantime, I hope this chapter can provide some guidance to those who are committed to teaching writing courses that are about writing.

APPENDIX 12.A

Course Readings

Bennett, Karen. 2009. "English Academic Style Manuals: A Survey." *Journal of English for Academic Purposes* 8:43–54.
Crewe, W. J. 1990. "The Illogic of Logical Connectives." *ELT Journal* 44:316–25.
Curzan, Anne. 2009. "Says Who? Teaching and Questioning the Rules of Grammar." *PMLA* 124:870–79.
Huckin, Thomas N., and Linda H. Pesante. 1988. "Existential There." *Written Communication* 5:368–91.
Hyland, Ken. 1998. "Boosting, Hedging and the Negotiation of Academic Knowledge." *Text* 18:349–82.
Hyland, Ken. 2002. "Options of Identity in Academic Writing." *ELT Journal* 56:351–58.
Kaplan, Robert B. 1966. "Cultural Thought Patterns in Intercultural Education." *Language Learning* 16:1–20.
Liu, Dilin. 2005. "Plagiarism in ESOL Students: Is Cultural Conditioning Truly the Major Culprit?" *ELT Journal* 59:234–41.
Sowden, Colin. 2005. "Plagiarism and the Culture of Multilingual Students in Higher Education." *ELT Journal* 59:226–33.
Thonney, Teresa. 2011. "Teaching the Conventions of Academic Discourse." *Teaching English in the Two-Year College* 38:347–32.
Vande Kopple, William J. 1985. "Some Exploratory Discourse on Metadiscourse." *College Composition and Communication* 36:82–93.
Wishnoff, Jennifer. R. 2000. "Hedging Your Bets: L2 Learners' Acquisition of Pragmatic Devices in Academic Writing and Computer-Mediated Discourse." *Second Language Studies* 19:119–48. http://www.hawaii.edu/sls/wp-content/uploads/2014/09/Wishnoff.pdf.

APPENDIX 12.B

List of Journals Frequently Consulted for Course Content

Across the Disciplines, wac.colostate.edu/atd/.
Composition Forum, compositionforum.com/.
Composition Studies, www.compositionstudies.uwinnipeg.ca/.
ELT Journal, http://eltj.oxfordjournals.org/.
English Journal, www.ncte.org/journals/ej.
Journal of Basic Writing, wac.colostate.edu/jbw/.
Journal of English for Academic Purposes, http://www.journals.elsevier.com/journal-of-english-for-academic-purposes/.

Journal of Second-Language Writing, www.jslw.org.

Teaching English in the Two-Year College, www1.ncte.org/store/journals/college/105397.htm.

Writing & Pedagogy, www.equinoxpub.com/WAP.

Writing Center Journal, www.english.udel.edu/wcj/.

Written Communication, wcx.sagepub.com/.

REFERENCES

Bain, Ken. 2004. *What the Best College Teachers Do.* Cambridge, MA: Harvard University Press.

Bartholomae, D. 1986. "Inventing the University." *Journal of Basic Writing* 5:4–23.

Casanave, Christine. 2003. "Multiple Uses of Applied Linguistics Literature in a Multi-Disciplinary Graduate EAP Class." *ELT Journal* 57:43–50.

David, Denise, Barbara Gordon, and Rita Pollard. 1995. "Seeking Common Ground: Assumptions for Writing Courses." *College Composition and Communication* 46:522–32.

di Gennaro, Kristen. 2012. "The Heterogeneous Second-Language Population in US Colleges and the Impact on Writing Program Design." *Teaching English in the Two-Year College* 40:57–67.

Downs, Doug, and Elizabeth Wardle. 2007. "Teaching about Writing, Righting Misconceptions: (Re)Envisioning 'First-Year Composition' as 'Introduction to Writing Studies.'" *College Composition and Communication* 38:552–84.

Gee, J. P. 1989. "Literacy, Discourse, and Linguistics: Introduction." *Journal of Education* 171:5–17.

Hairston, Maxine. 1992. "Diversity, Ideology, and Teaching Writing." *College Composition and Communication* 43:179–93.

Hyland, Ken. 2003. *Second Language Writing.* Cambridge: Cambridge University Press.

Lindemann, Erika. 1993. "Freshman Composition: No Place for Literature." *College English* 55:311–16.

Skehan, Peter. 1989. *Individual Differences in Second Language Learning.* London: Edward Arnold.

VanPatten, B. 1990. "Attending to Form and Content in the Input." *Studies in Second Language Acquisition* 12:287–301.

Wardle, Elizabeth, and Doug Downs. 2013. "Reflecting Back and Looking Forward: Revisiting 'Teaching about Writing, Righting Misconceptions' Five Years On." *Composition Forum* 27. compositionforum.com/issue/27/reflecting-back.php.

White, Ed. n.d. "What on Earth Has Happened to Freshman English?" http://www.upcolorado.com/about-us/blog/item/2816-freshman-english.

13
DEVELOPING A WRITING ABOUT WRITING CURRICULUM

Cat Mahaffey and Jan Rieman

> INSTITUTION TYPE AND SIZE: Urban public research university (one of sixteen in a state system); 29,000 students
> COURSE CONTEXT: Two-course sequence required for general education; first-year writing program
> STUDY DESIGN/METHODOLOGY: Faculty surveys, artifacts from program development over the last five years
> WAW PROGRAM OR NOT: Hybrid writing about writing curriculum—first in two-course sequence is WAW
> WAW COURSE OR SINGLE ASSIGNMENT/UNIT: WAW course
> INSTRUCTOR TYPE/POSITION: Both authors are non-tenure-track, full-time lecturers, now senior lecturers, and WPAs in a FYW program that is housed within a freestanding writing program
> KEY TERMS: Curriculum; professional development; assessment

ABSTRACT

Curricular shifts are messy, time-consuming, and sometimes heated. This chapter discusses how one first-year writing program at a large public urban university researched, piloted, and implemented a shift from a formalist approach to writing instruction to a social constructivist, writing about writing curriculum. Offered from the perspective of two WPAs, details include why, when, and how the WAW curriculum was adopted, how a responsive stance by WPAs helped in this shift, and how, ultimately, honoring the culture of our program helped strengthen it as a whole.

INTRODUCTION AND CONTEXT

We serve as WPAs in a first-year writing program at a large urban university that adopted a WAW curriculum five years ago. The work has been steady, fruitful, and immensely rewarding, but it's not been without challenges. Curricular shifts require time to take hold, and we've worked hard to be responsive to shifting faculty needs throughout the process. We hope that sharing our story can offer other writing programs some insight into professional development around WAW, faculty perceptions of the approach, and broader implications of adopting it.

As with assessment, curriculum design and professional development must be locally situated. We would be remiss not to mention that our adoption of a WAW curriculum coincided with our separation from the English department, bringing with it increased expectations of self-governance for our lecturer cadre. In many ways, these responsibilities fueled development, as instructors who once felt marginalized collaborated to visualize and build both a new program and a new curriculum that reflected values around writing studies in a way that perhaps wouldn't have been possible within the confines of the English department.

Ours is a freestanding writing program whose two-course first-year writing sequence of 1101 and 1102 satisfies the general education requirement for writing. We offer roughly 120 sections of first-year writing each semester with classes capped at twenty-two. Our faculty consists of twenty-nine full-time lecturers on three- to five-year contracts, about a dozen part-time faculty (fewer in the spring), and seven TAs. The majority of our faculty members hold MAs in English literature or a related field; there are a handful of MFAs in poetry and fiction, an MEd in elementary and middle school language arts education, four PhDs (none in composition and rhetoric), and three ABDs, one permanently, one still hopeful and wishful to finish, and one whose interest in composition and rhetoric has usurped the dissertation's original focus.

CATALYSTS FOR CURRICULAR CHANGE

The curricular shift from a largely formalist to a constructivist approach to teaching first-year writing was a response to a number of factors and, ultimately, a catalyst for significant cultural changes within our program. A driving force for the redesign was bringing our curriculum more in line with current research in writing studies. A secondary aim was to standardize the 1101 course, the first in our two-course sequence. Students were moving into 1102 with wildly disparate experiences from 1101 and landing in 1102 without even a shared vocabulary for how to talk about writing. While the 1102 courses were more similar in their aims as a whole, they, too, needed a shared focus around inquiry-guided learning.

Around the time we were imagining the new curriculum, Downs and Wardle's 2007 "Teaching about Writing, Righting Misconceptions: (Re)Envisioning 'First-Year Composition' as 'Introduction to Writing Studies'" article appeared, and some of us were intrigued and excited about the possibility of writing itself as the subject of a FYW course. This WAW idea became a guiding principle in rethinking 1101, whose course description eventually developed into the central claim that writing is both its "primary subject of inquiry and the primary activity."

DEVELOPING THE CURRICULUM

With a new course description drafted as a guide, the WPA at the time worked with a group of four faculty to pilot a year-long WAW approach in 1101. We focused our WAW efforts on 1101 for the pilot because the change was more radical there than in 1102, where the focus shifted from a formalist argument-based, academic essay approach to an inquiry-guided, semester-long project whose final product needed to be rhetorically responsive to intended audiences and the writer's purpose as opposed to a stock "argumentative essay." The four instructors piloting the courses were fortunate to have acquired a publisher-provided test copy of *Writing about Writing* (Wardle and Downs 2014) that our students used for one year. Having this shared textbook was immensely helpful in rethinking how to approach the class. While each faculty member developed his or her own version of the course, the pilot team and the WPA met regularly throughout the year to talk through the WAW approach, develop assignments, and share teaching experiences. Members of the group who piloted the course were then part of a curriculum redesign committee that revised the course descriptions developed for the pilot for our 1101 and 1102 classes: Writing and Inquiry in Academic Contexts I and II.

Faculty who piloted the 1101 WAW course shared their materials—including student compositions—and their take on the experience with the full faculty during the process of deliberation on the new curriculum. We did so through designated presentations and updates at faculty meetings. Faculty were given many opportunities to explore this proposed curriculum, talk with the WPA and the instructors who piloted the course, and provide feedback on the revised course descriptions. Once the FYW faculty were satisfied that this proposed curriculum was right for our program, the new course descriptions were approved and the proposal moved through all of the necessary departmental, college, and general education procedures for changes to a curriculum. There were several obvious advantages to this work, but one of the most significant was that each step of the process allowed (or forced) us to articulate our program's values and approach to teaching writing to the wider university, making our work more visible and reminding faculty across campus that literacy development does not begin or end with first-year writing. Another benefit of this work was that the course descriptions were shaped in response to faculty-articulated values rather than only what the WPA proposed, something that was forgotten later in the process.

Throughout the development work, there was an overall sense of curiosity and excitement about what this curriculum could look like. Resistance, interestingly enough, occurred *after* faculty approved the curriculum and were then expected to enact it. Despite the shared work and decision making, some faculty felt, after the fact, that the curriculum had been forced on them and resented what felt like top-down curricular mandates. We attribute a good bit of this resistance to larger issues within the program at the time—most notably, feelings of instability and insecurity. Soon after the curriculum was adopted, the WPA who had led the curricular shift stepped down, the chair of the English department became acting WPA, and two lecturers with little experience in WPA work were hired as "assistant directors," charged with the day-to-day operations of FYW. This period was before the split from English and tensions all around were high. As a response to this turmoil, the English department chair and the dean's office coordinated small-group meetings with associate deans and FYW faculty. While these provided an institutional platform for sharing frustrations, the real work of getting beyond these stances of anger and resistance were ongoing, self-initiated, one-on-one conversations between faculty who were at odds with one another. It's a testament to our professionalism and true respect for one another that through these conversations we were able to overcome the pervasive mode of divisiveness that was then the culture of the FYW/English department divide. Once the internal conflicts were in the process of resolution, the WPAs were able to focus on developing meaningful, intentional, and sustained professional development that honored our faculty culture.

PROFESSIONAL DEVELOPMENT

Thinking about the culture of our program—who we are, what we value, and how we like to work—played an important role in how we structured faculty development. We have never had a common textbook or common assignments. We value autonomy in our text choices and assignment design, which is wonderful, but also a challenge when trying to build a cohesive program or enact a new curriculum. Because of this established sense of instructor independence, it took perhaps more time for our faculty than it may have for others to adjust their thinking and situate their course designs around notions of inquiry into writing studies rather than the conventional modes that most of us had been teaching for decades. The shift was slow, requiring multiple approaches to professional development intentionally designed to complicate and destabilize deeply held beliefs about how novice writers develop and the role of the writing teacher in this process.

Faculty Thinking and Planning Groups

As we developed our plans for professional development, we were conscious of two main goals: in our newly autonomous program, (1) we needed to nurture an atmosphere of faculty ownership; and (2) we needed to facilitate what was for some a huge shift in pedagogy toward WAW. The first step toward meeting these two goals was to encourage collaborative development of syllabi and assignments by setting up course redesign groups. We started this process at the end of the spring semester of the pilot year in preparation for the implementation of the new curriculum in the fall so that groups could plan together over the summer. These groups continued meeting into the fall with the intention that they would gather weekly to confer and offer support as questions and stumbling blocks arose during our first semester teaching the new curriculum. Groups consisted of one faculty member who had been part of the pilot project, at least one part-time faculty member, and several full-time lecturers. These groupings were intended to make sure no one group was marginalized or lacked access to faculty already familiar with WAW. Our seven teaching assistants were peppered throughout. For adjunct faculty whose schedules prevented them from participating as actively as they would have liked in these redesign groups, the WPAs held a two-day summer institute as a substitute.

Some groups meshed well and continued to meet even into the spring semester and beyond (one group met for roughly two years, eventually presenting together at a regional writing conference about their collaboration), while others seemed to lack cohesion or discipline in their meeting schedules. Overall, this small-group approach proved successful in that every instructor had a network of several go-to contacts when advice was needed. This strategy also empowered the faculty to look to each other and experience a shared inquiry into development of the new curriculum instead of it being delivered top-down from the WPA. This work also ensured that multiple perspectives and ideas were generated rather than constraining the vision of what courses and assignments should look like through the lenses of a few leaders.

Ad Hoc Committee Work

By mid-spring of the first year, we were hearing from students in 1102 that they were being asked to repeat course assignments from 1101, a problem we had not anticipated. In response to this issue, we put together an ad hoc committee charged with clarifying the differences between the first and second semester of our two-course sequence. We needed to ensure that we all understood what each course aimed to do, what assignments were appropriate for each and, most important, why.

During the committee's first meeting, we discussed at length our goal of not constraining faculty by standardizing the curriculum, but nonetheless acknowledging that some consistency was necessary to honor the spiral nature of literacy development while also scaffolding coursework appropriately from 1101 to 1102. As you might imagine, discussions were rich and sometimes heated as faculty struggled to first define key concepts and learning outcomes for each course and then consider what types of assignments were most appropriate to reach those outcomes. We opted to survey the faculty to get a sense of how they saw the distinction between 1101 and 1102 and what their goals were for each course:

> Survey questions:
> What, in your understanding, are the goals of 1101 and 1102?
> What are your individual learning goals for students in these classes?
> How do you think 1101 and 1102 are connected? How do you think they are distinct?
> What assignments are you using in 1101 and 1102?
> What textbook or other readings are you using?

The committee used the data from this survey to map out distinctions. One of the bigger breakthroughs was a decision to push all secondary research into the second semester, reserving the first course for inquiries into writing studies, writing as dialog, and the writing self. We agreed that a primary research project, like an ethnography, was a better choice for the first semester to facilitate students' critical engagement with discourse communities of interest to them. The second semester would expose students to an extended research project driven by inquiry, with the final product taking many forms born out of rhetorical awareness of genre and purpose rather than a formulaic, thesis-driven academic essay.

Faculty Conference for Fall Orientation

One year in, we modeled our fall faculty orientation on a mini-conference where faculty presented ways they had implemented the curriculum the previous year or what they had planned for the coming year. We had a call for proposals in the spring, and in the fall, there were several concurrent sessions during two different time blocks that faculty could choose to attend. We had sessions on particular assignments, in-class activities, broad concepts like introducing genre, and several examples of how readings were being used in the course. In the afternoon there was a panel session on ePortfolios, and at the end of the day an engaging whole-group discussion. This day built upon the intentional culture that we as WPAs sought to nurture, the concept of shared inquiry that began with the curricular redesign groups and continued through the promotion of instructor agency and acknowledgment of expertise. We worked hard to balance being responsive to faculty feedback while also supporting everyone with the intellectual engagement required of this shift by providing articles to read, assignments to consider, and lots of small-group or one-on-one meetings. This approach to teaching writing was quite different for our faculty, and its implementation required concerted effort to help faculty wrestle with the shift in ways that made sense for them.

Throughout the first and second year, knowing that faculty still needed scaffolding and support as their thinking and teaching approaches continued to shift, we held in-house workshops and lunch 'n' learns that encouraged faculty to share what assignments, course designs, and texts were working (and which were not). Workshops typically lasted a full day and took place within our own space at no cost to the program. We provided breakfast and lunch as we could based on the program's contingency funds, and we even invited Elizabeth Wardle to host an all-day workshop when the first edition of *Writing about Writing* was released. This was atypical for our program since we don't have a common textbook and are rather wary of publisher influence. But because this was the only textbook of its kind, we took advantage of this opportunity. Lunch 'n' learns were much simpler in nature, lasting no more than two hours at a time, with faculty bringing their own food. While these gatherings expanded the faculty's thinking about WAW, they also provided safe spaces for faculty to raise questions and challenge each other and the WPAs, all in an effort to promote/facilitate buy-in from instructors, something we believed essential to the success of the curriculum and our program in general.

Finally, early in the process we created a writing program site in our course management system to house foundational readings for faculty, archive discussion forums, showcase sample assignments, and capture much of our program and professional development work. We envisioned that the site would be visited often as faculty reflected and redesigned their syllabi each semester, but in truth, as the shift moved forward, faculty visited it less frequently over time, and it now seems to be visited only by new faculty, remaining largely underutilized by everyone else in the program.

Realigning Our Student Learning Outcomes

Our program's most recent work has been to refashion our student learning outcomes for first-year writing. We have general education learning outcomes to meet, but we easily map our own more curriculum-specific ones on top. With the rollout of the new curriculum we revised our SLOs and now, with recent research on threshold concepts, we have revised them again to better match our curricular goals. This latest revision took a full year of discussion, drafting, and revising, with all faculty involved in the process at multiple levels. First, we introduced the idea of threshold concepts and spent the better part of a two-day, full-faculty retreat brainstorming what those might consist of. We relied heavily on the *CWPA Outcomes Statement for First-Year Composition* (Council of Writing Program Administrators. 2014), which had just been released the summer before our retreat in July 2014. After the retreat, we invited Jessie Moore from Elon University to our campus to work with our faculty in further clarifying the notion of threshold concepts and their relationship to transfer.

After we narrowed our faculty's goals down to five major programmatic threshold concepts, we handed the reins over to our Curriculum Committee for further discussion and drafting. It took the committee a full semester to delineate and sculpt those threshold concepts into what could be considered measurable learning outcomes for our program. Overall, this work pushed our program and its faculty into even deeper discussions about what we value and how to ensure student success, strengthening virtually every part of our university's first-year writing student experience. In addition, our new SLOs strive to strengthen our

WAW curricular goals by more directly defining for both students and faculty what skills, practices, and awarenesses should be complicated and shaped for students in our FYW courses.

FIVE YEARS IN: SUCCESSES AND CONTINUING STRUGGLES

The year we implemented the WAW curriculum was also our biannual program assessment year, which brought its own constellation of changes. Since one element of the new courses was that "grades are derived primarily from portfolios that include work generated throughout the term" (course description), WPAs had to revamp the previous assessment model. We had historically used a traditional biannual assessment of single-shot papers, and within the largely formalist curriculum, many faculty knew exactly the formal structures they would teach and could quickly evaluate whether students had filled in these formats correctly or not. The new assessment design would need to use portfolios instead since they were required for each course and represented the capstone work of the semester, and this required practice in rhetorical reading by faculty. This, of course, took some finagling, not only with the logistics of collecting ePortfolio links and distributing them to readers, but with helping faculty read these portfolios rhetorically while identifying what we value in our program.

Over the past five years we have tried a number of approaches to portfolio assessment and are still working on it, but a few substantive changes related to program assessment have resulted: (1) we now have a tradition of end-of-semester program assessment workshops at the end of *every semester*, not just on mandated program assessment years; (2) these workshops are grounded in collaborative inquiry into and dialog about what, how, and why we are enacting our curriculum and how we can best tell if it's working. We've looked at portfolio assignments, discussed the merits of various web-based platforms, and have had speakers like Bob Broad, who came to lead us in a dynamic criteria mapping (DCM) workshop that we applied in our most recent program assessment (see Broad 2003). The DCM workshop ultimately revealed a need to dig deeper into what we mean by reflection, or what we came to call critical reflection, and this concept became a focus of our PD for the following semester. By explicitly connecting program assessment, classroom practice, and critical reflection on both a micro and a macro level, we are able to develop ongoing PD experiences in response to faculty desires.

Overall, the curriculum shift has been transformative, both for faculty and students. There is still much WPA work left to do, but one particular benefit of our engagement with a WAW curriculum continues to be FYW faculty's increasingly visible role as collaborators across campus, involved in various general education initiatives related to writing. We've also noticed a marked difference in the number of faculty pursuing writing studies research and developing interest in the scholarship of teaching and learning. Because we were intentional about it, for the most part, our faculty express a sense of ownership and authority over their teaching and the program as a whole more and more each year.

Now that we are five years into our not-so-new curriculum, we often use the terms *WAW* and *writing studies* interchangeably because some faculty perceive WAW as too narrow an approach. We recently attempted to gauge our faculty's identification of the curriculum as WAW or writing studies through a faculty survey. The responses showed that 74 percent of faculty respondents consider it a writing studies curriculum while roughly 63 percent consider it WAW. In the survey, a few faculty shared this sentiment: "I see the 'writing about writing' approach as more directly connected to the Rhetoric & Composition field, probably because I was introduced to this term via the Elizabeth Wardle textbook [Wardle and Downs 2014]. I see 'writing studies' as a broader approach, more inclusive of other fields that study writing, and more open to an interdisciplinary approach." Another faculty member wrote: "For me, 'Writing studies' is an umbrella term while 'writing about writing' is an approach within the writing studies field, similar to 'writing to learn.'" The majority of our faculty respondents, however, saw no "difference between the two. It's two names for the same thing." We note this issue of terminology because it influences how we talk about and enact the curriculum within our program and describe it to the broader university (see figures 13.1 and 13.2). This difference in how strongly faculty identify 1101 as a WAW/writing studies approach compared with 1102 makes sense since 1101 is more directly WAW and, in some ways, points to success in our efforts to distinguish 1101 from 1102. As WPAs, we aren't greatly concerned about this on the practical side, since most of our faculty seem to be moving toward our goal of a consistent experience for our FYW students. An unexpected revelation in this survey was how strongly faculty identify as writing teachers. As one faculty member expressed it, "I have an MA in English Lit although I teach first-year writing now." This sense of identifying as writing teachers combined with a freestanding writing program has been a powerful confluence of identity shaping.

Far and away, we feel that our students have benefited most from our shift toward a writing about writing approach. We are helping student writers become more adaptive and agile as they move through various

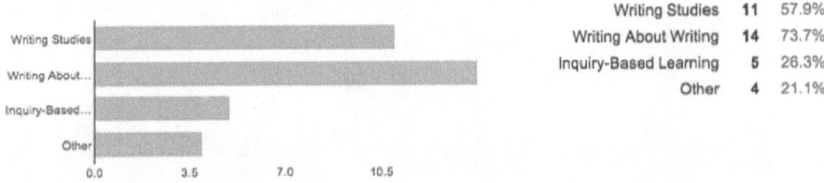

Figure 13.1.

writing situations. They are more flexible and inquisitive researchers who question and compose in rhetorically responsive ways rather than through formulaic compositions. In an effort to document this success more concretely, we are embarking on the first-ever longitudinal study of writing instruction on our campus. We anticipate that this will not only reveal how and when students are transferring the writing strategies from their FYW courses to other writing courses across the disciplines, but also help us hone down which aspects of our curriculum are effective and which need to be revisited.

While our narrative of transforming our FYW curriculum from a formalist to a social constructivist stance is complex, we can confidently say that the gains we've experienced—the growth in our faculty's engagement with writing studies research and their investment in and ownership of our first-year writing program, along with improvements in student writer competencies—are due for the most part to our having shared the journey through adopting, designing, and regularly revisiting the programmatic values of our writing about writing curriculum.

REFERENCES

Broad, Bob. 2003. What We Really Value: Beyond Rubrics in Teaching and Assessing Writing. Logan: Utah State University Press.

Council of Writing Program Administrators. 2014. CWPA Outcomes Statement for First-Year Composition (3.0). http://www.wpacouncil.org/positions/outcomes.html.

Downs, Douglas, and Elizabeth Wardle. 2007. "Teaching about Writing, Righting Misconceptions: (Re)Envisioning 'First-Year Composition' as 'Introduction to Writing Studies.'" College Composition and Communication 58:552–84.

Wardle, Elizabeth, and Doug Downs, eds. 2014. Writing about Writing: A College Reader. 2nd ed. Boston: Bedford/St. Martin's.

PART II

Process

14
Vignette

COMMUNITY COLLEGE COMPOSITION, CRITICAL LITERACY, AND THE WRITING ABOUT WRITING CURRICULUM

Shawn Casey

> INSTITUTION TYPE AND SIZE: 24,000-student regional community college
>
> COURSE CONTEXT: First-year writing course in a general education sequence
>
> STUDY DESIGN/METHODOLOGY: Case-based reflection
>
> WAW PROGRAM OR NOT: Stand-alone WAW approach to a first-year writing course
>
> WAW COURSE OR SINGLE ASSIGNMENT/UNIT: Single unit for a WAW course
>
> INSTRUCTOR TYPE/POSITION: Tenured associate professor, now assistant professor
>
> KEY TERMS: Critical literacy; community college; literacy narrative; first-year composition

At an open enrollment institution like mine, first-year writing is an introduction to almost every aspect of college work. This includes course and composition technologies, the formal and informal expectations of assessment and attendance, the physical and virtual campus environment, and college culture in general. Further, our courses are sometimes the first experience of college for a student's entire family. So we have a special imperative to meet the needs of our "generation one" students. Most recently, our courses have come to be viewed by our state legislature as an extension of the secondary school curriculum. Through concurrent enrollment partnerships ("dual credit" at our school) and curriculum alignment initiatives, our course objectives, teaching strategies, and textbooks are now shared as part of a statewide grade 7–14 "College Credit Plus" mandate. This means our composition courses are now sometimes taught in high schools and our students may enroll as early as middle school. These realities upset the binaries that shape our profession, as Miles McCrimmon (2010) argues in his survey of the political ecology of dual-credit writing courses (209). As the context of the "first-year" writing course evolves beyond the model of the four-year school, the content of the course should also adopt new strategies to do more than introduce students to a standardized image of academic writing.

In my own courses, using critical literacy maxims as loose guidelines to help keep students focused on investigating and building a critical perspective on their writing has helped me bring WAW pedagogy into alignment with our larger institutional guidelines and outcomes. Ira Shor, a compositionist who collaborated with the originator of critical literacy pedagogy, Paolo Freire, has described critical literacy as "literacy for questioning society" (Shor 1999). In the writing about writing classroom, it may be enough to say that critical literacy pedagogy allows students not only to research but to critique the conditions of their own experiences of literacy. So in my courses, we work to develop a "literacy for questioning literacy."

For example, for the last several years I have taught a literacy-themed assignment sequence in my developmental writing classes. Students write a brief narrative about a literacy they bring to the classroom, interview teachers or practitioners in their current field of study about literacy, and reflect on their learning about literacy at the end of the course. The critical literacy goals of the course are broad and experiential. The outcomes do not require students to develop a critical perspective on literacy as a culturally defined and institutionally mandated practice. Yet this is what happens. Students cross a threshold at some point during the semester. They move from puzzled incredulity at the requirement to write about "reading and writing" to a more sophisticated understanding of the growing reading and writing requirements of their world. They build a foundation for later work that requires a more sophisticated rhetorical understanding of literacy. And by recognizing and writing about how literacy is learned, or not learned, they begin to build a context for understanding why so much emphasis is placed on "processes" in their later courses.

This past semester, one student shared with the class her experience interviewing a clinical supervisor. As she worked through the questions about the literacy requirements for a counseling position, she noted that the supervisor became more and more evasive in her responses. The student observed that the counselor clearly hadn't given much thought to the literacy requirements of the job. The student shared how further questions concerning technology and software and reporting requirements revealed the unacknowledged literacy expectations that we had discussed in class.

In another example, I spoke with a department chair who had been interviewed by one of my students about literacy requirements in the healthcare field. She was curious about why some of the questions seemed to revolve around "basic" literacy when, from her perspective, her field required a much more sophisticated level of reading and writing from students. This is precisely the category mistake that Downs and Wardle (2007) describe—advanced or "college-level" writing expectations somehow come to subsume basic literacy requirements like careful and close reading or proofreading at the level of the sentence or word. These are the assumptions that critical literacy reveals, and writing about writing is a key tool in this process. Our conversation turned to one of the chair's key concerns: improving her students' work with citation formatting. To the chair, conquering citation styles and formatting was an "advanced" literacy skill associated with academic writing. Yet when we unpacked the actual value of this skill to her students, we began to talk about such "basic" concepts as the purpose of standardization, punctuation, and proofreading—all important concepts in the healthcare field.

The conversations initiated by this approach to WAW may not draw directly on writing studies scholarship, but they initiate a conversation that raises critical awareness of the literacy practices that underlie professional and academic writing. This assignment sequence helps bring critical concepts about literacy to the fore by asking students, and community members, to investigate and reflect on their own literacy practices. Mark Blaauw-Hara (2014) describes another example of how WAW concepts helped him align his own work as a WPA with the general education goals of his small community college (357). Blaauw-Hara admits his research data provides only a rough approximation of the effect of WAW pedagogy in his classroom. However, he also makes the important point that his results allowed him to "start a larger conversation about transfer and writing" at his institution. He describes how, by gathering institution-specific data, he was able to use the study as a "jumping-off point for several presentations and workshops for faculty" (359). When the focus is on "community" education, these conversations are an important step in developing a context where WAW makes sense for diverse institutional aims.

While the community college context may initially seem to present an obstacle to WAW pedagogies developed in universities or drawing on academic research on writing, this contrast can itself initiate important conversations among faculty. Thus, at an institutional level, even small steps toward critical conversations about the content and purpose of the first-year writing course can initiate a move toward WAW. These conversations can help administrators and instructors begin to think through how writing can become the content of the writing course, even in a context where academic research and writing about writing are not programmatic goals endorsed or even imagined by more-removed stakeholders.

After evaluating current first-year writing course content, it may become clear that critical writing-about-writing concepts are already available in community college contexts. For example, the literacy narrative is a popular course assignment in FYC. Similarly, most composition textbooks include significant attention to process work, and students may be familiar with the idea of drafting and editing when they enter a college composition course thanks to the widespread adoption of the process methodology. Since process has been the focus of a significant amount of writing research, supplemental research studies can help students investigate their own writing processes within a research-based, disciplinary framework. And finally, many writing studies scholars have recognized that the turn toward multimodal composition, far from diminishing the focus on written composition, promotes a critical understanding of the technologies and conditions of the construction, distribution, and reception of texts of all kinds. These common elements in contemporary writing classrooms help shift the focus away from the teaching of academic discourse as a monolithic practice dictated by the authority of a textbook or instructor and toward a critical understanding of context-contingent writing—goals that meet the aims of both WAW and critical literacy.

In my community college classroom, I adopt the focus on student experiences and the goal of articulating student "problems" with literacy that are hallmarks of Freirian critical literacy pedagogy (Shor and Freire 1987, 52). Acknowledging that literacy learning presents a set of problems that can be researched, rather than simply errors to be corrected, helps me connect the widely varying experiences of my students to the practice of academic research on writing and literacy. My aim is to help students see that problems with literacy can themselves become the subject of study. Developing this critical perspective on literacy as a legitimate aim in the first-year writing classroom means approaching reading and writing as activities embedded in institutions, processes, technologies, and rhetorical contexts that can be exposed, examined, and understood as part of the research and composing process. This critical perspective allows students to make connections between what Gwen Gorzelsky describes as procedural and conceptual understandings of literacy (2013, 399). When students begin to understand that how they learn has as much importance as what they learn, they begin to reframe their experiences of literacy within an expanded critical context. Researching, remembering, and reflecting on student experiences with writing is an important step in developing this critical perspective.

For example, when given the opportunity, my students often quickly connect the lessons of anthologized excerpts of Rose's (2012) "Blue-Collar Brilliance" or Kozol's (2012) "Fremont High School" to their own experiences of literacy learning. These connections arise in response to problems or challenges posed by the social inequalities addressed in critical literacy pedagogies and often on display in community college contexts. My students recognize, and write about, the undervalued intelligence of working people that Rose describes by providing narratives that reflect on their own experiences or the experiences of family members at work. This is an important step toward building the skills to observe and write about the process of developing college-level reading and writing skills. Similarly, when students read Kozol's description of an underfunded high school, they begin to reflect on and talk about the contexts of their own literacy learning. Significantly, these conversations often involve examinations of both positive and negative high school experiences. This allows me to extend the discussion to include our own physical and virtual campuses, and to discuss the differences between student access and the motivated use of different resources. In a critical context, one that draws on the authority of firsthand experience confirmed by writing research, students have the opportunity to view their own experiences of literacy not as examples of personal shortcomings or limitations, but as acknowledgment of the context-specific experience of literacy and learning.

These are just two mentor texts that have helped me build a critical perspective on literacy that prepares students to research and write about writing in their future assignments. In another assignment, I ask students to interview peers, teachers, or practitioners about the literacy requirements of the courses in their field of study. Each step of this assignment requires students to think about writing in a new way and to develop a vocabulary that helps them describe and investigate the technology, rhetoric, and processes associated with writing in their field. Again, this assignment is grounded in critical literacy pedagogy—it draws on student experience and interest first, and it makes students the authority on literacy, rather than subjecting them to the research findings of others. Building a disciplinary vocabulary but asking students to extend their investigations beyond the writing classroom is one way that I try to encourage the transfer aims of WAW pedagogy. However, I also keep in mind that many of my students will be moving on to four-year schools. In the case of the dual-credit students in our courses, some will probably leave their high schools and move directly to colleges and universities where they will work with professors and grad students with active research agendas in the areas of writing and literacy. So I also justify my focus on critical literacy by emphasizing to students and administrators and other faculty that the purpose of the course is not only to provide appropriate "training" in the reading and writing required at my school but to align student learning with larger trends in higher education.

This critical reflection on literacy borrows from critical literacy studies by emphasizing a focus on students' experiences of literacy. But it also augments that reflection in a way that should be recognizable to the proponents of WAW. When we bring the experience of literacy learning and literate activity into the realm of academic inquiry, students are encouraged to examine not only their own experiences but also the myriad functions, meanings, and processes of literacy itself. This approach, hopefully, allows students to begin to develop a critical perspective on literacy that brings them across a threshold, to borrow a currently popular term, because it offers a new understanding of how to think critically and actively about reading and writing as subjects of research, inquiry, and ongoing examination.

REFERENCES

Blaauw-Hara, Mark. 2014. "Transfer Theory, Threshold Concepts, and First-Year Composition: Connecting Writing Courses to the Rest of the College." *Teaching English in the Two-Year College* 41 (May): 354–65.

Downs, Douglas, and Elizabeth Wardle. 2007. "Teaching about Writing, Righting Misconceptions: (Re)Envisioning 'First-Year Composition' as 'Introduction to Writing Studies.'" *College Composition and Communication* 58 (June): 552–84.

Gorzelsky, Gwen. 2013. "Experiential Knowledge: How Literacy Practices Seek to Mediate Personal and Systemic Change." *College English* 75 (March): 398–419.

Kozol, Jonathan. 2012. "Fremont High School." In *The Norton Reader*, edited by Linda Peterson et al., 367–71. New York: Norton.

McCrimmon, Miles. 2010. "Contesting the Territoriality of 'Freshman English': The Political Ecology of Dual Enrollment." In *College Credit for Writing in High School*, edited by Kristine Hansen and Christine R. Farris, 208–26. Urbana, IL: NCTE.

Rose, Mike. 2012. "Blue-Collar Brilliance." In *The Norton Reader*, edited by Linda Peterson et al., 393–400. New York: Norton.

Shor, Ira. 1999. "What Is Critical Literacy?" *Journal of Pedagogy, Pluralism and Practice* 1 (4). http://www.lesley.edu/journal-pedagogy-pluralism-practice/ira-shor/critical-literacy/.

Shor, Ira, and Paulo Freire. 1987. *A Pedagogy for Liberation: Dialogues on Transforming Education*. New York: Palgrave.

15
Vignette

FYC STUDENTS AS WRITING STUDIES SCHOLARS
Promoting Procedural Knowledge through Participation

Andrew Ogilvie

> INSTITUTION TYPE AND SIZE: 5,000-student, Jesuit liberal arts university
> COURSE CONTEXT: Hybrid writing-speaking course as part of first-year requirement in core curriculum
> STUDY DESIGN/METHODOLOGY: Case-based reflection
> WAW PROGRAM OR NOT: Stand-alone WAW course in a core curriculum
> WAW COURSE OR SINGLE ASSIGNMENT/UNIT: Sequence of WAW assignments in WAW course
> INSTRUCTOR TYPE/POSITION: Staff lecturer, now assistant professor
> KEY TERMS: Discourse community; genre; enculturation; declarative knowledge; procedural knowledge

It is perhaps orthodoxy among writing studies scholars today that student writing experience is improved when writing tasks are situated within authentic rhetorical environments and meaningfully align genre with audience, content, and purpose (Soliday 2011; Downs and Wardle 2007). Developing authentic, contextualized genres and environments within the classroom, however, is no doubt a complex challenge. The WAW approach that informs my FYC course attempts to address this challenge by providing students with a simulation of the experience of writing oneself into a discourse community—in this case, the discipline of writing studies. In doing so, students develop both declarative and procedural knowledge of writing that becomes a framework, or language, from which they can approach future writing situations. To achieve this outcome, the course's central assignment asks students to contribute to an ongoing debate within writing studies over the notion of a universal academic discourse, using their disciplinary majors as a case study. Students do a corpus analysis of their discipline's academic discourse and then, using our field's genre features and rhetorical strategies, stake a claim over the stability and uniformity of writing across disciplines. The course's emphasis on helping students think about how they approach writing, as opposed to focusing on teaching a set of closed writing skills, echoes the conception of a WAW course set forth by LaRiviere in this volume. Students' experience of writing themselves into an academic discipline provides them with a way of integrating new knowledge of writing and understanding how they might enlist this experience and knowledge in future courses.

In the first few weeks, students and I discuss their perceptions of writing and how students sometimes come into college with somewhat limited understandings of writing. I note that a key goal of this course is to encourage them to begin thinking about writing as a more complex social activity with critical stakes for human pursuits and goals. I also explain how this course provides them with a "theory" and language for writing that is made up of disciplinary concepts. These core concepts are Beaufort's (2004, 2007) five knowledge domains—discourse community, genre, rhetorical, subject matter, and process. Together, we identify examples of these concepts and talk about the relationships between them. We read Gee (1989) to understand how language practices are situated in discourse communities, and we talk about how membership in our own communities (soccer player, family member, son, Latinx) involves knowing a particular discourse. Gee's theory of enculturation explains the apprenticeship process of entering a discourse community, and we connect this concept to students' own experiences of becoming a cashier, waiter, or dancer. Importantly, I discuss how the curriculum of their college major is designed as an enculturation process.

To initiate the project, I first provide a short overview of ecology theory and describe how texts perform functions within systems. An academic article, I note, is part of a complex set of networks comprised of universities, departments, and disciplines. Professors' roles within this ecology are twofold—to teach and to create new knowledge. To create new knowledge, professors do research, identify a gap or debate in existing research, and then argue their own position in the genre of an academic journal article. This short overview of the relationship between texts, professors, and academia ideally provides students with a more contextualized and demystified understanding of a journal article.

Having established this ecology, I then introduce them to a central debate in our field involving whether a single academic discourse exists, and whether writing instructors should or could teach a set of "general" writing skills. We read Theresa Thonney's (2011) article "Teaching the Conventions of Academic Discourse," identify her central claim, the evidence, and the "how" of the article. Telling students that they are apprentices in my discipline as part of an enculturation process, I then explain that they are being asked to create new knowledge, as a professor would, in composing their own academic article within the field of writing studies. The students then collect five articles from journals within their major, replicating Thonney's corpus analysis method, and evaluate the articles using Thonney's six "moves of academic discourse" as an analytic tool. Their article then addresses several questions. Is Thonney's claim accurate? Are the six moves evidenced in your field's writing? Is there hedging in your field? How might these features connect to the discipline's content and epistemologies? Ultimately, what portrait can we draw of writing in your major from our analysis?

Students ask about the generic features of their own article, and I tell them they should try to assimilate not only the structure of Thonney's article but also the lexical bundles, the hedging, and how she uses evidence. This explicitly assimilative process is designed to enact Bakhtin's (1986) notion of *ventriloquation*. The assimilation they do here, I make explicit, is the kind of approach they will need in their major. Ultimately, the course's overarching aim is to move students recursively between knowing *what* and knowing *how*, to go from understanding a genre as situated and purpose-driven to actually being situated and driven by a purpose in knowingly acting within a genre.

REFERENCES

Bakhtin, M. M. 1986. *Speech Genres and Other Late Essays*. Translated by V. W. McGee. Austin: University of Texas Press.

Beaufort, Anne. 2004. "Developmental Gains of a History Major: A Case for Building a Theory of Disciplinary Writing Expertise." *Research in the Teaching of English* 47:136–85.

Beaufort, Anne. 2007. *College Writing and Beyond: A New Framework for University Writing Instruction*. Logan: Utah State University Press.

Downs, Douglas, and Elizabeth Wardle. 2007. "Teaching about Writing, Righting Misconceptions:(Re)Envisioning 'First-Year Composition' as 'Introduction to Writing Studies.'" *College Composition and Communication* 58:552–84.

Gee, James Paul. 1989. "Literacy, Discourse, and Linguistics: Introduction." *Journal of Education* 171:5–17.

Soliday, Mary. 2011. *Everyday Genres: Writing Assignments across the Disciplines*. Carbondale: Southern Illinois University Press.

Thonney, Teresa. 2011. "Teaching the Conventions of Academic Discourse." *Teaching English in the Two-Year College* 38:347–62.

16
Vignette

PROCESSES OF ENGAGEMENT
A Community College Perspective

Olga Aksakalova and Dominique Zino

> INSTITUTION TYPE AND SIZE: 20,000-student urban two-year college
>
> COURSE CONTEXT: Stand-alone FYW and required general education course
>
> STUDY DESIGN/METHODOLOGY: Pedagogical reflection
>
> WAW PROGRAM OR NOT: WAW-enhanced first-year writing course
>
> WAW COURSE OR SINGLE ASSIGNMENT/UNIT: Single unit
>
> INSTRUCTOR TYPE/POSITION: Tenure-track assistant professors, now associate professors
>
> KEY TERMS: Two-year college; voice; identity; writing process; community of practice

LaGuardia Community College is one of the largest two-year colleges in the City University of New York system, with close to 20,000 full-time students who hail from over 150 different countries. The majority are first-generation college students (51 percent, which is 15 percent higher than the national average). As teachers, we understand our composition classrooms as borderlands between the comforts of nonacademic discourse and unfamiliarity with academic communities. We have found that some students perceive the writers they read in college classrooms as "naturally" talented, exempt from fumbling through a writing process. In fact, many college students seem to have the impression that to be a good writer means simply to be *beyond* process, which may lead to a lack of motivation. A writing about writing disposition heightens our awareness of students' struggles to recognize the centrality of writing processes; at the same time, it points to ways for students to work productively within these struggles and to learn to navigate them.

DOI: 10.7330/9781607328421.c016

Early in a semester, when the students begin to concretize the laboriousness of a composing process through both language and practice, we introduce two texts in the same class period: Katherine Schulter's (2011) "Why I Write: Q. and A. with Seven *Times* Journalists" (suggested in Wardle and Downs' [2014] *Writing about Writing*) and Anne Lamott's (1994) "Short Assignments" from *Bird by Bird: Some Instructions on Writing and Life*. Read together, these texts illustrate that even professional writers experience writing as an unwieldy and at times anxiety-producing process. Students identify with journalist Simone S. Oliver when she admits, "I often get overwhelmed by all the information I've gathered," and smirk in disbelief when Michael Luo describes his habit of "sketch[ing] out a couple of different versions" of a text (Schulter 2011). Faced with a writing process that is much more elaborate than they anticipated, students take comfort in Lamott's "Short Assignments," which suggests a way out of anxiety and procrastination: dividing a seemingly overwhelming project into manageable small tasks. As writers like Lamott, Oliver, and Luo acquire a presence in our classrooms, the uncertainty they express becomes an invitation for students to verbalize their current experience with drafting. They also help to remind students that prewriting activities scaffolded into their assignments are not "busy work" but necessary steps toward thinking as writers that ultimately generate the essay content. As a result of this initial writing about writing work, many students produce increasingly nuanced descriptions of their composition processes as the course unfolds, suggesting their deeper engagement with revision.

Later in a semester, sometimes writing about writing moments emerge organically as the students respond to challenges presented by course readings and assignments. As teachers, we aim to provide models of how writers "self-scaffold" to foster learning experiences that neither we nor our students could have written into a syllabus. Take, for example, the following scenario: At 1:30 a.m., midway through the semester in a first-year writing course, a student struggling to respond to an assigned course text—Sherry Turkle's *Alone Together* (2011)—emails her professor. The class is in the midst of refining research topics related to how technology impacts human relationships. With all the enthusiasm and exhaustion that spurs a late-night/early-morning email, this student dashes off a multiparagraph explanation of how she thought her paper would be about "concentration," yet she was unable to find her own take on the topic after rereading passages from Turkle's book. Frustrated, she turns to another author, Nicholas Carr, who writes about technological change and human cognition. Sensing a stylistic difference between

Carr's (2008) scientific arguments and Turkle's often anecdotal evidence, the next thing she does takes her from a novice writer to an innovative *writer about writers*: she turns to one of Carr's recorded public lectures on *YouTube* and starts to transcribe about sixteen minutes of it. She sends the professor her transcription along with an explanation about why hearing Carr's voice is helping her find a way to loosen Turkle's expert grip and insert herself into the discussion about concentration (and why, as you may have already guessed, she needs an extension to finish her draft). Stepping back from both authors, the student feels ready to declare a new research focus: not "concentration" exactly, but "the interrupted life"—a phrase that, for her, now rings with potential examples and associations, whereas the previous phrase fell flat. By stepping away from the course text, she has made space for her own voice to begin to emerge.

The next time the student and professor meet, the professor asks her to record, in her own speaking voice, her late-night email about her thinking and writing process, calling it a "process podcast." The professor senses that the act of recording an unwieldy process could help both herself and the student get underneath a dulled sense of a research topic as a static, preexisting entity and illuminate, in the student's own words, how a research focus can emerge from a writer's productive struggle with others' voices. Moreover, in following semesters, listening to the process podcast becomes a valuable model for other students at the moment when they are preparing to do the critical thinking necessary to generate research topics. By slowing down and drawing attention to students' metacognitive awareness of their own thinking processes, these recorded commentaries themselves become writing about writing texts.

Writing about writing strategies enable us to widen our classrooms to include voices that our students could not hear previously: those of more experienced writers and their own inner voices on the subject of writing, perhaps externalized for the first time. To dispel the myth that strong writers have moved beyond a process, we try to summon the presence of a writing community into the classroom early on in the semester. Then, as students gain more facility with the writing process, we try to stay primed to how their own innovative approaches to writing challenges might emerge and inform our teaching methods.

REFERENCES

Carr, Nicholas. 2008. "Is Google Making Us Stupid?" *Atlantic*, July/August. http://www.theatlantic.com/magazine/archive/2008/07/is-google-making-us-stupid/306868/.

Lamott, Anne. 1994. "Short Assignments." In *Bird by Bird: Some Instructions on Writing and Life*, 16–22. New York: Anchor Books.
Schulter, Katherine. 2011. "Why I Write: Q. and A. with Seven *Times* Journalists." *New York Times*, October 17. learning.blogs.nytimes.com/2011/10/17/why-i-write-q-and-a-with-seven-times-journalists/.
Turkle, Sherry. 2011. *Alone Together: Why We Expect More from Technology and Less from Each Other*. New York: Basic Books.
Wardle, Elizabeth, and Doug Downs, eds. 2014. *Writing about Writing: A College Reader*. 2nd ed. Boston: Bedford/St. Martin's.

17
Vignette
ENGINEERING WRITING ABOUT WRITING IN ENGINEERING
Experiments in Technical Writing and Collaborative Design

Andrew Lucchesi

> TYPE AND SIZE: 16,000-student public liberal arts university
> COURSE CONTEXT: Second course in a two-course writing program; required general education sequence
> STUDY DESIGN/METHODOLOGY: Case study
> WAW PROGRAM OR NOT: Individual WAW course design
> WAW COURSE OR SINGLE ASSIGNMENT/UNIT: WAW course
> INSTRUCTOR TYPE/POSITION: Graduate student instructor, now assistant professor.
> KEY TERMS: Engineering; technical writing; genre analysis; digital composition; advanced composition

For three years I have taught first-year and advanced composition courses for declared engineering majors at an urban STEM-focused four-year college. As a PhD student specializing in writing studies and digital composing, I have used these courses to experiment with WAW approaches to technical writing and writing in the disciplines (WID) instruction. While I retain the standard learning goals established by the English department, which administers the two-course WID-inspired writing sequence for the engineering majors, my approach to incorporating WAW content into the curriculum is far from the norm.

For the instructors who teach these Writing for Engineers courses—many of whom are graduate students in the college's English MA programs—the English department recommends a mishmash of two equally current-traditional curricula. The first suggested curriculum uses textbooks featuring prescriptive definitions of technical genres, with model assignments requiring students to practice lab reports and technical memos based on hypothetical engineering scenarios; the second variant asks students to compose conventional assignments on science topics (for example, compare and contrast essays about ethical technology research).

While novice instructors with little or no engineering background could easily teach these recommended curricula, the curricular emphasis on hypothetical genre performance and textbook authority asks little of students' technical knowledge of engineering or its discursive practices, thus limiting their creative abilities to combine these coexisting professional practices and consequentially apply them. Elsewhere in the university and in the work world, engineers write lab reports, memos, and technical specifications, and they do so from a position of deep professional investment that emerges from their own hands-on work in the laboratory, building site, or design studio. These courses, however, are not linked with engineering labs or engineering content courses—they are stand-alone four-credit writing courses—and as a result, the curriculum lacks the rhetorical specificity and authentic problem solving that characterize engineering as a field.

Based on Wardle and Downs's writing about writing (WAW) approach (2011), I developed a more student-centered, discipline-concentrated writing course for engineers. I designed the curriculum I describe in this chapter for a second-level advanced writing for engineers course; however, I have also employed many of these assignments in introductory-level courses as well. I call my approach "writing for engineers about writing in engineering" (WEAWE). By focusing on concepts of *genre, discourse communities*, and *writing process*, the WEAWE approach places students in the position of writing researchers. Throughout the course, students constantly investigate engineering language usage, experimenting with the scholarly tools of composition/rhetoric and applying those heuristics and strategies to discover the nature of disciplinary discourses and composing practices within the field of engineering.

At the beginning of the term, I ask students to explore John Swales's (2009) definition of *genre*. Many students enter the course with an expectation that genre conventions are dictated wholly in advance by authorities (such as textbooks). In Swales's model, however, genres emerge from the professional and rhetorical aims of writers (14). Accordingly, Swales argues that we learn to master new genres through a process of "consciousness raising" by which we come to understand both the traditional forms and the local exigencies that "color" each genre performance (5). This more nuanced and rhetorically connected model of genre allows students to frame their "consciousness raising" about genre conventions within their burgeoning understanding of the professional lives of engineers.

In the culminating project for this first unit, students work in groups to research a genre of writing used by professional engineers. After gathering real-world examples of the genre from online searching and a survey of a range of technical writing handbooks, students work in groups to produce a website aimed at an audience like themselves, novice engineering students on their own campus. After debating possible genres to focus on, students mine a wealth of text resources (analog and digital) to create well-researched and eminently usable genre guides about lab reports, technical memos, grant proposals, and other genres key to science and engineering professions.

Rather than emphasizing the coverage of certain prescribed technical genres—as the department-recommended curriculum does—this approach centralizes the metacognitive processes of genre acquisition. Rather than trusting one authoritative source, students learn to analyze genre models, to make generalizations, and to formulate plans for performing in unfamiliar genres. Further, the genre tutorial websites students create are themselves group experiments in genre consciousness raising, as they must consider the usability, conventions, and design of sites like the Purdue OWL in order to achieve their goals. Throughout this project, students do the research, planning, and design thinking that engineers regularly do on the job, but they also become metacognitive about engineering language practices in the process.

In the final unit of the course, students use the concept of *writing process* to experiment with primary research in the classroom. After we read a range of writing studies research from Wardle and Downs's (2011) second chapter, "Writing Processes: How Do *You* Write?" I ask students to propose their own studies aimed at providing primary evidence about how engineers use writing under professionally defined and disciplinary-imposed circumstances. The projects students develop require them to gather real-world data about the writing lives of engineers, either by studying the texts of professional engineers, which they must gather, or by staging experiments where they can study the writing habits of engineering students of varying experience levels on their local campus.

Students propose a wide range of process experiments, which we debate and vet through a series of written and in-class assignments. Every student is asked to design a group project idea and prepare a two-part proposal for the study. First, they use the class blog to publish a written proposal that lays out a writing process–related question and a proposed method for study. To do this, they must both cite precedent from the writing studies research we read earlier in the unit and lay out a clear and feasible plan for conducting their research in the remaining weeks of the semester. When all the proposals have been posted, students present "lightning pitches," two- to three-minute versions of their proposals. These allow students to discuss the feasibility of each project and to state their interests in one another's projects. Often, the public vetting process allows the class to both winnow out the weaker project ideas and add sharper detail to the strongest ones. After this week of debate and idea sharing, I ask students to select the projects they think are the strongest and to rank their own preference for group placement. My only requirements are that every group have at least three members and that all members of the group agree to a final action plan, which they must submit to me a week after the groups are solidified.

In the most recent semester, five proposals were approved by the class, including a study of the usefulness of focused freewriting for solving calculus questions; a study of effective and ineffective approaches to writing building instructions in prose; and a study of how technical writers revise their building directions based on consumer feedback. We use class time to stage experiments, recruiting volunteers both from within the class and from the wider school of engineering, allowing us access to more advanced engineering students and graduate-level scientists. Through this focus on experimentation and primary research, students not only developed their knowledge of engineering genres, as the more traditional curricula had suggested, but also found audiences to "test" our products that would then lead to more problem solving (and text revision).

Of course, in a semester where we can devote only five weeks to a single unit, a project like this can produce only limited results. In their final research reports and in-class presentations, all five groups from this semester recognized that further research would be necessary to make any definitive recommendations about the benefits of freewriting for math classes, or how to make technical building instructions more user-friendly. Because their writing throughout this unit tied directly into the ambitious experimental projects the students designed, students were able to rehearse the rhetorical challenges of writing as engineers, including balancing technical detail with convincing, intelligible dialog with readers.

In the end, this Writing *for* Engineers *about* Writing *in* Engineering curriculum has been successful because the WAW approach demands students to actively engage in producing the writing knowledge at the center of the course and to make it explicit for themselves. I am hopeful that the model could be scaled up for broader application across the department in the future. For engineering students who thrive on experimentation, design, and collaborative problem solving as a professional habit of mind, a discipline-specific WAW course can offer ways to draw in students from STEM fields who might otherwise find current-traditional writing courses alienating and counterproductive to their field's disciplinary aims.

REFERENCES

Swales, John. 2009. "World of Genre—Metaphors of Genre." In *Genre in a Changing World*, edited by Charles Bazerman, Adair Bonini, and Débora Figueiredo, 1–16. Fort Collins, CO: WAC Clearinghouse and Parlor.

Wardle, Elizabeth, and Doug Downs, eds. 2011. *Writing about Writing: A College Reader*. Boston: Bedford/St. Martin's.

18
Vignette

WRITING ABOUT WRITING PEDAGOGY IN A MIXED MAJOR/NONMAJOR PROFESSIONAL WRITING COURSE

Gabriel Cutrufello

> INSTITUTION TYPE AND SIZE: 4,400-student private liberal arts college
>
> COURSE CONTEXT: Introduction to the major for professional writing majors; required writing course for hospitality management majors
>
> STUDY DESIGN/METHODOLOGY: Case-based theorizing
>
> WAW PROGRAM OR NOT: WAW promoted and encouraged but not required
>
> WAW COURSE OR SINGLE ASSIGNMENT/UNIT: Semester-long single assignment
>
> INSTRUCTOR TYPE/POSITION: Tenure-track assistant professor
>
> KEY TERMS: Business writing; professional writing majors; nonmajors; genres; self-reflective writing

The professional writing program at York College of Pennsylvania, now in its thirteenth year, offers a course entitled Communication in Professional Cultures that serves both the professional writing major and the recently created general education program as an advanced communication course; prior to fall 2015, the course served only professional writing and hospitality management majors. Therefore, sections have a mix of second-, third-, and fourth-year students in various stages of their professional development, which requires a responsive approach to instructional design. In this institutional and course context, writing about writing (WAW) pedagogy meets student needs through a course content that fosters awareness of writing in a variety of professional contexts. Similar to the use of WAW in the first-year composition classroom, a WAW-focused business writing course can show students that "writing is . . . content- and context-contingent" (Downs and Wardle 2007, 558), even as it helps the instructor stay abreast of the many contexts for professional writing students encounter at multiple stages of their education and professional development without the instructor serving as an expert in the variety of disciplines students bring into the classroom. Due to the variety of student majors and career choices, a WAW-focused business course addresses individual student needs by providing an analytical framework that illuminates the various writing practices and social contexts. Usually, business writing courses tend to focus on the genres of professional writing, such as the memo, report, and resume, which are presented as static forms, but this approach is not adequate in the varied context outlined above. Furthermore, integrating a WAW approach with the commonly taught recommendation report genre develops students' ability to communicate as professionals by having them investigate the writing activities in their chosen majors and professions and recommend potential changes to the course based on their research, which fosters students' metacognitive awareness of writing.

WAW pedagogy introduces students to writing studies terminology, critical perspectives, and research activities, and these elements help students construct a meaningful understanding of writing, which fosters a metacognitive awareness that they are more likely to transfer to future writing situations. Sarah Read and Michael J. Michaud (2015) argue that students take generalizable knowledge about writing, rather than specific, discrete writing skills, across the college/work boundaries and suggest that WAW pedagogy can potentially foster transfer of knowledge across those boundaries (428–29). Similar to students reported on in Read and Michaud's article, students enrolled in FCO210 are taught as "*professionals-who-write*" (430). The course assignments stress that students are responsible for applying the generalizable theories of writing to the specifics of their career fields. This approach is combined with more overt reflective moments that help foster the transfer of writing knowledge. For example, students are asked to reflect after each major assignment on how their research informs their understanding of their discipline and what writing strategies they imagine they will have to use in the future. Integrating reflective writing into the recommendation report assignment, making it a central part of the writing experience, develops students' metacognitive awareness and supports the transfer of knowledge from one context to another. Recommendation reports are particularly good at fostering this work because they connect research to real-world needs. In this way, the course adopts reflective writing to activate metacognitive awareness (Walwema and Driscoll 2015, 40).

During the semester-long project, students investigate the writing practices of a career of their choice by interviewing a professional in the field, gathering and analyzing sample documents, and reporting their findings to their classmates in a formal report and presentation. Their research then informs a recommendation report, a common genre in business writing courses. As a cumulative experience, the recommendation report genre requires students to integrate their knowledge of professional writing with the writing studies content of the course, which communicates information and then "offer[s] suggestions about what the readers ought to do next" (Markel 2012, 513). The forward-looking orientation of the genre also challenges students to connect their research with writing studies concepts because they must use their knowledge of professional writing scenarios to imagine the most salient contexts and genres that student writers should familiarize themselves with in a business writing classroom. Markel suggests that the recommendation report follow a "problem-solving model" to identify a need or problem, establish criteria for responding to the need or problem, determine possible courses of action by evaluating them using a critical framework, and formulate recommendations (514–15). In my classes, students do often suggest new examples or genres based on their experiences and use writing studies concepts to explain and substantiate their choices.

Using WAW pedagogy transforms student learning of common business documents from a genre approach focused on form to an exploration of writing as a communal activity facilitated by genres. The students' recommendation report results from their research into genre and the knowledge they gain about writing through reflection. Similar to Read and Michaud's (2015) student letters to upcoming graduates (451), students in the class consider how their work could potentially be applicable to others. The recommendation report requires that students consider what they have learned through research in relation to their future plans, the course goals, and the needs of their classmates. Not only do they study genres in their professional fields, students use the recommendation report genre to enact change that takes into account future students in the course. This work is facilitated by WAW pedagogy, which Downs and Wardle suggest "encourages . . . self-reflection and mindfulness" (2007, 577). The recommendation report genre explicitly requires students to reflect on their learning, the various professional contexts for writing, and the effect of those contexts on writing. Furthermore, as Amy Devitt argues, it is important to keep "generic form and generic contexts united" (2004, 200); having students use the genre of the recommendation report highlights that concept for students and fosters transfer of learning by matching the form of the report with the content and context of the course.

Since a WAW approach helps students to become writing researchers, their findings are essential for the instructor to respond to an ever-changing variety of writing experiences. The recommendation report findings augment future course examples and topics and help to develop the instructor's awareness of the potential contexts and various genres students may experience in the future. Each academic year and major offers different types of student experiences that inform their research. For second-year students who have not completed an internship, the project is a chance to begin to make connections in the professional world and consider areas of interest in their field. For third- and fourth-year students, it is an opportunity to engage more thoroughly with a current internship or to reflect upon a recent internship experience. For professional writing majors, the use of WAW pedagogy introduces and reinforces central concepts of the field, and for nonmajors this approach introduces them to a flexible set of theoretical concepts useful in making sense of diverse writing situations. Each of these experiences is further informed by choice of major, and the resulting recommendation reports can be quite varied and useful for developing the course. For instance, the genre examples can be incorporated into future activities, and the increased awareness of writing contexts has helped the instructor to develop better ways to introduce students to writing studies research methods. Since the college has shifted to a WAC/WID model of writing instruction, several programs now require FCO210 for their majors; given the diverse student and institutional needs this course serves, the use of WAW pedagogy both promotes student research of writing in various fields and helps faculty use student findings when planning future iterations of the course.

REFERENCES

Devitt, Amy J. 2004. *Writing Genres.* Carbondale: Southern Illinois University Press.

Downs, Douglas, and Elizabeth Wardle. 2007. "Teaching about Writing, Righting Misconceptions: (Re)Envisioning 'First-Year Composition' as 'Introduction to Writing Studies.'" *College Composition and Communication* 58:552–84.

Markel, Michael H. 2012. *Technical Communication.* 10th ed. Boston: Bedford/St. Martin's.

Read, Sarah, and Michael J. Michaud. 2015. "Writing about Writing and the Multimajor Professional Writing Course." *College Composition and Communication* 66:427–57.

Walwema, Josephine, and Dana Lynn Driscoll. 2015. "Activating the Uptake of Prior Knowledge through Metacognitive Awareness: An Exploratory Study of Writing Transfer in Documentation and Source use in Professional Writing Courses." *Programmatic Perspectives* 7:21–42.

19
NEGOTIATING WAW-PW ACROSS DIVERSE INSTITUTIONAL CONTEXTS

Sarah Read and Michael J. Michaud

> INSTITUTION TYPE AND SIZE: Various Carnegie institutions
> COURSE CONTEXT: Widely varied
> STUDY DESIGN/METHODOLOGY: Online surveys and follow-up interviews
> WAW PROGRAM OR NOT: N/A
> WAW COURSE OR SINGLE ASSIGNMENT/UNIT: Varies
> INSTRUCTOR TYPE/POSITION: Varies
> KEY TERMS: Multimajor professional writing course; writing about writing–professional writing; diverse institutional types; weak WAW-PW; strong WAW-PW

ABSTRACT

In this chapter, we build on our previous work investigating the intersections of writing about writing (WAW) pedagogies and the multimajor professional writing (MMPW) course by sharing four case studies of MMPW instructors engaged in what we have called a WAW-professional writing, or WAW-PW, instructional approach. We find that multiple factors influence implementation of WAW-PW, including institution type, curricular situation, and instructor training. We argue that as a result of the high variability in pedagogical and institutional conditions surrounding MMPW instruction, scholars in the field of writing studies must weigh "weak" and "strong" definitions when consolidating what we mean by WAW-PW. At stake in the scope of a definition is the inclusivity of a diversity of institutional and curricular situations in which a WAW-PW approach can and does flourish.

INTRODUCTION

Over the years that we were writing our article "Writing-about-Writing and the Multimajor Professional Writing Course" (Read and Michaud

DOI: 10.7330/9781607328421.c019

2015), we frequently speculated that the approach to teaching multi-major professional writing (MMPW) that we were proposing, one in which instructors treat professional and/or technical writing as the *content* of a professional writing course, was one that was likely already in practice in MMPW classrooms across the U.S. Our purpose was not so much to propose a new approach to MMPW instruction as it was to consolidate a vision for MMPW that we imagined already existed in many instantiations.

As we shared our thinking with colleagues at professional conferences, we soon learned that our surmise was, at least anecdotally, correct. We met scores of writing instructors who told us stories of their WAW-inspired classrooms. These narratives often identified common elements of a WAW approach to the teaching of PW—reading (and writing about) academic research in professional writing, projects that positioned students as professional writing researchers, and a focus on reflection that sought to encourage in students new transfer-focused ways of thinking about writing in professional contexts. These instructors were already doing something resembling what we were calling WAW–Professional Writing (WAW-PW) and they were hungry for the opportunity to talk more about their experiences. It was invigorating for us, too, to learn that, in approaching the MMPW course from a WAW framework, we were not alone. What we lacked, however, was ground-level data on the actual experiences of instructors teaching with a WAW-inspired approach.

We also conducted follow-up interviews (ten as of the writing of this chapter) with select respondents to try to better understand their experiences. The case studies reported in this chapter, which are only a portion of the interviews done and transcribed, are products of those interviews. These case studies were selected for inclusion because of their engagement with WAW-PW. The main criterion that we used to identify survey respondents as interview candidates of possible interest to a study about WAW-PW was survey respondents' answers to a question about their *primary* approach to teaching the MMPW course. Those who indicated as a primary approach that they (1) taught students how to do their own research about writing in workplace contexts (twenty-three respondents); or (2) engaged students in reading scholarly texts (thirteen respondents) were selected to be recruited for an interview about WAW and the MMPW. We felt that respondents who identified either of these approaches were likely to have elements of WAW in their teaching philosophy, pedagogy, course design, and/or course content (*even if* they otherwise might not explicitly identify with a WAW approach). In choosing respondents with whom to follow up, we also considered institutional type, in order ensure that our institutional representation was broad.

As our case studies illustrate, instructors' experiences with WAW-PW are highly variable, dependent on myriad factors that vary across institutional type, curricular situation, and instructor training, a point we take up at the end of our chapter as we consider implications of our research and attempt to articulate a consolidated definition of WAW-PW.

PARTICIPANT PROFILE: ABIGAIL ETTINGER
>   Type of institution and region: Research-intensive public university (Midwest)
>   Instructor rank: Full-time, tenure track (pre-tenure)
>   Highest degree: PhD
>   Primary field of graduate training: Writing studies
>   MMPW course number/title: English 303: Scientific and Technical Writing
>   Textbook: *Writing in the Sciences: Exploring Conventions of Scientific Discourse* (Penrose and Katz)
>   Primary approach to teaching MMPW course: Teaching students how to do their own research about writing in workplace contexts

Teaching Philosophy and Motivation

Abigail is a new assistant professor, about to enter her second year on the tenure track. Her pedagogy is informed by her recent graduate training; her dissertation research, which investigated writing across disciplinary contexts; and her experience with WAW pedagogies. Abigail is highly aware of the situational nature of all writing and of the pedagogical value of investigating literacy practices and their social contexts. In the case of teaching technical or professional writing, Abigail asks, "How can I tell students, 'Write an instruction manual'? It just seems so arbitrary. Better for them to investigate, in a particular place, what genres are used and analyze those." Abigail's major pedagogical objective is for her students to develop transferable knowledge about writing in their discipline and future workplace(s).

Experience with WAW-PW: "Born" WAW

When asked to teach ENGL 303, Abigail brought no prior experience with teaching technical or professional writing and no industry background. She did have experience implementing a WAW approach to teaching first-year composition, though, and it was to this experience, as well as her work in writing across the curriculum (WAC), that she turned when she first started to plan her course. "I really valued a writing about writing approach," Abigail explained. "I felt empowered. I felt like I could teach [ENGL 303] if I made it a WAW course." The WAW curriculum that Abigail ultimately devised for ENGL 303 reflects her knowledge of and commitment to WAW (as well as her experience with WAC).

Assembling a "Hybrid" MMPW Course

One of the challenges Abigail has faced in teaching ENGL 303 is understanding the purpose of the course itself. Having taught the class only twice and having played no role in its origination, Abigail must work with the description and outcomes she has been given. What has been especially difficult is understanding how to integrate the two key terms in the course's title. "The course is called Scientific and Technical Writing and that's interesting because those two things might be similar but they might also be different sometimes," Abigail explained. "The students are not scientists who are in the early stages of learning to write in the discipline and they're not in a technical communication BA program." The course draws students from engineering, business, and science/pre-med programs. As a result, Abigail has tried to create a class that integrates both the scientific and the technical, creating a "hybrid" course that offers something to everyone.

Building a WAW-PW Course Sequence

Abigail's ENGL 303 curricular sequence might serve as a model for others looking to experiment with WAW-inspired approaches to professional and technical writing. Students interview a professor in their discipline to learn about scientific research and writing, analyze a scientific article in their field, interview a professional in their future field and study his or her writing, and write a reflective letter on course learning. This sequence moves outward, from academic to professional writing, and asks students to investigate writers, genres, and contexts. "Since there is no way to know what kind of writing [the students] will need to do," Abigail explained, "I decided the responsibility would be theirs—to research the writing that interested them and that they might possibly be doing in the future."

PARTICIPANT PROFILE: BARBARA BELLWOAR

TYPE OF INSTITUTION AND REGION: Baccalaureate college (mid-Atlantic region)

INSTRUCTOR RANK: Full-time, tenure track (pre-tenure)

HIGHEST DEGREE: PhD

PRIMARY FIELD OF GRADUATE TRAINING: Writing studies

MMPW COURSE NUMBER/TITLE: EN 272: Introduction to Professional Writing

TEXTBOOK: None

PRIMARY APPROACH TO TEACHING MMPW COURSE: Teaching students how to do their own research about writing in workplace contexts

Teaching Philosophy and Motivation

Barbara's goals for all of the writing courses she teaches focus on raising students' awareness about writing and teaching transferable skills and knowledge. "I want students to be aware of what they already know about writing and about how the kind of writing they're learning in [a] particular course is different from what they already know about writing," she explained. *Context* is a key term in Barbara's teaching philosophy. In EN 272, for example, she works to help students understand "the differences between writing at school and writing at work." During their workplace research projects, students ask, "What are people writing at work? How are they doing this kind of writing? What are they finding important? How do they acquire these skills so that they can keep using them?" In EN 272 and all her classes, Barbara helps students better understand the situated nature of all writing.

Experience with WAW-PW: Managing Student Expectations

Finding ways to create buy-in among students for the WAW-inspired MMPW course that Barbara has designed has been a challenge. In class and on her syllabus, Barbara works to prepare students for what to expect in the course, "Each organization in the 'real world' is different and will require different kinds of writing. The primary focus of the course will *not* be to teach you the skills you need to write for a professional organization, but to teach you how to learn the skills you need once faced with a professional writing situation." Despite her efforts, Barbara has received push-back from her students on her approach to the course. Whereas Barbara wants to teach them "how to learn the skills [they] will need," they frequently just want her to teach them the skills themselves. One specific point of tension comes from course readings which, Barbara reports, challenge the students to the point where they sometimes disengage with the course and question her authority. To mediate this problem, Barbara has begun to investigate textbooks that will allow her to continue to innovate but also, she hopes, lend the course a sense of authority that she feels it may be lacking in a WAW-PW-inspired approach.

Institutional and Professional Pressures

While Barbara has been encouraged by colleagues in her department to develop courses that draw on her specialized training (they know nothing of WAW and there is no institutional support for this approach to teaching writing), there is no doubt that the institutional situation in which she finds herself at this point in her career impacts her curricular thinking and planning to a considerable extent. Negative comments on student evaluations of instructors at a small, residential, highly student-centered liberal arts college are not tolerated. As Barbara has learned, her efforts to pursue unique pedagogical approaches to teaching writing as a nontenured faculty member may come at a cost. Add to all of this her status as a young, female instructor at an institution where under half of the faculty are female, and it's not hard to understand why Barbara is reconsidering her teaching approach as she approaches her tenure year. Her perceived lack of authority and status as an untenured faculty member, the weight of her students' sometimes traditional expectations, and the reality of the highly student-centered ethos of her institution are pushing her to find ways to mediate some of the more challenging aspects of implementing a WAW-inspired approach to teaching MMPW.

PARTICIPANT PROFILE: MANDY GOODALL

> TYPE OF INSTITUTION AND REGION: Two-year public technical institute/trade school (Plains state)
> INSTRUCTOR RANK: Full-time, non–tenure track
> HIGHEST DEGREE: MA
> PRIMARY FIELD OF GRADUATE TRAINING: English/literature
> MMPW COURSE NUMBER/TITLE: Workplace Communications 110
> TEXTBOOK: *Successful Writing at Work* (Kolin)
> PRIMARY APPROACH TO TEACHING MMPW COURSE: Teaching students to do their own research about writing in the workplace

Teaching Philosophy and Motivation

Mandy's approach to teaching MMPW courses is heavily informed by her concern for the transfer of the more generalized rhetorical knowledge that students learn in a classroom to the very specific applications that they will encounter in their trades. She approaches each element of the course curriculum with the question "How is this relevant?" She works hard to bring relevant writing examples from industry into the classroom and she is explicit about getting students to think about how what they are learning on a specific assignment, such as writing a technical description, will transfer into the context of their particular trade. Mandy's explicit concern for learning transfer shapes how she plans her lessons and how she presents the assignments.

Experience Teaching WAW-PW: Researching Workplace Writing

While overall Mandy's syllabus presents a conventional genre-driven approach to MMPW, her defining WAW-type course element is to send her students out into industry to collect samples of writing, such as brochures, instructions, or even blank incident report and work order forms. In the classroom the students "talk about what they are, how they work . . . and what they need to know and communicate on those documents." Mandy's industry-focused approach and "Aristotelian approach to teaching" are in contrast to some of her colleagues who teach in a lecture-heavy "Just believe what I tell you" mode. Some students expect this approach and respond to her invitations to share their own industry experience with an attitude of "We don't have any experience. That's why we're here, you're supposed to tell us what to do." Overall, student attitude is a constraint that Mandy sees in a trade school environment, but she is optimistic that attitudes "will come back around."

Impact of Department Culture

One of the challenges Mandy cited in developing her WAW-inspired MMPW course is the divergent backgrounds of instructors. For example, instructors from a K-12 background bring with them an expectation of standardized curriculum and teaching practices. They also view standards at the trade college as a step up from their previous experience. In contrast, instructors such as Mandy who come from a "liberal arts" background in higher education have an expectation of "quite a bit of autonomy and instructional license," and view the trade school standards as a step down. Another line of delineation among instructors is industry experience: "The instructors who've been in industry are talking about and using information, drawing on that knowledge. And the instructors who haven't are drawing upon the textbook."

Mandy has experience in industry prior to teaching, which she feels is useful in helping her understand what industry partners need students to be able to do. Teaching load is also an issue; Mandy recently taught four sections of the MMPW course in one term, each with a cap of thirty-two students.

Course Outcomes and Objectives

Mandy's MMPW course is designed around a standardized set of outcomes that were developed by looking to other universities for examples. It is difficult to find precedence, however, for a course that accommodates students from many trades, so, she concedes, "we're guessing." The objectives are on file with the higher learning commission for accreditation and all instructors have to be able to demonstrate in assignments and via assessment that they are being met. Despite some support for professional development around the course from the dean of instructional design, Mandy still feels challenged about the types and structures of the lessons that are standard to the course: "I'm not sure I feel totally confident about knowledge transfer when they [students] go to apply it to the job."

PARTICIPANT PROFILE: AMANDA GEISER
   TYPE OF INSTITUTION AND REGION: Two-year multicampus community college (Pacific Northwest)
   INSTRUCTOR RANK: Tenure track
   HIGHEST DEGREE: PhD
   PRIMARY FIELD OF GRADUATE TRAINING: Composition and rhetoric
   MMPW COURSE NUMBER/TITLE: English 227: Technical/Professional Writing
   TEXTBOOK: *Scenes of Writing* (Devitt, Reiff, Bawarshi)
   PRIMARY APPROACH TO TEACHING MMPW COURSE: Teaching students how to do their own research about writing in workplace contexts

Teaching Philosophy and Motivation

Amanda draws on her strong background in rhetorical genre theory to inform her writing pedagogy. She adopted *Scenes of Writing* for her first section of English 227 after listening to advice from colleagues to "teach the course according to her expertise." Since, unlike some of her colleagues, Amanda doesn't have formal experience with writing in industry, she decided to go with the approach that is "most meaningful to me." Her overall course design first prompts students to choose and analyze a genre relevant to their work/career ambitions, followed by a multistage project in which they produce that genre using what they have learned from analysis. In order to balance students' expectations for a more conventional approach to the course, Amanda also includes a module in the middle of the course on preparing job application materials.

Experience Teaching WAW: Student Expectations

Amanda knew that she would need to prepare students to expect an unconventional approach to her MMPW course. She put language in the syllabus warning that the class would be atypical and encouraging students to adopt a spirit of openness. Despite her efforts to mitigate student expectations, students did push back about wanting a more explicit and conventional curriculum.

Teaching Online

The challenge of enacting an unconventional MMPW curriculum was compounded for Amanda because the course was fully online. One limitation was that Amanda couldn't fall back on in-person and informal explanations of readings and assignments as she could in a classroom setting. Given that students rarely took advantage of office hours or phone conferences, their primary access to the material was text-based. Amanda reported that this created confusion about what kinds of genres they should choose to study. While the textbook mainly used as examples everyday genres such as restaurant menus, many students were training to enter technical trades. The relative isolation of students in an online course setting also meant that they were less likely to learn from each other's experiences.

Course Outcomes and Objectives

Amanda spoke extensively about problems with the outcomes for this course. As head of the department assessment committee, she is invested in assessable writing outcomes. She found the existing outcomes to be so broad that meeting them in a single ten-week course would be impossible. For example, the outcomes include "Read, interpret, analyze, and evaluate complex technical and professional documents and visuals" and "Design and produce the most commonly used business/professional communications." Amanda recognized that they were the product of "a lot of finagling" to get them through the department curriculum committee, but she critiqued the lack of definition of the differences between professional, business, and technical writing and what seemed to be a heavy emphasis on production at the expense of process and analysis.

To design her own section of the course, Amanda used the department outcomes as a starting point, but she plans to start a departmental conversation about improving the outcomes for English 227. While some of her colleagues agree that the professional/technical writing sequence should be longer and that the outcomes need to be improved, a large department (over 100 faculty), a reliance on contingent faculty (75 percent), and the lack of money and incentives make coordinated curricular change difficult. In the case of English 227, many instructors have their courses well-established and view any change in outcomes or curriculum as a question of "how would I fit that in" rather than as an opportunity to rethink the course.

FACTORS THAT INFLUENCE THE TEACHING OF WAW-PW

Our case studies suggest that a number of critical factors influence the teaching of MMPW in U.S. higher education. These factors inevitably impact instructors' ability to design and teach WAW-inspired professional writing courses. In what follows, we identify and discuss several of these critical factors.

Department/Program Standardization

MMPW courses serve many masters. Nonwriting departments and programs, other colleges within the institution, colleagues in other disciplines, and even accreditation agencies of non-writing-based disciplines and fields all influence the design and teaching of MMPW courses. Even in situations where faculty are encouraged to "teach to their strengths," as in the cases of Abigail, Barbara, and Amanda, instructors sometimes confront syllabi, course descriptions, course outcomes, and objectives/standards that often they played no role in creating and that are frequently outdated, misguided, confusing, and/or simply impossible to accommodate. Faced with such standardization, which is sometimes combined with departmental cultures that work against curricular experimentation, innovative instructors may find that implementing new or different approaches to teaching MMPW, such as WAW-PW, can be challenging.

Student Expectations

As we have seen in the stories above, and especially in the cases of Barbara and Amanda, student expectations can impact the design and teaching of MMPW courses to a considerable degree. There is, we feel, a current-traditional approach to teaching MMPW, characterized by a focus on teaching generalized genres of professional communication (e.g., memos, letters, proposals, instructions, reports), that impacts almost all elements of the course. Students learn about this current traditional approach from other students, advisors, textbooks, other instructors, and course descriptions. Faculty attempting to implement WAW-PW approaches to teaching MMPW must inevitably manage student expectations for the current-traditional approach. In some instances, such management may prove successful, even fruitful. In other instances, unsuccessful management can lead to negative implications for faculty.

Lack of Traditionally Sanctioned Teaching Materials

The fact that there are no WAW-PW textbooks or other teaching materials impacts instructors' ability to deliver WAW-PW instruction effectively and persuasively. While some instructors, like Abigail, may find the dearth of such materials invigorating, even liberating, in that they are encouraged to innovate and experiment, others, like Amanda, work to adapt materials that may not be ideally suited to MMPW instruction, and others still, like Barbara, long for the imprimatur and sense of authority that officially sanctioned course materials can bestow upon a course.

Other Critical Factors

Given the constraints of space, we will only briefly identify several additional factors that influence the potential for a WAW-inspired approach to MMPW instruction. Certainly, instructor status is one such factor, as we see in the case of Barbara. Faculty members who are at critical professional/career junctures may avoid WAW-PW approaches, feeling that "playing it safe" is the best option given their liminal status. Teaching load also functions as a critical factor, as we see in the case of Mandy Goodall. Faculty teaching multiple sections of MMPW and large numbers of students may opt for pedagogical approaches that better lend themselves to high-volume teaching. Mode of delivery is another factor impacting WAW-PW instruction. As we see in the case of Amanda, instructors teaching MMPW courses in online formats may face challenges articulating the rationale for a WAW-PW approach to their students or may opt for a more traditional, textbook-driven approach to the course, given the lack of face-to-face opportunities for explanation and contextualization.

CONSOLIDATING OUR DEFINITION OF WAW-PW

The wide range of factors across institutional types that shape and constrain our case study instructors' implementations of WAW-PW in the multimajor professional writing classroom deeply problematizes the project of consolidating what we mean by WAW-PW. With such a diversity of factors shaping the experience of instructors, it is difficult to see how it is possible to develop a set of curricular rationales (Downs 2010, 21), outcomes (i.e., WPA Outcomes Statement), or even a definition that is sensitive to institutional and curricular situations as divergent as a trade school (Mandy Goodall) and a research university (Abigail Ettinger).

Taking the project forward, given the available data from these case studies, we propose that a consolidated notion of a WAW-PW approach include two elements: (1) the instructor places an explicit, although not necessarily formal, emphasis on knowledge transfer in the sense of developing students to become learning transformers of rhetorical knowledge (Read and Michaud 2015, 429); and (2) some elements of the course, including lesson plans, assignments, and/or readings, render professional and technical writing as "studyable" and develop students, either formally or informally, as "researchers" of writing in professional and/or technical contexts. A definitional rubric including just these two elements presents a broad umbrella for WAW-PW that enables instructors from different institutional settings and with different types of training, such as Mandy and Abigail, to fall under the banner of WAW-PW.

However, despite the satisfyingly democratic impulse behind what we might call the "weak" definitional rubric for WAW-PW, we acknowledge that it risks leaving out definitional elements of the WAW approach that are born of the effort to effect substantive change in how writing is conceived of and taught in higher education (Downs and Wardle 2007, 552). For example, a "strong" definitional rubric for WAW-PW would also include elements such as students learning disciplinary knowledge about professional and technical writing from scholarly sources and that the instructor's concern for developing students as learning transformers is formally enacted by assignments that promote forward-reaching structured reflection (445).

We feel that what is at stake for scholars of WAW between a weak and a strong rubric for WAW-PW is an honest consideration of how inclusive WAW can really be across all institutional types. If we define WAW-PW and/or WAW in terms of a few high-level and adaptable elements (such as an undetermined notion of transfer), then there is a lot of potential to broaden the conversation about WAW to include all institutional types, such as community colleges and trade schools. If a WAW-PW approach requires elements that run counter to the various curricular and institutional structures encountered by many instructors, WAW can be an approach accessible only to instructors with a high degree of autonomy over their course outcomes and curriculum and institutional structures that support this autonomy.

We cannot settle the relative value of either a "weak" or a "strong" definitional rubric for WAW-PW in this short chapter. However, when it comes to knowing where to look for and how to identify WAW approaches to teaching writing at work, we feel that there is value for members of the WAW scholarly community to continue to weigh the relative value of a more inclusive "weak" version of what a WAW approach means against the less inclusive but more substantive "strong" version for teaching writing in the MMPW course and beyond.

REFERENCES

Downs, Doug. 2010. "Teaching First-Year Writers to Use Texts: Scholarly Readings in Writing-about-Writing in First-Year Comp." *Reader: Essays in Reader-Oriented Theory, Criticism and Pedagogy* 60:19–50.

Downs, Doug, and Elizabeth Wardle. 2007. "Teaching about Writing, Righting Misconceptions: (Re)Envisioning 'First-Year Composition' as 'Introduction to Writing Studies.'" *College Composition and Communication* 58:552–84.

Read, Sarah, and Michael Michaud. 2015. "Writing about Writing and the Multimajor Professional Writing Course." *College Composition and Communication* 66:427–57.

20
Vignette

A UNIQUE PAIR
Pairing WAW in a First-Year Writing Sequence as the First Step in Academic Research

Frances Johnson

> INSTITUTION TYPE AND SIZE: PhD-granting, Hispanic serving institution; 11,234 students
>
> COURSE CONTEXT: First course in a two-course FYW; required general education sequence
>
> STUDY DESIGN/METHODOLOGY: IRB-approved study of first-year learning communities program with the individual course situated in a discipline-specific learning community
>
> WAW PROGRAM OR NOT: WAW version of a FY learning-community course
>
> WAW COURSE OR SINGLE ASSIGNMENT/UNIT: Sequence of WAW assignments focusing on the introductory freshman writing course
>
> INSTRUCTOR TYPE/POSITION: Professional track assistant professor, now professional track, associate professor.
>
> KEY TERMS: Primary research; learning communities; assignment sequences; FYC

The first low-stakes writings my freshmen do deal with their high school experience with research and writing. Few students write about developing a research question, finding credible sources, and writing using manuscript style; most students' responses tell quite a different story. These responses paint a bleak research picture of being given a question to answer based on a work of literature and then having one class period to "research" in the library. Students' library research experience involves the librarians having arranged a section of books and pre-chosen websites for use. This is why my first semester course's aim is to provide students, who are declared science majors, an introduction into conducting primary research by using the broad area of writing studies as their research basis.

Critical to my creation of a research-based writing course is the inclusion of composition as a course comprising the first-year learning communities. The university enrolls all college students with no college-level transfer courses (FTIC-0) in groups of classes where the students all attend the same large lecture(s) and break-out sections of first-year seminar and first-year composition. While most of the FTIC-0 sections are mixed-major enrollment, my learning community's construction is reserved for declared science majors. Students enroll in four classes: first-year composition (FYC), seminar, biology, and chemistry. In the first-semester composition writing assignments, students use themselves as research subjects and engage with primary source scientific journal articles to conduct a content analysis.

Inspiration for the course came from Russell's (1995) and Wardle's (2009) work indicating that students should engage in writing activities mirroring writing done in legitimate discourse communities. Both scholars call for a reimaging of first-year composition, challenging students to examine writing as a communication tool used in specific ways in specific discourse communities. For Russell and Wardle, the current configuration of FYC was not meeting this challenge.

My original course redesign began in 2006 as a solo effort to tie FYC into the biology and chemistry courses at a time when those teaching the science courses believed that *composition had nothing to offer science students*. I initially focused my composition course as a writing in the discipline (WID) course. With the adoption of the *Writing about Writing* textbook (Wardle and Downs 2011) and concept in the FYWP (supported by my WPA and a dedicated adjunct), I reenvisioned the course. Still focusing on the genres of the scientific discourse community, the new course used writing studies/research as the content for these genres.

Reading foundational scholarship on writing and writing studies supports all FYC courses, and I vary the readings by semester to keep the course fresh for me (see appendix 20.A for a listing). Typically, students read scholarship on research methods, rhetoric, discourse communities, genres, and the place of authentic genres in FYC. These are difficult readings for the students, so I must always keep in mind their reading abilities and metacognitive skills.

One reading I use every semester is Swales's insights into the construction of introductions, the CARS model (1990, 137). Students first read the excerpt in the *WAW* book (Wardle and Downs 2011), then review the entire section from Swales's original text. I begin with Swales because of his work's student-reader friendly nature. Swales provides the opportunity for discussion and practice of *how* professionals compose introductions to research articles. Supporting Swales's blueprint for writing an introduction, I follow up the textbook extract with his original work in order to provide students with an insight into writing as the basis for research. Additionally, students have web-based resources available to them from the course wiki page on Swales's CARS model. I use this work because it provides guidance for these novice students and makes writing introductions a bit less intimidating.

I begin with an auto-ethnography in which the students examine their writing process. The next assignment is a variation; in an ethnography, the students record the writing process of other students, either from the class, the science learning community, or a roommate. The last assignment examines the artifacts produced by the scientific discourse community. For this, the students use the introductions of primary source journal articles found for a research project in their seminar class. I arrange the sequence in this manner to have students begin with looking at writing by using themselves as participants, then easing into a wider participant pool by using the same topic—writing process—but on a larger scale. The concluding work provides the students with the opportunity to apply skills developed in the first two projects by looking at an authentic work of the scientific discourse community, which also ties in with their exposure to Swales's CARS model.

Prior to beginning the auto-ethnography, students read Perl's (1979) research article as a grounding for their methods. For the data set, students record themselves using the talk-aloud/think-aloud method while working on a writing assignment from any class. Students transcribe their recordings and code using a modified version of Perl's coding. The resulting paper is formatted as introduction, materials/methods, results, and discussion (IMRaD). While this may seem formulaic, the IMRaD format is the accepted way to communicate primary research within the scientific discourse community and thus helps introduce these students into how the community exchanges information among its members.

The next assignment, an ethnographic exploration of the writing processes of others, involves more student interaction with research design and research participant, and is supported by having students read more scholarship, such as Greene (2001). I obtained IRB approval because the students are using human participants, and I believe it's necessary to introduce students into the rigor of obtaining permission to use human participants as well as the participant protection such research projects involve. Not only were students given/read the informed consent document, they were required to obtain one for any participant outside of the science learning community. As with the first assignment, students complete an IMRaD-formatted report on their results.

The final assignment involves more scholarship, such as Swales's (1990) work on discourse communities. Students use the methodology of content analysis for examining introductions to primary source journal articles found for a science-based project in their seminar class. The students develop a research question based on language use (for example, how many times are pronouns used), collect and analyze the data, and then compile another IMRaD-formatted article. While this may seem like an extreme sequence for incoming freshmen, students rise to the challenge and produce some remarkable work, as validated by the number of students writing in this genre who win the outstanding writing award in the category of freshman composition presented by our English department.

This vignette illustrates the concept of writing about writing in the freshman composition classroom and its uses as a springboard for teaching students about academic research within a learning community. Because students are working in genres they will encounter in a specific discourse community, such assignments provide grounding for skills that perhaps will transfer into other writing opportunities. While I developed these assignment sequences within a specific discourse community, I believe the foundational principles of writing about writing are applicable in FYC courses inside and outside of a learning community.

APPENDIX 20.A

Course Readings

Greene, Stuart. 2001. "Argument as Conversation: The Role of Inquiry in Writing a Researched Argument." In Wardle and Downs 2011, 10–20.

Haas, Christina, and Linda Flower. 1988. "Rhetorical Reading Strategies and the Construction of Meaning." In Wardle and Downs 2011, 122–37.

Harris, Joseph. 1989. "The Idea of Community in the Study of Writing." In Wardle and Downs 2011, 582–93.

Hyland, Ken. 2004. "Disciplinary Discourses: Social Interactions in Academic Writing." In Wardle and Downs 2011, 700–703.

Kleine, Michael. 1987. "What Is It We Do When We Write Articles Like This One—And How Can We Get Students to Join Us?" In Wardle and Downs 2011, 23–32.

Lamott, Anne. 1994. "Shitty First Drafts." In Wardle and Downs 2011, 301–4.

Penrose, Ann M., and Cheryl Geisler. 1994. "Reading and Writing without Authority." In Wardle and Downs 2011, 603–16.

Perl, Sondra. 1979. "The Composing Process of Unskilled College Writers." In Wardle and Downs 2011, 192–214.

Porter, James E. 1986. "Intertextuality and the Discourse Community." In Wardle and Downs 2011, 87–97.

Rose, Mike. 1980. "Rigid Rules, Inflexible Plans, and the Stifling of Language: A Cognitivist Analysis of Writer's Block." In Wardle and Downs 2011, 237–49.

Swales, John. 1990. "The Concept of a Discourse Community." In Wardle and Downs 2011, 468–79.

Tomlinson, Barbara. 1988. "Tuning, Typing, and Training Texts: Metaphors for Revision." In Wardle and Downs 2011, 252–69.

Wardle, Elizabeth. 2010. "Identity, Authority, and Learning to Write in New Workplaces." In Wardle and Downs 2011, 521–35.

Wardle, Elizabeth, and Doug Downs, eds. 2011. *Writing about Writing: A College Reader*, 1st ed. Boston: Bedford/St. Martin's.

REFERENCES

Greene, Stuart. 2011. "Argument as Conversation: The Role of Inquiry in Writing a Researched Argument." In *Writing about Writing: A College Reader*, edited by Elizabeth Wardle and Doug Downs, 10–20. Boston: Bedford/St. Martin's.

Perl, Sondra. 1979. "The Composing Process of Unskilled College Writers." In *Writing about Writing: A College Reader*, edited by Elizabeth Wardle and Doug Downs, 192–214. Boston: Bedford/St. Martin's.

Russell, David R. 1995. "Activity Theory and Its Implications for Writing Instruction." In *Reconceiving Writing, Rethinking Writing Instruction*, edited by Joseph Petraglia, 51–78. Mahwah, NJ: Lawrence Erlbaum.

Swales, John M. 1990. *Genre Analysis: English in Academic and Research Settings*. Cambridge: Cambridge University Press.

Wardle, Elizabeth. 2009. "'Mutt Genres' and the Goal of FYC: Can We Help Students Write in the Genres of the University?" *College Composition and Communication* 60:765–89.

Wardle, Elizabeth, and Doug Downs, eds. 2011. *Writing about Writing: A College Reader*. Boston: Bedford/St. Martin's.

21
Vignette

RESEARCHING ABOUT RESEARCH, WRITING ABOUT WRITING FROM SOURCES

Elizabeth Kleinfeld

> INSTITUTION TYPE AND SIZE: 22,000-student, urban, modified open-enrollment public university; emerging Hispanic-serving institution
>
> COURSE CONTEXT: Upper-division rhetoric elective for English majors and minors
>
> STUDY DESIGN/METHODOLOGY: Participant research
>
> WAW PROGRAM OR NOT: Not a WAW program
>
> WAW COURSE OR SINGLE ASSIGNMENT/UNIT: Single assignment in a rhetoric, not writing, course
>
> INSTRUCTOR TYPE/POSITION: Tenured associate professor, now full professor
>
> KEY TERMS: Professional writing; WAW; WAW-PW; co-op; STEM

The assignment I describe here is from an upper-division rhetoric course on authorship studies that examines Western concepts of authorship and originality and covers topics including copyright, plagiarism, collaborative authorship, and theories of invention. Rather than assign a typical research paper, I formulated an assignment that uses a WAW approach to help students understand the complexities and nuances of source use. Instead of talking about what students *should* be doing when they write from sources, I have them study how source material is actually integrated into writing by themselves and others. This WAW assignment does what di Gennaro argues in her chapter: "enables and empowers students," engaging them in "analyzing writing for their own uses and contexts."

A key goal of the course is to expose students to the research on writing from sources. To get a sense of how writers refer to and cite sources, students read work by Karen Burke LeFevre (1987) on invention, Rebecca Moore Howard (1999) on source use, and James Porter (1986) on intertextuality. I follow up these readings with an assignment in which students analyze their use of sources, both cited and uncited, in a piece of writing they did for another class; most choose papers from their first-year writing or literature courses. The assignment was inspired by Paul Parker's (2013) suggestion that students study a piece of their own writing for patterns of source use. I ask them to identify moments of intertextuality; cited source use, using the terms and definitions used by the Citation Project (summary, paraphrase, quotation, patchwrite); and other, perhaps more ambiguous, collaborations with texts and/or people.

This assignment asks students to learn about how they as writers write from sources. Rather than trying to teach students *how to write*, the assignment teaches them "*about [their] writing*" (Downs and Wardle 2007, 553) and the effects of the choices they have made in citing sources. The resulting papers are in-depth analyses of specific instances of, as Howard (1999) might say, collaborations with source material.

Students share their conclusions from these analyses with each other in class, noting, for example, that they had overrelied on quotation, they had not cited sources for some of the ideas presented, and that it was often unclear where the cited material ended and their own ideas began. Interestingly, students have also noted that there seems to be little correlation between their finesse with using sources and the grades they earned on the papers. Students also report that they often choose quotation over paraphrase to avoid charges of plagiarism.

As students' metacognitive awareness of their source use develops, their writing from sources becomes more nuanced and rhetorically complex. For example, last semester, in the reflective letters accompanying their final course projects, in which students research a particular aspect of authorship that interests them, every student made an attempt to explain how works not cited in the final paper shaped their thinking about their topic. Nearly every student discussed a challenge they faced in giving enough context for a source reference in their paper, indicating an important move away from cherry-picking quotations from a source to support a point, a move common to the papers analyzed by the Citation Project (Jamieson and Howard 2011). Several students detailed frustrations they felt with the length of one or more of their source quotations, suggesting a desire to move away from overreliance on quotation that perhaps has outpaced their writing skills.

Overall, the assignment helps students see writing from sources as much more than a simple matter of plunking quotations that support their argument into their own writing. As students closely examine their own source use strategies, they build an understanding of the effects of their choices and broaden their repertoire of techniques for integrating source material into their writing.

REFERENCES

Downs, Doug, and Elizabeth Wardle. 2007. "Teaching about Writing, Righting Misconceptions: (Re)Envisioning 'First-Year Composition' as 'Introduction to Writing Studies.'" *College Composition and Communication* 58:552–84.

Howard, Rebecca Moore. 1999. *Standing in the Shadows of Giants: Plagiarists, Authors, Collaborators*. Stamford, CT: Ablex.

Jamieson, Sandra, and Rebecca Moore Howard. 2011. "Phase 1 Data." *The Citation Project*. http://site.citationproject.net/results/phase-i-data/.

LeFevre, Karen Burke. 1987. *Invention As a Social Act*. Carbondale: Southern Illinois University Press.

Parker, Paul. 2013. "From Rules to Judgment: Exploring the Plagiarism Threshold in Academic Writing." In *Critical Conversations about Plagiarism*, edited by Michael Donnelly, Rebecca Ingalls, Tracy Ann Morse, Joanna Castner Post, and Anne Meade Stockdell-Giesler, 46–63. Anderson, SC: Parlor.

Porter, James E. 1986. "Intertextuality and the Discourse Community." *Rhetoric Review* 5:3 4–47.

22
Vignette

THE FYW WAW COMPOSITION CLASSROOM REIMAGINED
Threshold Concepts through Gamification

Samuel Stinson

> INSTITUTION TYPE AND SIZE: 29,000-student Midwest public research university
>
> COURSE CONTEXT: Required general education FYW course
>
> STUDY DESIGN/METHODOLOGY: Teacher reflections on a games-based assignment involving one section of FYW
>
> WAW PROGRAM OR NOT: Stand-alone WAW course in FYW program
>
> WAW COURSE OR SINGLE ASSIGNMENT/UNIT: Sequence of WAW assignments in WAW course
>
> INSTRUCTOR TYPE/POSITION: Graduate teaching assistant, now full-time Lecturer
>
> KEY TERMS: FYW; threshold concepts; games; gamification; pedagogy

INTRODUCTION

I will discuss insights from an assignment in which first-year composition students over the course of seven weeks composed digital and in-person games for the class to play that reinforced WAW-curriculum threshold concepts.[1] Students were given this gamification assignment at the beginning of the summer semester and then signed up for available presentation days during those seven weeks. This assignment showed that games provide a mechanism for students to surface latent gamelike structures within the WAW classroom, such as victory conditions (successful completion of learning objectives), player positions (what students are able to do as participants), and strategies for gameplay (what choices are available within the class to best complete learning objectives) that benefit students in learning WAW threshold concepts. These composition games also invoke what I am calling trans-situational identities that allow students to learn concepts in one situation, playing a game, that transfer to other situations outside the game. When students become players and game designers, these new identities allow conceptual transfer of metaknowledge from playing and designing games to other domains. That is because, as James Gee (2003) has argued, games are rhetorical constructs that facilitate learning and transfer through student engagement, indirection, and play.[2] Gamifying the FYC WAW classroom by having students create and play composition games is one means by which we may help students better understand and transfer their understanding of threshold concepts.

In-class games can make use of this power to help students gain agency and practice threshold concepts in FYC by maintaining student attention and engagement as they provide procedural ways for students to learn declarative knowledge. As WAW approaches to teaching composition are meant to expose threshold concepts in order to teach declarative knowledge about writing from the field of rhetoric and composition, games provide procedural methods by which students may engage with these concepts in the WAW classroom.[3] Having students compose games also requires them to make rhetorical decisions about game design and implementation, and practice engaging their peers in play.[4] As a result, students learn both through playing games and through composing games for other students to experience.

The first student work group in my class appropriated and adapted the existing game Jeopardy and created a digital board of questions covering threshold concepts from course readings.[5] For this game, students played in groups on one computer per group, identifying concepts from that day's readings and earning points for each correct answer. In a group reflective writing on the assignment, the students explained their rationale for choosing Jeopardy by noting that the class is "already familiar with the rules and conditions" of the game, which "allows the player to not only apply learn[ed] knowledge, but also analyze what they have learned." A second student group adapted a well-known high school class game called Trashketball to have the class play among groups. Trashketball is a game in which students answer questions in order to gain the chance to shoot a wadded piece of paper into the classroom's trash bin. In this particular version of the game, students answered questions, which asked them to identify and explain threshold concepts, in order to earn the right to throw the trashketball into the wastebasket. Due to the course's summer schedule, groups presented week by week throughout the class. Each group had twenty minutes to present a brief exploration of the readings' main points and threshold concepts and then another fifteen minutes to have the class play the game.

As the first group had the class play its game, it became apparent that the game questions the groups were writing would require tweaking in order to focus less on facts (such as the Jeopardy game's "Malcolm X 10" category question "Where was Malcolm [X] born?" based on the Malcolm X (1965) reading "Learning to Read") and more on threshold concepts such as literacy sponsorship itself. The first group did include a question in which the answer was literacy sponsorship, but it was too basic: "What was the foucus [sic] of Brandt's [1998] reading?"("Brandt 10" question in Downer, Frank, and Black [2015]). This point, getting students to focus on concepts rather than just facts, was a continual process. But this was something that the students themselves were interested in doing in order to make their games more challenging to the other students.

Often during class, the students' attempts at creating questions would inspire the class to discuss how the question could have been phrased differently in order to better represent the concepts under discussion. For example, during the second group's presentation on Laura Carroll's (2010) article "Backpacks vs. Briefcases: Steps toward Rhetorical Analysis," I could tell that the students came prepared to play. When the class played the group's game, one student answered the group's question by repeating from memory the article's description of what constitutes emotional appeals, and in response another briefly debated Carroll's use of examples in that section. Although simple in design, the games provided students an interest in acquiring metaknowledge and iterative transfer of that knowledge to gain greater advantages in the game. At any moment during play, WAW threshold concepts became a type of currency in circulation that allowed students to better compete against their fellow players while also fostering teamwork in order to more accurately reflect that knowledge during play.

The third student work group created a quiz-show game that asked individuals in the class ten yes/no questions. At the end of the activity, the groups formed and averaged their quiz scores to award one group bragging rights. At first I had a reservation with this approach, since binary questions often fail to encapsulate the complexity that discussion questions afford. Yet even with this reservation I noticed that the students were intently participating and competing among the groups. The fourth group adapted bingo and was able to adjust the rules while the game was being played, allowing additional rounds of play to emphasize concepts that had not yet been discussed.[6]

In games, rhetoric operates under step-by-step procedures in which players interact by making choices that affect how a game algorithm responds, whether in victory or defeat or in adding to or subtracting from a running score. For instance, a player in *Super Mario Brothers* taking on the identity of Mario learns that the game algorithm rewards not directly touching enemy turtles except for jumping on the shells. If a player touches an enemy turtle, a procedure is invoked by the game's controlling algorithm that causes Mario to jump off the screen in defeat. Players learn to trigger desirable procedures through dying and retrying. In playing a WAW composition game, students better understand WAW threshold concepts as the game's step-by-step procedures get students to demonstrate their understanding of declarative knowledge by competitively answering questions. In this way the interaction among students and the group running the game constitutes a complex interaction of procedures that mirrors the complexity of actions in a video game algorithm. Answering questions incorrectly allows students to work together to make new attempts at correct answers. WAW threshold knowledge becomes necessary to understand in order for students to gain some other unrelated reward.

While designing composition games, I did not have students at first analyze their audience of peers using ethos, pathos, and logos. Instead I provided the class instructions to create a game that achieved a rhetorical effect through audience analysis that utilizes game theory–based rhetorical assessment through game design and play. From the handout I provided the class, here is how I stated this in the instruction: "For your group activity I would like for you to design and implement a simple game using the four-part definition [game player identities, a list of available moves, a list of rules and conditions, and game goals/objectives, including victory conditions]. Write several paragraphs that describe the game with this definition and provide this to the class. Then have the class play the game. What type of game could you create? You should focus primarily on helping students learn the threshold concepts from our readings and should be familiar with the arguments and main points that each article author presents." Gaining threshold knowledge in WAW courses largely comes from reading and understanding class articles. This threshold knowledge then allows the creation of a classroom-specific lexicon. Games that help students learn threshold concepts therefore largely focus on reading comprehension to help students gain this knowledge.

Because games are comprised of rules and conditions, I explained to students that they should provide an overview of which physical materials would be used to construct their games so that players would know how to interact with rules in order to meet game conditions. Only one of the games created in this class was digital; the rest were verbal games played in class through interaction and participation. The first group used an existing game template available online to compose their game.[7] The other groups wrote lists of questions and provided material to play their game: group 2 asked questions and rewarded those who answered correctly with a wadded piece of paper to throw into the room's trash can; group 3 kept score of questions answered correctly on the chalkboard; group 4 provided customized photocopy bingo boards adapted from an online template and used this to allow players to compete for a candy prize.[8]

Students generally adapted existing familiar games that required very little new instruction in rules, facilitating focus on concepts instead of game mechanics. Game questions were challenging, a necessary quality of good games (Gee 2004, 57), as challenge inspires student participation. In each case games-based learning initiated by students puts students in control of mastering WAW conceptual knowledge, a key step in transferring that framework to noncurricular rhetorical situations. Students gain this control by becoming engaged through gameplay and achieving indirect goals as they earn points in the game by answering questions. Students also investigated online tools that allowed them to modify the games based on the classroom rhetorical situation, demonstrating increased interest in creating challenging experiences for their peers. When I asked a student what he thought the difference was in discussing threshold concepts through gameplay rather than through regular class discussion, he told me, "The difference is that when we're playing games to learn these ideas, we are smiling when we do that." While smiling is not always a necessary step in learning, it is an aspect of play that often affords student engagement. Engaged students in this class seemed generally more interested in discussing the meaning of threshold concepts in order to perform better in their peers' games, at times speaking up and qualifying other groups' answers in attempting to compete for points. This increased engagement is a unique aspect of games, allowing students to learn threshold concepts through indirect activities.

Overall, students selecting and implementing games in class not only demonstrated eagerness to participate in the other groups' games but also showed greater familiarity with WAW threshold concepts as a result of this interaction. I reached this conclusion after informally following up with the class after playing each game. I would lead the class into a group assessment of the game's effectiveness, also introducing classical rhetoric terminology, and asking the class to provide oral feedback to the presenting group. Earlier games such Jeopardy emphasized factual knowledge, while later games were targeted more at defining, exploring, and further discussing threshold concepts. This change in focus occurred after each subsequent group used feedback from earlier sessions to further rhetorically position their game based on previous group peer review. Having groups provide a rationale for their game allowed me to see students further reflecting upon their understanding of their game's rhetorical qualities. For example, the students who created the Jeopardy game noted that in their design of questions "we focused on facts surrounding the life of Malcolm X, such as 'At what grade did Malcolm X leave school?' The rule[s]and conditions of Jeopardy, such as the player answering in a form of a question, allows the player to not only apply learned knowledge but also analyze what they have learned. By answering the statement above, the player may relate it to Brandt's [1998] theory of how economics relates to literacy sponsorship." While the connection between testing knowledge and understanding WAW threshold concepts may be tentative, the exploration these students attempt opened up a student-initiated space in classroom discourse for this topic to emerge. Additionally, discussing facts from student-designed games provided students a springboard from which to make other connections to the course readings. Weeks later in the class, students could frequently recall and use threshold concepts in class conversation that had received this additional attention through in-class gameplay.

NOTES

1. It is my hope that projects such as this one will further encourage compositionists to apply game studies to surface unacknowledged gamelike assumptions at play in order to change how we think about learning, rhetoric, and the presentation of knowledge in the WAW classroom. Acknowledging and surfacing these assumptions may allow students opportunity to perform new roles as they gain genre knowledge in situated, constructed gamelike environments.
2. Literacy also figures significantly in games-based learning since games prominently use verbal text to convey key aspects of character development and story (Garrelts 2013, 30–31).
3. Many thanks to Matthew Vetter for his thoughts on procedural knowledge and our conversations about this topic.
4. Games have an "expressive power" that "comes from procedural representation" (Bogost 2007, 197).
5. Interested readers can visit http://www.superteachertools.us/jeopardyx/jeopardy-review-game.php?gamefile=1433299#.VikYTWtyyW7 to view the first student work group's Jeopardy game.
6. Students co-creating the classroom experience through constructing group games and activities gain further insight into the situatedness of the composition

classroom. That is because students have the opportunity to reflect on what aspects of games/activities help their peers build conceptual metaknowledge through choice-making and game-situated play (Gee 2003, 108).
7. This template is available at http://www.superteachertools.us/jeopardyx/.
8. Interestingly, the candy itself was not the lure: students seemed equally fascinated and engrossed in playing the other three games that did not offer candy.

REFERENCES

Bogost, Ian. 2007. *Persuasive Games*. Cambridge, MA: MIT Press.

Brandt, Deborah. 1998. "Sponsors of Literacy." *College Composition and Communication* 49 (2): 165–85.

Carroll, Laura Bolin. 2010. "Backpacks vs. Briefcases: Steps toward Rhetorical Analysis." In *Writing Spaces: Readings on Writing*, edited by Charles Lowe and Pavel Zemliansky, 1:45–58. West Lafayette, IN: Parlor.

Downer, Jade, Zakary Frank, and Troy Black. 2016. "Malcolm X." Super Teacher Tools, July 6. http://www.superteachertools.us/jeopardyx/jeopardy-review-game.php?gamefile =1433299" \l ".VikYTWtyyW7.

Garrelts, Nate. 2013. "The Pencil Shaped Joystick." In *Rhetoric/Composition/Play through Video Games*, edited by Richard Colby, Matthew S. S. Johnson, and Rebekah Shultz Colby, 25–32. New York: Palgrave Macmillan.

Gee, James Paul. 2003. *What Video Games Have to Teach Us about Learning and Literacy*. New York: Palgrave Macmillan.

Gee, James Paul. 2004. *Situated Language and Learning: A Critique of Traditional Schooling*. New York: Routledge.

Malcolm X. 1965. "Learning to Read." In *Writing about Writing: A College Reader*, 2nd ed., edited by Elizabeth Wardle and Doug Downs, 119–27. Boston: Bedford/St. Martin's, 2014.

23
CURRICULAR REVIEW IN WAW
Involving Alumni, Students, and Faculty in Writing about Writing in Technical Fields

Jennifer deWinter

> INSTITUTION TYPE AND SIZE: 6,000-student polytechnic university
> COURSE CONTEXT: Undergraduate curriculum with senior thesis
> STUDY DESIGN/METHODOLOGY: IRB-exempted; alumni and exit survey, focus groups, interviews, and course evaluations
> WAW PROGRAM OR NOT: Writing and rhetoric program with WAW emphasis in courses and projects; professional writing major
> WAW COURSE OR SINGLE ASSIGNMENT/UNIT: Curriculum review
> INSTRUCTOR TYPE/POSITION: Tenure-track associate professor, director of writing and professional writing; now associate professor and director of interactive media and game development program
> KEY TERMS: Curricular review; professional writing; methods; senior thesis; rhetorical analysis

ABSTRACT
This chapter provides a summary of a three-year curriculum review of WAW in a writing and rhetoric program that houses the professional writing major. Program faculty distributed alumni surveys, conducted focus groups with current students, interviewed industry representatives, and met with affiliated faculty. Results from alumni and industry professionals indicated clear support for WAW and rhetorical analysis skills; students still indicated more interest in instrumental approaches to writing (i.e., technical reports, cover letters, and seminar papers). Ultimately, the writing and rhetoric program introduced/strengthened both WAW and rhetoric courses in all four levels of the undergraduate degree.

INTRODUCTION
Writing about Writing is often discussed in the context of first-year composition programs in which composition is a required course for all

DOI: 10.7330/9781607328421.c023

incoming students. However, WAW can be implemented in writing programs and degrees that do not serve first-year composition, and as our self-study indicates, the importance and professional benefits of WAW are well respected among professionals, alumni, and faculty trained in rhetoric and composition (this includes affiliated faculty in other degrees who have completed professional development in rhetoric and composition). In this chapter, I outline a three-year curriculum review of the writing and rhetoric (WR) program and its primary major, professional writing (PW), that resulted in curricular and project-based revisions, supporting greater integration of WAW principles and approaches.

Because this approach is based on data collection within and about certain academic communities, the results may not transfer, but the method can be applied in most institutional settings. In our interactions with all stakeholders, we were careful to ask questions about WAW, rhetoric, and genre courses (such as technical communication or business writing). Thus we were able to collect a rich data set that shaped our curriculum but also gave the program rhetorically effective quotations from alumni and industry representatives, counterbalancing on-campus assumptions and demands from faculty and students concerning a more skills-based approach to writing and rhetoric. And to be clear, the faculty were ready to revise the curriculum based in direct response to the collected data, which in this case led to a strengthening of WAW and rhetorical analysis.

INSTITUTIONAL CONTEXT

Worcester Polytechnic Institute (WPI) is an engineering school with additional strengths in biomedical and business research, located in central Massachusetts. Perhaps unusually, WPI has no writing class requirement. Instead, it has a project-based curriculum with a project in each year: the Great Problem Seminar, the Humanities and Arts (HUA) Inquiry Seminar, the Interactive Qualifying Project (applying social science methods to real-world problems where science/technology meets society), and the Major Qualifying Project (a senior thesis in the student's declared major). Writing in these projects and other writing-intensive courses is supported by the director of communication across the curriculum and the writing center.

Additionally, we offer a robust number of writing and rhetoric courses that students can take to fulfill the humanities and arts requirement (five courses plus an Inquiry Seminar project) to earn a minor in writing and rhetoric or to major in professional writing. In 2009, courses offered were Elements of Writing, Professional Writing, Technical

Writing, Writing about Disease and Public Health, Peer Tutoring in Writing, Rhetorical Theory, Visual Rhetoric, Digital Rhetoric, and Study of Writing—a total of nine writing courses, all at the 2000 and 3000 level.

CURRICULUM REVIEW

In 2009, the writing and rhetoric program started a five-year review of the major in professional writing intended to bring cohesion to the curriculum and provide data for resource allocations. The major has both rhetoric and analysis courses and also writing and production courses.

We knew that we needed to significantly revise the curriculum to reflect demand, capacity, and growth potential as well as to create a major that would attract targeted giving. Further, while courses tended to fill, our major numbers remained low, with only about twenty students with a declared professional writing major at any one time, or about five per year. In preparing for our review, we read the WR course evaluations, which all strongly indicated that students wanted more writing and production courses—a skills-based approach that complements engineering curricula—rather than rhetoric and theory courses.

Borrowing from Salvo and Ren's (2007) participatory assessment approach, which adapts participatory design principles concerning user involvement into assessment practices, we identified all of the possible stakeholders who could provide feedback in the review process. For us, this meant faculty, close administrators, students, alumni, community service partners, and target industries that would likely hire our students. Linking our approach with literature concerning best practices in curricular reviews, we conducted the following:

> An alumni survey of previous majors from the professional writing major and the writing and rhetoric major, and students involved with the writing center as peer tutors, with a response rate of 16 out of 33 (Evans et al. 1993; Dalton and Wright 1999);

> Creation of four focus groups with students who have taken WR courses and four focus groups with those who have not taken any WR courses to fulfill the HUA Inquiry Seminar project (Salvo and Ren 2007; Hendershott and Wright 1993; Fishman, Marx, and Best 2003);

> Regular meetings with WR and affiliated faculty to discuss outcomes and goals in classes and work to come to consensus about programmatic goals and outcomes (Stark et al. 1997);

> Interviews with human resource managers from ten representative area industries, including biomedical, information technology, supply chain management, and engineering/manufacturing.

In addition to this, we pulled course reports and exit surveys that we collect at the time of graduation. Data collection took approximately eighteen months to complete. During this time, we also reviewed similar programs in writing, technical and professional communication, information, and communication.

FINDINGS AND DISCUSSION
Student Responses
Student responses from the focus groups mirrored a lot of what we were finding in course evaluations. Students who had not taken WR courses explained that if they did choose to take such courses, they wanted to learn practical writing skills. Students who had taken writing courses such as Elements of Writing (similar to first-year composition), business writing, and technical writing were split; some wanted more focus on "how to" and less emphasis on research skills and analysis, while the other half liked the material as presented. There were a small number of people in the focus groups who had taken rhetorically focused courses in addition to writing courses, and they expressed an interest in either more rhetorical analysis in the class or a course on rhetoric in writing theory and scholarship. Students who were writing and rhetoric and professional writing majors were most interested in rhetoric courses and Study of Writing, the only writing course that studied the primary literature of rhetoric and composition and conducted original studies on writing. These students drove demand for rhetorical theory and practice-based inquiry seminars to fulfill the sophomore Humanities and Arts project.

Some of these findings may be accounted for by awareness and popular representation. Those students who had not taken writing were talking about writing as a tool, necessary to do other things. This echoes Downs and Wardle's (2007) summary of common misconceptions concerning college writing in popular discourse: that writing could be learned once and applied multiple times. Transfer of writing skills is assumed in this model. This also mirrors the student population; almost all students at WPI are majoring in STEM disciplines, so their perceptions of writing tend toward what Katz (1992) disparagingly refers to as an ethic of expediency. Students who had taken WR courses talked about writing as a process, and identified the need to study different writing concepts, such as plagiarism, audience, medium, and so forth, because these are contested ideas rarely talked about in different writing contexts. Students who aligned with our rhetoric classes all talked about how they didn't know what "rhetoric" was; the course just fit into their schedules, but they discovered a passion for the field that led to increased enrollments in the writing and rhetoric concentration, the minor, and the two majors. Nevertheless, overwhelmingly, students wanted more practical courses in writing for science and engineering, particularly looking to Technical and Business Writing.

Alumni Survey

We anticipated that the alumni survey would come back with similar feedback, reinforcing what we heard in the focus groups. After all, we pulled ten years of course reports, which provided data from when alumni were still students. Alumni survey data showed that the respondents found the rhetoric courses—those courses that analyzed communication strategies—were more influential in their professional life. They also indicated strong support for both the Study of Writing course (a 3000-level methods course) and the senior project (MQP)—both of which focus on writing about writing—noting that these experiences provided them with additional analysis and information literacy skills that were widely applicable to different writing and communication contexts.

When we benchmarked these responses to the literature, we were pleased to find that this is consistent with workplace research. For example, in "Novice and Insider Perspectives on Academic and Workplace Writing: Toward a Continuum of Rhetorical Awareness," Leydens found that students turned professionals tended to develop their rhetorical awareness and were able to express the role and importance of rhetoric when they became experienced and reflective practitioners (2008, 259). And this finding is not new. Winsor's 1996 book *Writing Like An Engineer: A Rhetorical Education* explores the awareness that practicing engineers have concerning rhetorical strategy and genre affordances. It is likely, then, that our alumni entered professional writing positions and were called upon to use reflexive rhetorical tools more often to respond to particular situations and needs. Further, our alumni reported that they were often called upon to write in genres that they had not encountered before; one alumnus explained that he was required to create new forms of documents and genres to respond to emergent media demands.

At the time of running our surveys, we had only started teaching our first-year composition equivalent, Elements of Writing, as a writing about writing course, so only students who graduated after 2009 were able to speak to the value of this part of our curriculum.

Meetings with Associated and Affiliated Faculty

The professional writing program is an interdisciplinary program that requires students to have technical or scientific competency in addition to writing courses and projects. As such, our affiliated faculty come from more traditionally aligned programs, such as English and philosophy, but also STEM disciplines such as mechanical engineering, biomedical engineering, social science, aerospace engineering, robotics, and interactive media and game development. Affiliated faculty serve as co-advisors on student projects, often as content experts. The associated faculty is an interdisciplinary group of six people who meet regularly to steer the program; they come from writing and rhetoric, mechanical engineering, and philosophy.

Our affiliated faculty proved the largest stumbling block when revising for a rhetoric- and WAW-focused curriculum because they wanted more skills-based writing courses. Their concern is that students can't write in their classes, and they believe that more writing classes in general will fix this problem. In retrospect, we should not have been surprised because many of the concerns and desires that faculty expressed align closely with what WAC initiatives have been reporting for years. Thus, even though these faculty co-advise the senior project and see the process of analyzing and writing about writing within the field of rhetoric and composition (often praising the process for its rigor), they are often driven by their frustrations in their own courses. Once we realized this, we refocused our meetings on our writing-intensive initiatives and used this as an opportunity to educate nonwriting faculty on writing pedagogy and process. Many of these affiliated faculty have subsequently taken the Teaching with Writing faculty training that we offer through the communication across the curriculum program.

Associated faculty reported that students responded well in their classes to different rhetorical analysis tools, writing about writing, and data analytics. We saw that there was little overlap in the different courses where concepts could be repeated and reinforced, so during a one-year period, we attempted to define opportunities for programmatic cohesion around these three strengths that we already knew.

Corporate Interviews

Corporate interviews mirrored much of the feedback that we were receiving from our alumni. The HR representatives said that the company valued the ability to assess particular (and often ambiguous) situations and respond accordingly. Further, they explained that clear communication appropriate for the technical expertise of the group was important, and people who were able to navigate those changes tended to be more successful. This mirrors recent reports noting that students with liberal arts degrees and/or background have important skills in synthesis, research, communication, attending to ambiguity, and attending to human systems (Segran 2014; O'Shaughnessy 2015). Among these proficiencies, communication skills tend to be most in demand.

CURRICULAR CHANGES

After synthesizing and discussing this data, the associated faculty revised the curriculum to reinforce our current strengths and add depth in medical writing and data literacy and analytics. Further, we ensured that our classes took a rhetorical approach to writing, with a focus on the research questions and literature in rhetoric and composition.

Previously, we had no 1000-level first-year writing courses. During our revision, we moved Elements of Writing to the first year, thus creating a gateway WAW course in which students synthesized academic work from the field then added to one of the major disciplinary keywords debates (grammar, audience, literature, plagiarism, and so forth). After learning summary, critique, and synthesis (students synthesize ten academic articles around their keywords), students write an argument in which they enter a disciplinary debate about writing.

While there is no significant difference in the numerical data on student course evaluations when comparing sections that employed WAW principles to those courses that had alternative themes, the written comments indicate that students are engaging with the concepts differently. Before the course revisions, students commented on writing as a process, and they often discussed the value (or lack of value) of peer review. In the writing about writing courses, students would engage in a brief metaconversation about writing topics. For example, one student wrote, "I was explaining plagerism [*sic*] to my sorority, and we all thought that WPI needs to change the policy. Right now, we are treated like we stole something, but it's harder than that." Another student wrote: "My group studied peer review and we also did peer review. We were able to tell each other what we needed. When [one of my group members] wasn't doing his job, we talked to him as a group . . . We learned team work and collaboration because we knew what we needed and talked about it."

Recent alumni who took Elements as a writing about writing course also discussed the long-term positive effects of this course. One student, an electrical and computer engineering/computer science double major who took a writing about writing Elements course in the fall of 2009, wrote effusively:

> Taking Elements was a pivotal moment for me because it was the first time I was reading academic literature (and a lot of it), synthesizing it, and using it to form my own arguments. My topic was the nebulous concept of "style," and I'll never forget the first reading you ever gave me was Paul Butler's "Style in the Diaspora of Composition Studies" . . . I remember being struck by the depth of the author's analysis of how style is important to so many genres of writing. There was a part about how style fits into the construction of a syllabus. I remember thinking, frustrated at the author for having to read it all, "Why is this so important? Why does anyone care about how a syllabus is constructed? Why does it matter how it uses pronouns? It's just an outline of course topics." But as I read further into the paper (and many others), I began to understand the rhetorical implications of what I thought were small stylistic choices in writing. This helped me see the complexity in writing . . . well, anything . . . and how important concepts like word choice and sentence structure were to creating an argument. I believe that the time I spent reading and writing about writing helped me understand why these concepts are important to creating arguments.

Another student, who received her dual degree in chemical engineering and professional writing, reflected on her experience in Elements, where she researched the role of literature (or not) in first-year composition classes:

> Now that I have become a professional engineer, I find narratives as prominent as ever—they are at the beginning of any quality excursion meeting, as fellow engineers begin to explain what went wrong with the tool and set the backdrop for continuous improvement projects. [Narratives are] ever-present in the corridor conversations and lunch time chats, which are subtly sometimes the most important conversations of all, as office politics are the ever-present hidden current influencing the business and its people. From this exposure to narratives in composition, I have learned to communicate in these meetings more effectively, and network more successfully—exchanging narratives with others in order to form stronger connections that will help me create a stronger network of support as I learn and advance in my career.

This may read as a ringing endorsement for literature in the classroom, but underlying it was the WAW principles that asked students to read *CCC*, *College English*, and related journals in rhetoric and composition and engage with the ideas and values of narratives as discussed in the field.

In addition to this, we instituted a Writing about Science and Technology course in the first year, which is functionally Elements with a different content focus. It's important to remember (1) there is no first-year writing requirement, so students opt into these classes; and (2)

WPI is a science and technology university, so this topic would naturally appeal to incoming students.

In the second year, we introduced a course entitled Elements of Style in which students studied disciplinary work on style and linguistics to write about style and conduct stylistic analysis. This provided a pathway for students to take courses such as Cross-cultural Communication at the 3000-level and Academic Science Writing, in which students write about STEM-based disciplinary writing at the 4000-level.

Further, based on feedback that we received concerning Study of Writing, we decided to move that course to the 4000-level and retitle it Methods in the Study of Writing to reflect what alumni and students said they valued. This course asks students to define writing-specific research questions and create studies with replicable methods from composition and social studies, which provides the foundation for the Major Qualifying Project, or senior thesis. Because students need to have a technical competency in this major, students had to define writing questions within technical fields, marry those questions to how rhetoric and composition think about communication strategies, and then write about writing in chemical engineering, video games, and bio-tissue engineering, for example.

Students have done a number of projects in which they must analyze and write about writing before performing in the genre and situations on which they focus. The typical MQP asks students to define a topic, define research questions in the topic, and write a literature review, a method, results and discussion, writing in action, and then a reflective conclusion. These typically run 80–100 double-spaced pages. For this project, one student translated technical information to a nontechnical audience in scientific journalism. She conducted her study on the generic conventions with a focus on metaphor and then wrote a piece that explained new advances in rocket engines. Another student wanted to write grants for cultural institutions, so she ran a study on integrating images and visuals into grant writing and then wrote a grant for the American Antiquarian Society as her practical component. In all of these cases, we asked students to situate their questions in the field of rhetoric and composition and act from the knowledge generated by their literature reviews and results.

FINAL THOUGHTS

These curricular changes have taken a long time to instantiate and were not adopted until the spring of 2014. Nevertheless, we have already seen their positive impact on the students. First, students perceive writing as a discipline with disciplinary methods and approaches, and they are able to articulate the value of this. Second, we found that students and alumni appreciated courses and opportunities that allowed them to talk about writing in a critically informed way with others, and we revised the curriculum to reinforce these opportunities in all four years of the undergraduate curriculum. And third, we have used this as an opportunity to educate our academic peers about the value and discipline of writing not as a service tool that communicates their material but as an object of study in its own right. The challenge comes with disseminating our WAW curriculum across campus so that our academic peers understand the value of the field writ large, a challenge that colleagues at other institutions often face.

In this case, the curricular review acted rhetorically as a process. Those involved were by and large convinced that the results would strengthen the program regardless of what their preconceived notions were. Further, because we were able to involve alumni and industry professionals in this process, we effectively created an opening for greater development with these communities, either through alumni relations or our office of development, a strategy that would work in many institutions. Thinking of WAW as a strength in a curriculum that is identified and supported through the process of curricular revision enables multiple stakeholders to feel invested in the outcomes and implementation of these core disciplinary and curricular concepts.

I would like to end with a quotation from an exit survey given to recent graduates. One of our students finished the professional writing degree and was accepted into a PhD program in rhetoric and composition. She wrote: "Learning about rhetoric and composition (as opposed to simply researching the topic of proposal writing) was tremendously valuable for me because I was able to communicate my ideas more effectively and clearly, not only in terms of my academic research paper, but also in terms of my oral presentations and for the actual proposal writing exercises. Even outside of fields directly related to rhetoric and composition, I find the same skills to be useful in discourse and research because these skills deal with ways of communicating, whether it be for written, oral, or visual media." And in an employment era when "excellent communication skills" appears constantly in the job requirements, such an endorsement of a writing about writing curriculum with a focus on rhetorical awareness, coupled with the research questions and methods of rhetoric and composition, validates and promotes the important intellectual work our field does.

REFERENCES

Dalton, Bruce, and Lois Wright. 1999. "Using Community Input for the Curriculum Review Process." *Journal of Social Work Education* 35 (2): 275–88.

Downs, Douglas, and Elizabeth Wardle. 2007. "Teaching about Writing, Righting Misconceptions: (Re)Envisioning 'First-Year Composition' as 'Introduction to Writing Studies.'" *College Composition and Communication* 58 (4): 552–84.

Evans, D. L., G. C. Beakley, P. E. Crouch, and G. T. Yamaguchi. 1993. "Attributes of Engineering Graduates and Their Impact on Curriculum Design." *Journal of Engineering Education* 82 (4): 203–11.

Fishman, Barry J., Ronald W. Marx, and Stephen Best. 2003. "Linking Teacher and Student Learning to Improve Professional Development in Systemic Reform." *Teaching and Teacher Education* 19:643–58.

Hendershott, Anne, and Sheila Wright. 1993."Student Focus Groups and Curricular Review." *Teaching Sociology* 21 (2): 154–59.

Katz, Steven B. 1992. "The Ethic of Expediency: Classical Rhetoric, Technology, and the Holocaust." *College English* 54 (3): 255–75.

Leydens, Jon. 2008. "Novice and Insider Perspectives on Academic and Workplace Writing: Toward a Continuum of Rhetorical Awareness." *Professional Communication, IEEE Transactions on Professional Communication* 51 (3): 242–63.

O'Shaughnessy, Lynn. 2015. "New College Grads: Who Employers Want to Hire." *CBS News*, January 20. http://www.cbsnews.com/news/new-college-grads-who-employers-want-to-hire/.

Salvo, Michael J., and Jingfang Ren. 2007. "Participatory Assessment: Negotiating Engagement in a Technical Communication Program." *Technical Communication* 54:424–39.

Segran, Elizabeth. 2014. "Why Top Tech CEOs Want Employees with Liberal Arts Degrees." *Fast Company*, August 28. http://www.fastcompany.com/3034947/the-future-of-work/why-top-tech-ceos-want-employees-with-liberal-arts-degrees.

Stark, Joan S., Malcolm A. Lowther, Sally Sharp, and Gertrude L. Arnold. 1997. "Program-Level Curriculum Planning: An Exploration of Faculty Perspectives on Two Different Campuses." *Research in Higher Education* 38 (1): 99–130.

Winsor, Dorothy A. 1996. *Writing Like an Engineer: A Rhetorical Education.* Mahwah, NJ: Lawrence Erlbaum.

PART III

Engagement

24
TRANSFER OF WRITING-RELATED LEARNING

Rebecca S. Nowacek

In writing studies, the disciplinary preoccupation with transfer of learning grows out of the fact that our profession is intellectually and institutionally bound up with the teaching of writing—often in the context of required courses. Writing instructors, writing program administrators, and researchers in writing studies all feel very keenly the fact that we cannot, in one or two semesters, prepare students for all the genres and situation-specific demands that they will face in earning their degrees, much less in the course of their careers. What we must do instead, then, is prepare students to face those various futures by helping them develop the capacity to exercise reflective judgment under conditions of uncertainty. When we say we want to "teach for transfer" what we often mean, I propose, is enabling students to successfully navigate new and uncertain situations by helping them to cultivate the abilities to perceive a degree of similarity to prior experience while also reflecting critically on differences. This particular formulation of what it might mean to teach for transfer summarizes some of the most important beliefs about transfer that have emerged within writing studies and related fields but can also make visible some of our collective blind spots. In the pages that follow, I elucidate those beliefs and blind spots, then turn to considering more directly how this working definition of transfer might connect with the descriptions of WAW curricula that make up this volume.

To think of transfer as an exercise of reflective judgment under conditions of uncertainty suggests that transfer is more than mere application—a view in keeping with developments in writing studies and elsewhere. In the field of cognitive psychology, there has been a long tradition of research conducted under experimental lab conditions following what has been called the "two problem transfer paradigm." Research taking this approach has been particularly interested in the degree to which subjects are able to take lessons from source Problem

X and apply them to target Problem Y (see Gick and Holyoak's [1980] quintessential study in this tradition). Researchers often found that participants did not make connections unless they were prompted or had a certain degree of expertise that allowed them to perceive structural similarities in the problems despite surface differences.

However, research conducted in more naturalistic settings demonstrates that an individual's experience of sameness and processes of connection-making can be far more dynamic than the unidirectional connotations of the term *application* suggest. Rather than focusing solely on the application of learning from Problem X to Problem Y, researchers taking a more sociocultural approach to studying transfer in naturalistic settings note that not only might an experience in Situation A lead a person to understand Situation B differently, Situation B might change an individual's understanding of the earlier Situation A and the learning associated with it. Further, perceiving a connection between the two situations might even lead a person to understand herself differently; the experience of connecting previously disparate contexts can be transformative rather than a matter of mere application. In large part because of this changing view of transfer, many scholars have proposed alternate terms, including expansive learning (Engeström 2014), critical transitions (Beach 1999), and creative repurposing (Wardle 2012, invoking Prior and Shipka 2003 and Roozen 2010). Nevertheless, the word *transfer* continues to function as a big-tent term for many acts of connection-making.

A second advantage of describing transfer as an act of exercising reflective judgment under conditions of uncertainty is that it expresses an optimism that transfer is indeed possible. Across a variety of fields, scholars have expressed concern about the degree to which transfer fails to occur, sometimes questioning whether transfer of learning is even possible (Detterman and Sternberg 1993; Dias et al. 1999; Freedman, Adam, and Smart 1994). To think of transfer as an exercise of reflective judgment under conditions of uncertainty, however, is to adopt a more hopeful outlook. Recognizing that transfer often involves transformation, not just application, research in writing studies and educational psychology increasingly suggests that it may be our research methods, not our students, that are to blame for our inability to identify instances of transfer. This approach takes to heart Brent's (2012) illumination of the persistent if subtle presence of what he calls "transformable rhetorical knowledge," Nowacek's (2011) argument that students make more connections than instructors are aware of, and Wardle's (2007) admonition that "focusing on a limited search for 'skills' is the reason we do not recognize more evidence of 'transfer.'" We are looking, she notes, "for apples when those apples are now part of an apple pie" (69).

Third, this formulation implies that transfer can and does happen across multiple domains. While much of the research on transfer in writing studies has focused on how students make use of what they've learned in FYC in subsequent courses, to think of transfer as an exercise of reflective judgment under conditions of uncertainty tacitly acknowledges that the experience of connection-making can extend in multiple directions. Writers can make connections that stretch both forward and backward in time; students might make connections between classes they are taking simultaneously; writers might also forge connections between writing assigned in school and writing that's undertaken for work or as part of other extracurricular writing experiences and identities. In the context of this volume, it is particularly helpful to affirm that when we attend to transfer of writing-related knowledge, we might attend not only to how effectively a FYC curriculum prepares students to exercise reflective judgment under future conditions of uncertainty, but also how our writing classes at various points in the curriculum afford opportunities to connect with prior learning, concurrent learning, and the writing individuals do at home, at work, and for pleasure.

Finally, this formulation highlights the roles reflection and metacognition play in promoting transfer of learning—a focus that grows in part from a long-standing commitment to reflection in the field of writing studies and that is highlighted in Perkins and Salomon's much-cited definition of high-road transfer as requiring "deliberate mindful abstraction" (1988, 25). And indeed, metacognition has frequently been recognized as a powerful facilitator of transfer. "Meta-awareness about writing, language, and rhetorical strategies in FYC," Wardle writes, "may be the most important ability our courses can cultivate" (2007, 82). Drawing from their case study of Clay, a student in a WAW course they describe as adopting a Teaching for Transfer (TFT) curriculum, Yancey and colleagues conclude, "Through reflection, Clay was able to develop knowledge about writing and use it appropriately both inside and outside FYC" (2014, 93). And according to Beaufort, "Reflection in action . . . if part of a writer's process, will increase the ability of the writer to learn new writing skills, applying existing skills and knowledge appropriately" (2007, 152).

However, in our efforts to teach for transfer we should remember that even as the lens provided by this formulation brings some elements of transfer into focus, it obscures others. For instance, to define transfer as an act of exercising reflective judgment under conditions of uncertainty doesn't quite account for the proposition that metacognitive awareness does not seem to be necessary for all instances of transfer. Donahue reports that preliminary results from her research "indicate that mature practices might indeed develop without an accompanying meta-awareness" and require "less meta-awareness than is usually recognized" (2012, 155). My own research (2011) similarly indicates that meta-awareness, although a powerful facilitator of transfer, is not necessary for all instances of transfer. How might a more robust understanding of this more routinized, more tacit type of transfer enhance our understanding of transfer of writing-related knowledge?

Nor would a focus on an act of exercising reflective judgment under conditions of uncertainty necessarily highlight the role various habits of mind and types of knowledge might play in facilitating transfer—an area of inquiry that has garnered increasing attention in writing studies scholarship on transfer. The inclination to engage in reflection and metacognition, discussed above, might be seen as one of these facilitating habits of mind—but there are several others that are obscured by a definition that focuses so heavily on reflective judgment. For instance, researchers in writing studies have increasingly begun to identify dispositions as a means of facilitating (or inhibiting) transfer. Driscoll and Wells (2012) focus on dispositions as "individual, internal qualities that may impact transfer" and associate them with the habits of mind identified in the WPA Framework for Success in Postsecondary Writing. In particular, Driscoll and Wells focus on motivation, self-efficacy, attribution, and self-regulation as dispositions that can "determine students' sensitivity toward and willingness to engage in transfer." While Driscoll and Wells acknowledge that dispositions do not operate independently of context, Wardle (2012) goes even further in her explication of problem-exploring and answer-getting dispositions. Although dispositions may present as internal traits of individuals, Wardle argues, they are very much a function of a larger habitus; drawing on Bourdieu, Wardle points to the influence of "extended participation in . . . educational settings with an obsessive focus on standardized tests" as responsible for the inclination of "participants to act and react to problems by seeking quick and formulaic answers . . . what I am calling answer-getting dispositions." Whatever their genesis, dispositions are a growing area of inquiry.

The potential for genre knowledge to facilitate transfer has also been a focus of recent writing studies research. Genre might serve as an "exigence for transfer" (Nowacek 2011), carefully selected antecedent genres might invite transfer of learning across contexts (Devitt 2004), and the concept of uptake can provide a richer conceptualization of how those genred discursive spaces invite translation across heterogeneous and even contradictory memories (Rounsaville 2012). Reiff and Bawarshi's (2011) discussion of boundary crossers and boundary guarders also highlights the very particular ways in which boundary crossers talk about their genre knowledge. Rather than applying antecedent genre knowledge wholesale, they break it up—repurposing it through "not talk," a process elsewhere described as bricolage (Nowacek 2011). Genre knowledge, then, is often seen as a crucial means of facilitating transfer.

A fourth consideration has focused on how much more transferable expert knowledge might be. Beaufort (2007), for instance, identifies five domains of knowledge (rhetorical, genre, subject matter, writing process, and discourse community knowledge) upon which expert writers draw; when they can, she argues, their knowledge is much more likely to be repurposed in ways that avoid what she calls negative transfer. In a distinct but related vein, the recent effort to identify threshold concepts of writing has emphasized the ways in which the more expert view of the phenomenon of writing provided by the lens of threshold concepts is troublesome, transformative, and perhaps irreversible. Although Adler-Kassner and Wardle (2015) do not explore the question of transfer explicitly or in depth, the very premise—that the lens of a threshold concept might be transformative and irreversible—suggests that expert knowledge may be more portable knowledge, capable of transforming an individual's understanding of writing across many contexts. Threshold concepts are also, of course, liminal, so the relationship between expert knowledge and transferable knowledge is complex, but worth further exploration.

To summarize, instructors interested in creating educational experiences that will encourage students to make connections among their various experiences of writing and learning and to reflect critically on those connections may read the chapters in this volume with an eye towards several factors. Is transfer conceptualized as a dynamic experience crossing multiple domains rather than reduced to an unidirectional act of application from an earlier class to a later one? Is a focus on the value of reflection and metacognition for facilitating transfer complemented with inquiry into more routinized transfer of writing-related knowledge and skills? Are other means of facilitating transfer—including dispositions, genres, and the nature of expert knowledge—also considered?

With these beliefs and blind spots in mind, I'd like to raise one additional point to consider when designing (or reading about) WAW curricula: what exactly can or will transfer? Despite extensive exploration of what might make dynamic transfer possible, writing studies scholars have said surprisingly little about exactly what types of writing-related learning will transfer. In part this has been a reasonable, perhaps even necessary, response to the persistent misconception that a single writing course can transmit a set of skills that will then be applied (note here the return to the language of "application") in future classes. Such writing skills read more like qualities of an ideal text (e.g., "clear writing" and "good organization") and take little heed of disciplinary or other contextual differences in "good" writing. In the attempt to alter the terms of the conversation and the expectations of our colleagues, writing studies has offered a much richer portrait of the process of transfer, emphasizing dynamic connections and mindsets that might facilitate those connections. A trade-off, though, is that we have not systematically explored what writing-related knowledge is involved in those connections.

This lack of clarity is exacerbated in discussions of the WAW curriculum by the intentionally close match between declarative knowledge and procedural knowledge. (Declarative knowledge is content knowledge, knowledge of what; procedural knowledge is knowledge of how to.) For instance, if one goal of a writing class is to help students learn to undertake significant revision, a WAW approach to curriculum design might likely ask students to read research on revision. The course then not only sets out to teach the how of revision; studies of revision also become the subject matter, the what, of the course. Such confluence between the declarative and procedural knowledge of a course, Wardle and Downs (2013) have argued, "will vastly improve learning transfer of this declarative and procedural knowledge to new writing situations . . . For the purposes of transferable writing knowledge, the concept of 'rhetorical situation' itself seems vastly more applicable to other writing tasks than, for example, learning to write a memoir that will move an English teacher to tears." In this example, teaching a concept (rhetorical situation) is privileged over teaching a particular genre (memoir). Elsewhere, another WAW proponent writes that "while we may not be able to teach students *transferable writing skills*, we can provide them with *transferable writing knowledge* that they can take with them to help them work through any writing/communication assignment" (Scott Warnock, quoted in Downs and Wardle 2012, 134, emphasis added). Here the distinction is between skills and knowledge. Perhaps both cases imply that it is threshold concepts of writing that need to be taught, threshold concepts that offer a transformative and thus transferrable way of thinking about writing.

Certainly Yancey and colleagues have provided compelling evidence that focusing on a short list of key concepts and including repeated opportunities for reflection can do just that (2014, 73 and throughout). But as promising as this early study is, we have not, as a field, sufficiently grappled with the question of what types of writing-related learning transfer. Are writing concepts (threshold concepts, key concepts) transferrable writing-related knowledge? Are they somehow preferable to other types of writing-related knowledge? What other types of transferrable writing-related knowledge might we identify? In my own analysis of how students talk about their writing (Nowacek 2011), I identified four types of transferrable writing–related knowledge: content knowledge, mechanics and style, writing processes and analytical approaches, and genre knowledge. Might a repertoire of routines (like engaging in peer review, doing a reverse outline, etc.) be transferrable knowledge? Is genre knowledge not just an exigence for transfer but also part of the writing-related knowledge that is involved in an act of transfer?

Ultimately, it is not within the scope of the chapters in this volume to answer these questions, but I raise them in closing as a potential focus for those of us reading these contributions and imagining our own curricula (and, perhaps, our own future inquiries into student learning). Meanwhile, the contributions to this volume help us to imagine ever-broader and more ambitious ways to approach the challenges of helping students to move successfully among the multiple demands of their current and future writing lives.

REFERENCES

Adler-Kassner, Linda, and Elizabeth Wardle, eds. 2015. *Naming What We Know: Threshold Concepts of Writing Studies*. Logan: Utah State University Press.

Beach, King. 1999. "Consequential Transitions: A Sociocultural Expedition beyond Transfer in Education." *Review of Research in Education* 24 (1): 101–40.

Beaufort, Anne. 2007. *College Writing and Beyond: A New Framework for University Writing Instruction*. Logan: Utah State University Press.

Brent, Doug. 2012. "Crossing Boundaries: Co-op Students Relearning to Write." *College Composition and Communication* 63:558–92.

Detterman, Douglas K., and Robert J. Sternberg, eds. 1993. *Transfer on Trial: Intelligence, Cognition, and Instruction*. Norwood, NJ: Ablex.

Devitt, Amy J. 2004. *Writing Genres*. Carbondale: Southern Illinois University Press.

Dias, Patrick, Aviva Freedman, Peter Medway, and Anthony Pare. 1999. *Worlds Apart: Acting and Writing in Academic and Workplace Contexts*. Mahwah, NJ: Lawrence Erlbaum.

Donahue, Christiane. 2012. "Transfer, Portability, Generalization: (How) Does Composition Expertise 'Carry'?" in *Exploring Composition Studies: Sites, Issues, and Perspectives*, edited by Kelly Ritter and Paul Kei Matsuda, 145–66. Logan: Utah State University Press.

Downs, Doug, and Elizabeth Wardle. 2012. "Reimagining the Nature of FYC: Trends in Writing-about-Writing Pedagogies," in *Exploring Composition Studies: Sites, Issues, and Perspectives*, edited by Kelly Ritter and Paul Kei Matsuda, 123–44. Logan: Utah State University Press.

Driscoll, Dana L., and Jennifer Wells. 2012. "Beyond Knowledge and Skills: Writing Transfer and the Role of Student Dispositions." *Composition Forum* 26. http://compositionforum.com/issue/26/beyond-knowledge-skills.php.

Engeström, Yrjo. 2014. *Learning by Expanding: An Activity-Theoretical Approach to Developmental Research.* Cambridge: Cambridge University Press.

Freedman, Aviva, Christine Adam, and Graham Smart. 1994. "Wearing Suits to Class: Simulating Genres and Simulations as Genre." *Written Communication* 11:193–226.

Gick, Mary L., and Keith J. Holyoak. 1980. "Analogical Problem Solving." *Cognitive Psychology* 12:306–55.

Nowacek, Rebecca S. 2011. *Agents of Integration: Understanding Transfer as a Rhetorical Act.* Carbondale: Southern Illinois University Press.

Perkins, David N., and Gavriel Salomon. 1988. "Teaching for Transfer." *Educational Leadership* 46 (1): 22–32.

Prior, Paul, and Jody Shipka. 2003. "Chronotopic Lamination: Tracing the Contours of Literate Activity." In *Writing Selves/Writing Societies*, edited by Charles Bazerman and David Russell, 180–238. Fort Collins, CO: WAC Clearinghouse.

Reiff, Mary Jo, and Anis Bawarshi. 2011. "Tracing Discursive Resources: How Students Use Prior Genre Knowledge to Negotiate New Writing Contexts in First-Year Composition." *Written Communication* 28:312–37.

Roozen, Kevin. 2010. "Tracing Trajectories of Practice: Repurposing in One Student's Developing Disciplinary Writing Processes." *Written Communication* 27 (3): 318–54.

Rounsaville, Angela. 2012. "Selecting Genres for Transfer: The Role of Uptake in Students' Antecedent Genre Knowledge." *Composition Forum* 26. http://compositionforum.com/issue/26/selecting-genres-uptake.php.

Wardle, Elizabeth. 2007. "Understanding 'Transfer' from FYC: Preliminary Results of a Longitudinal Study." *WPA: Writing Program Administration* 31 (1–2): 65–85.

Wardle, Elizabeth. 2012. "Creative Repurposing for Expansive Learning: Considering 'Problem-Exploring' and 'Answer-Getting' Dispositions in Individuals and Fields." *Composition Forum* 26. http://compositionforum.com/issue/26/creative-repurposing.php.

Wardle, Elizabeth, and Doug Downs. 2013. "Reflecting Back and Looking Forward: Revisiting 'Teaching about Writing, Righting Misconceptions' Five Years On." *Composition Forum* 27. http://compositionforum.com/issue/27/reflecting-back.php.

Yancey, Kathleen Blake, Liane Robertson, and Kara Taczak. 2014. *Writing across Contexts: Transfer, Composition, and Sites of Writing.* Logan: Utah State University Press.

25
Student Voice
WRITING ABOUT WRITING FOCUS
A Roundtable

Kimberly Hoover with Elle Limesand,
Maggie Hammond, and Max Wellman

> INSTITUTION TYPE AND SIZE: State research-extensive university, 16,000
> COURSE CONTEXT: First-semester required college composition course
> STUDY DESIGN/METHODOLOGY: Focus group interview from longitudinal study of student learning transfer from FYC to later courses
> WAW PROGRAM OR NOT: WAW used in most first-semester courses
> WAW COURSE OR SINGLE ASSIGNMENT/UNIT: WAW course
> INSTRUCTOR TYPE/POSITION: Non-tenure track faculty now PhD student
> KEY TERMS: Learning transfer, reflection, threshold concepts, identity, WAW

INTRODUCTION

This chapter will report on the experiences of three former writing about writing students involved in an ongoing longitudinal study examining the impact of WAW pedagogy. The interview discussed here is part of a research design funded by two grants, the MSU Faculty Excellence Grant (2014) and the Conference on College Composition and Communication's Research Initiative Grant (2015), and is conducted by a research team at Montana State University. Our MSU team selected participants from among a sample of nearly 400 FYC students over two semesters who gave us consent to be contacted about this study, with selection based on demographics such as gender, major, and final grade in their FYC course in order to create a representative group of students for the study. Our project has also recruited several students to follow throughout several years of their college lives, which is how we found the three students for this interview. We had already collected writing from and/or interviewed Elle, Max, and Maggie individually in prior stages of

DOI: 10.7330/9781607328421.c025

the research, and each responded to my request for a group interview in fall 2015. Once we got all three in the same room and the interview began, I was particularly curious about the positive experiences they had to report on. These three have, noticeably, exceptionally optimistic reactions to writing about writing pedagogy, and though this isn't representative of every student's experience in our study, their responses reveal some commonality as to why these three had such profound WRIT 101 (FYC) encounters.

Of our three students, Elle and Max came from the same class with the same teacher, while Maggie had a different teacher with a somewhat different curriculum. Currently sophomores in different majors—Max a writing major, Elle a potential business major, and Maggie a psychology major—the three have varying amounts and types of writing required in their current classes. But as they and I reflected back on their WAW experiences, we found some consistencies in what their writing classrooms looked like. Constants in all three interviewee's course curricula included readings and major writing assignments from Wardle and Downs's (2014) WAW textbook, a portfolio grading system, and emphasis (to varying degrees) on themes such as reflection, rhetoric, and metacognition—themes also discussed in this chapter.

Our interview session focused on themes designated by the editors of this collection, including transfer, reflection, threshold concepts, the use of WRIT 101, and identity. Though it has been several semesters since their WRIT 101 experiences, each of the three contributed insights to the themes of the roundtable and even some surprising comments that went beyond the scope of my expectations as interviewer. Perhaps the most profound theme I saw imbue the students' responses was a sense of relaxation and freedom in writing fostered by the WAW classroom, and how that shifted the students' perception of writing studies *and* their very identification *as* writers. Though this is an extremely condensed report of Elle's, Max's, and Maggie's interview, we hope this chapter provides an honest reflection of WAW student experiences in their own words, and represents the possible transfer of intellectual and personal skills that WAW instruction can foster.

TRANSFER

Our first theme was *transfer* which, as Rebecca Nowacek explains in greater detail earlier in this collection, is the ability to take skills and habits of mind fostered in one environment and apply them in new environments. Of course, writing instructors are thinking specifically about how students' perception of writing in one environment may shape their perception of writing in a new environment beyond the writing classroom. This section will show the effect of transferability from WAW classes, as the students I interviewed were already showing evidence of transfer in their responses before I could even ask if they were conscious of specific examples that occurred.

I began the discussion with this question: "If I said the word *transfer* aloud, what do you think of as the main skills or habits of mind that you have *transferred* out of writing class?"

Maggie exhibited rhetorical awareness in new writing situations: "I think the biggest thing is looking at, depending on which class, who I'm writing it for. And then . . . instead of just focusing on the purpose of the paper again looking more at . . . who I'm writing for, what my goal is for the paper and stuff instead of only caring about the format, which is what I used to do before. So I think that's what I took from the class."

Maggie also later elaborated on being able to interrogate the origin of her thought, a form of metacognition, as another transferrable habit of mind: "I guess the ability to be able to see . . . what led up to that point where I started thinking a certain way . . . I feel like a lot of times in my classes . . . I'll really begin to understand something but then there's always kind of my bias towards it and I kind of have to figure out why I'm thinking that way and I feel like we discuss a lot in the writing class about what setting was the author writing in? What led them to write a certain way? And what is leading us to perceive it a certain way. And I feel like that's really transferred to all my classes."

Like Maggie, Max was also keen to describe a heightened rhetorical awareness while also demonstrating a new perception of writing studies as a whole. To the initial questions of *what transferred*, he responded: "Maybe like, manipulating an assignment . . . to keep with the academic guidelines but make it funner for you to write . . . So, integrating humor or metaphors, or something that I enjoy writing, into the paper [so] that I could just drone on about the topic." To get a little more detail, I asked Max how he would go about gauging when these kinds of adaptations are appropriate or not. He offered these examples: "It's hard to say. This year at least I've just kind of dipped my toes and saw what happened or I, like, really did it and just submitted a paper that I kind of went a little overboard with it maybe, so it's just kind of testing to see what the instructor, your professor is going to feel about that . . . And just how they word the assignment could be another way to gauge, but I think I do kind of base the assignment . . . [on] who they are as a person from, like, what I've gotten from being in the class."

After this demonstration of sophisticated rhetorical awareness, I had to ask if this was an awareness that was fostered in WRIT 101 or if he had already been paying attention to this detail. His response: "I might have been paying attention to it but I think I really realized in WRIT 101 and I followed up the next semester with another class with the same instructor and it kind of built on that again."

A final note from Max includes the increased relaxation and comfort he found with a form of college enculturation: the willingness to speak up in class. "I think maybe engaging the classroom . . .'cause it was a smaller class. You can really work on your ideas before writing a paper when you're bouncing your thoughts off your peers and having an actual conversation. And then having a teacher or professor moderating that, it's really helpful. So I've tried to take that into my other classes and just not be afraid to talk and say what I think."

Elle, comparable to Max and Maggie, also showed a refined understanding of the adaptability of a rhetorical situation, and also expressed her transferable habit of making writing meaningful and fun for herself every time. She says it's "the idea of doing everything you can to get yourself more excited about the assignment. So, not just for getting a grade but what can I learn from this? How is this going to be useful to me in the future? . . . So usually what I did was looked at the prompt and tried to think of how that could tie into my major or an experience I've had and then try to make it as fun as possible." Here, she shows a comfortable attitude with making writing relevant to her life rather than just worrying about the academic expectations. She also elaborates on her advanced understanding of the importance of shifting tone depending on the context: "I think writing is kind of the foundation of being successful in any non-science- or math-based subject, whether it's sociology or . . . anything like English or business. It's kind of how you express what you're trying to get across and there's just so many different ways to do it. With business you're going to want to be directive, you're in something creative and in the arts you're going to want to draw on as much personal experience as you can and kind of go for more of an emotional stance rather than educational. But I guess the biggest transfer for me too was just how prevalent writing is and how much you can do with it."

USE OF WRITING ABOUT WRITING

Closely related to transfer, the students also discussed very practical *uses* of their FYC courses, focusing on the adaptability and relevance of WAW beyond the writing classroom. The interviewees mentioned many theoretical and practical ways they were able to use habits of mind and skills after their writing courses. I began by asking them if they could think on a more practical or utilitarian level of how they have used their writing courses since they've completed them.

Max responded with some practical tools, indeed: "Learning how to cite things properly, practic[ing] that for the first time in that class. And . . . then writing an abstract and reverse outlining process. So, like, writing processes that I still use after that class that I learned there."

Elle had some very interesting and relevant examples as well. "One thing I used it for was to help me with cover letters this summer. I kind of used reverse outlining. Using a different style of voice, and it helped me get an incredible job this summer that I don't think I would have gotten otherwise without the cover letter." Of course, I was compelled to ask how exactly she managed to design the cover letter so effectively, and she elaborated with these sharp rhetorical details: "I was modeling the style of writing that they were using in their wanted ads and anything like that. I was talking about myself but also including their values and just kind of a perfect balance between them and me."

Maggie followed up with another affirmation of the relaxed attitude she has adapted to the writing process itself and how useful this is: "I've kind of already said it . . . but kind of being more lax on the process of writing . . . Before [I'd] . . . totally freak out and feel like I can't do it . . . I still kind of, when I start writing I'll have an outline but I'm not so, 'I first have to write the intro and I can't write the next paragraph until the intro is done.' I kind of just start letting things come and flow and stuff before I start worrying too much about it."

As I asked for any last follow-up comments on uses of WAW, both Max and Elle echoed experiencing newfound comfort in freewriting. Max said, "I kind of picked up on a similar thing like that. Just getting over the super-structured, just getting a draft, sit down for an hour or two and write no matter how bad it is. You can come back and fix it later and work on it long as you like . . . flesh out those ideas a little bit." And Elle finished the series of questions with this response: "Well, then yeah, definitely, I think in this class . . . I would just sit down for an hour or two hours without going back and reading, I would just sit and mindlessly type until all the ideas were out. Usually you'd go back and read it and be like, that wasn't that bad, and just fix it up a little bit rather than stare at a sentence for an hour and not move on until that was complete."

This new comfort, or relaxation, as I refer to it throughout the chapter, really was one of the most unexpected themes I encountered in the interview. To me it seemed all three students had picked up an ability to *trust* in the writing process—the drafting, the revisions, the imperfect composition—in a way unprecedented until their WAW experiences, which is why I interpret this as a form of relaxation or comfort in the writing process itself.

REFLECTION

At the editors' behest, students also discussed their perceptions of the *reflective* element in WAW classrooms. By studying reflection and to what degree it is fostered in WAW, we are partially concerned with creating mindful and situationally aware writers able to more skillfully adapt to new writing situations. But reflection also plays a role in education not traditionally academic: self-growth and self-awareness. By fostering mindful *thinkers*, we foster students who can intellectually interrogate the beliefs, customs, and constructs that would otherwise direct their lives unconsciously. To begin this series of discussion, I asked the students: "In terms of the reflective element of the course, how much did that course seem like a place to practice reflection—self-reflection or reflection on anything in general?"

Maggie explained the strong emphasis of reflection in her course: "I feel like in our class in particular since [we] were focusing a lot on metacognition . . . it kind of geared us to . . . think that way and I think that was kind of the first time in any of my classes that we were really encouraged to kind of reflect and include more of ourselves in our academics . . . and not be so focused on the grade and that kind of thing. I don't know, I feel like being able to reflect in that class and be kind of free to just include whatever I wanted and just let it be really authentic definitely has helped me in other areas of my life too and kind of figure out why I do something a certain way, or why I behave a certain way and what led up to that. So I feel like it's helped me not only in writing and other areas of school, but personally too. Like growing as a person, emotionally and stuff."

And as the discussion ensued, we brought up the course portfolios required to revise written work for the semester. Maggie explained she found this conclusion to the course "really enlightening." She continues, "Because [I wanted to] kind of figure out why I included something . . . If that was important, try to figure out why it was important then. So it was really informative for me. Gave me a lot of insight to myself. My process of writing."

Elle agreed; her course also deeply revolved around reflection: "I would say knowing there was so much reflection in that class it felt like

I always had a second chance so I definitely took more risks in my writing. Kind of trying different things rather than doing the cookie-cutter style of exactly what the professor is looking for. It was more, 'This is what feels good to me. This is how I want to express this idea. Give it a shot.' I feel like most of the time it worked out better and now my writing has kind of shifted more towards what I like to do rather than fitting the mold."

As she explained this interesting effort with taking risk and second chances, I asked her if she continues to see this possibility of liberty elsewhere. She was resolute: "I would say I've definitely . . . continued with it. I think professors like it when you tie in those personal aspects and relate it to you and don't just write what every kid is writing since it's the stereotypical thing to do."

And, finally, Max reinforced Maggie's and Elle's observations that reflection encouraged taking risks and relaxing as a student: "I just thought that it kind of fostered the ability to stop writing as a student so much as writing just to write. So I thought that for me it personally made me realize how much I like writing. It made me want to pursue writing. I switched majors like halfway through that class from business to writing. So . . . for me personally, it reflected, made me realize that's what I enjoyed to do."

The relationship of revision to second chances discussed in this section is another intriguing outcome the students seemed to agree about. In a way, the knowledge of having a second chance, because of the requirement of revising your work seems to add to the effect of relaxing into and trusting the writing process.

THRESHOLD CONCEPTS

The terminology of *threshold concepts* allows us a way to target major, pivotal learning moments in the interviewed students' WAW experiences. As I asked the students to identify threshold concepts in their writing classes, it became evident that their obvious examples were closely related to several other themes of our discussion. Though threshold concepts are relative to the individual, the interwoven nature of this conversation—not just in this section but throughout this chapter—shows some similar epiphanies reached by all three students taking WAW courses. To the question of which profound threshold concepts the students could remember, they responded with the following insights.

Max really demonstrates here, as throughout this interview, his understanding that revision is central to developing writing, reminiscent of a crucial theme in the edited collection *Naming What We Know: Threshold Concepts of Writing Studies* (Downs 2015, 66). Max began, eventually citing by memory "Shitty First Drafts" by Anne Lamott (1994), to supplement his revelation about learning to let go and just enjoy writing: "So before like, most of the writing I did was for my high school classes and it was like a book review or . . . something. And I liked doing it but I'd . . . draft a paper, read it over once, do some copy editing maybe and then turn it in. So . . . coming from that to drafting a paper three or four times before I turn a paper in and having . . . actual stages of drafting and revising and copy editing. I think that there's more to it than just getting your thoughts out onto paper. And you're not going to get it perfect every time. Even professional writers aren't drafting a chapter in a book and, oh, that's perfect, and handing it to their editor . . . So I just kind of realized that I wasn't, that there's more of a process to it than just writing something for thirty minutes and turning it in."

For Maggie, the memory of a profound threshold was somewhat frustrating, actually, and for very interesting and important reasons. She cited "All Writing Is Autobiography" by Donald Murray (1991) to explain her initial discomfort with the idea that we are a part of what we write. In her words, "I felt . . . there was a point where I got really frustrated and angry with writing. Because it was like I remember during writing class realizing . . . how much of ourselves are in our writing. It doesn't matter what we're writing about, we're always in it and even if it's . . . a really formal paper, there's still parts of ourselves in it. And I was really mad about that because . . . I wanted to keep myself out of my academics. I wanted to turn in a paper and not have me a part of it. And, that's not possible. And I still kind of feel pressured because . . . I've learned that; I can't go back like how it was seen before the class."

Our third respondent, Elle, revisits a threshold concept she and the other interviewees had connected to several questions: feeling freedom and fun in what they write. Elle demonstrated a personal transformation as she reiterated this crucial threshold: "I think just the biggest thing for me was the concept of freewriting . . . once I got over that barrier of even though it's not perfect, keep writing. You don't have to have the perfect opening paragraph. It doesn't have to be eloquent and flow well. As long as you get the ideas out, then it's going to be that much easier to go back and fix it from there. And now that has completely changed my style of writing and made the process a lot more enjoyable along the way, too."

IDENTITY

I place the students' discussion of *identity* at the close of this chapter, as it seemed to carry a unanimous theme from our interviewees: that they identified, not necessarily before the WAW course but during and after the course, *as* writers. As you read this final section, you may notice the resolution in these students' comments that WAW allowed them to find a voice worth expressing, despite not being professional or paid writers. I really noticed here a shift in these students' self-perception of agency and confidence to express themselves. My final question to the students was: "Is there anything specifically that you could say that WRIT 101 did to help shape or alter your identity as a writer?"

The answer was obvious to Max, as during the course of his writing semester he switched his major to writing. Max said, "Well, it made me realize that's what I wanted to do with my career, with my life. That's what I'm passionate about. So I think it shaped that I'm more serious about all the writing I do now. It's something I want to pursue in the future." It was evident to me in this response that he now saw the possibility, or probability even, of being an editor or author, and so I asked if he saw himself as an author or editor before the writing course. He responded, "No, I don't think so. I really wasn't sure what I wanted to do. And thus, like, as the course started I realized I wanted to do something with writing."

Elle concluded on a familiar theme of the interview, for her and the other participants. "I think the biggest thing is that it just kind of reminded me that writing is enjoyable. It's a relaxing, fun activity for me. I think I can communicate things most efficiently through writing. So this summer I was going through an experience of moving to a new town and new people and I was so excited about it but couldn't verbally get people to understand. So I started writing . . . mock articles . . . that you'd find in *Outside* magazine. I wanted to get people to be on that basis with me and understand what I'd been doing for the past couple of months. So that kind of sparked my interest in journalism as well. It's something I'm still kind of curious about."

And Maggie eloquently wrapped our final round of questions with this inspiring response about the agency that belongs to even *students* of writing: "I feel like I've always been interested in writing, but I would never identify as a writer . . . like I wouldn't say, 'Yes, I'm a writer,' until after the class. And I feel like it's given me the confidence to know that I'll always be growing . . . But that doesn't mean I can't still be a writer now. It's kind of liberating to know that you don't have to be perfect but . . . that doesn't mean that you're not important. So what you say is important. So I think that's definitely helped me and I've been able to write more openly because I don't have the idea that someday I can be a writer. Once I'm published. All those things. Like once I am, but *now* I can do that."

And here, perhaps, we see another of the most profound themes that arose in this conversation: that prior to WRIT 101, Elle, Max, and Maggie may never have explicitly seen themselves as writers. I by no means want to claim this is an inevitable effect of writing about writing; however, it does seem like WAW classrooms are creating an opportunity for students to trust the writing process so much that they trust themselves to be writers, too.

CONCLUSION

It is clear that we cannot generalize that all student experiences in WAW courses have such profound outcomes and useful, transferrable habits of mind as in the cases of Maggie, Max, and Elle. What we can see, however, are some unexpected outcomes enabled by focuses on rhetoric and reflection in composition pedagogy. As an instructor who has taught writing about writing pedagogy for only three years, I rarely get to see or hear about how my students' perceptions of writing as an activity or art have shifted into their new writing environments, which is why listening to how these students actually transfer WRIT 101 outward is so interesting to hear. It's amazing to see, for example, that despite the classroom conversations that happen during the semester about how rhetoric may be mistaken as only a means of manipulation—and all the fears we may have as instructors that this is all students will remember about rhetoric—these students paradoxically feel more authentic and free as writers now because they know so much about how to change text to fit their own and their audiences' goals simultaneously. Elle's use of rhetoric to write a cover letter for a job, and Maggie's use of metacognition to understand herself better in any area of her life are not results we can guarantee as an instructor, but they are some of the most ideal outcomes to hear of. Finally, as a busy teacher of writing about writing, advocating relaxation or comfort with the writing process is not always at the forefront of my agenda, but if these examples of developing peace with the process are a byproduct of what we teach, then that is perhaps the most gratifying outcome a writing instructor can hope for.

REFERENCES

Downs, Doug. 2015. "Revision Is Central to Developing Writing." In *Naming What We Know: Threshold Concepts of Writing*, edited by Linda Adler-Kassner and Elizabeth Wardle, 66–67. Logan: Utah State University Press.

Lamott, Anne. 1994. "Shitty First Drafts." In *Writing about Writing: A College Reader*, 2nd ed., edited by Doug Downs and Elizabeth Wardle, 527–31. New York: Bedford/St. Martin's, 2014.

Murray, Donald. 1991. "All Writing Is Autobiography." *College Composition and Communication* 42 (1): 66–74.

Wardle, Elizabeth, and Doug Downs, eds. 2014. *Writing about Writing: A College Reader*. 2nd ed. New York: Bedford/St. Martin's.

26
FINDING A WAY INTO WAW
Extending Invitations across Disciplinary Lines

Matthew Bryan, Kevin Roozen, and Nichole Stack

> INSTITUTION TYPE AND SIZE: 63,000-student public university
> COURSE CONTEXT: Two-course FYW; required general education sequence
> STUDY DESIGN/METHODOLOGY: Retrospective program reflection
> WAW PROGRAM OR NOT: WAW-focused first-year writing program
> WAW COURSE OR SINGLE ASSIGNMENT/UNIT: WAW-focused first-year writing program
> INSTRUCTOR TYPE/POSITION: Full-time lecturer, tenured associate professor, and full-time lecturer now associate lecturer, tenured professor, and instructor and first-year composition director
> KEY TERMS: Disciplinarity; interdisciplinarity; first-year writing; stakeholders

ABSTRACT

This chapter elaborates strategies that a team of first-year composition WPAs has found useful for inviting three stakeholders from across the university to engage productively with WAW: student editors of a journal of first-year writing, graduate students preparing to teach first-year composition, and instructors and administrators affiliated with programs that serve English-language learners. These stakeholders often have their own disciplinary preconceptions as to what writing instruction looks like, and WAW can run contrary to those expectations. Ultimately, we argue that inviting stakeholders to draw upon their disciplinary orientations is crucial if they are to find their way into WAW.

INTRODUCTION

Discussions about writing about writing (WAW) pedagogies frequently center around what Downs and Wardle called the "elephant in the room" (2007, 575), the particular disciplinary expertise and preparation teachers need to effectively teach a WAW curriculum. In a later article, Wardle and Downs (2013) revised their original assertion that "instructors must be educated in writing studies to teach the [WAW] curriculum" (Downs and Wardle 2007, 575), arguing that their "experiences have demonstrated a wide variety of ways for current writing instructors with degrees in other fields to gain that familiarity in programs where idealistic insistence on rhet/comp degrees would result in gridlock" (Wardle and Downs 2013).

As a team of first-year composition WPAs, we are especially invested in this latter point. While our FYC program transitioned to a WAW approach five years ago (see Wardle 2015, "Intractable Writing Program Problems"), questions of disciplinarity remain a central issue, both within and outside of the department in which we teach. Since our FYC program serves as the entry point into the writing curriculum at the second-largest public university in the United States, we frequently find ourselves describing WAW to many different stakeholders who have their own preconceptions of what a writing course looks like. It is often the case that WAW runs contrary to these expectations. Where other curricula might be modeled by sharing student work or key assignments, the focus of WAW is less on the texts students produce and more on the learning that occurs as students take up writing as a central topic of study. How, then, can we make sure we are having coherent conversations about WAW with those less familiar with writing studies?

In this chapter, we argue that stakeholders' disciplinary backgrounds are a central consideration in inviting them to engage productively with a WAW approach to writing instruction and literacy learning more broadly. We focus on our experiences with three distinct groups of stakeholders: Matt's efforts with the student editors of our department's peer-reviewed journal of first-year writing, Kevin's work to prepare graduate students from different programs to teach first-year writing, and Nichole's collaborations with instructors and program administrators affiliated with intensive English programs (IEPs) and teaching English to speakers of other languages (TESOL). These three groups represent a variety of disciplinary and professional identities, but each interaction calls on us to negotiate anew a WAW approach to writing instruction. As Charles Bazerman argues, working at the interstices of different disciplinary perspectives "can help make visible the home discipline's core assumptions as well as the core assumptions of the other disciplines one engages with . . . When we see an intersection of concerns or when the other discipline might provide a resource, we have an intellectual obligation to learn what the other discipline knows and how it knows it" (2011, 19). In our experiences, discussions about WAW across disciplinary lines serve as invitations to reexamine what writing instruction can be, with interesting and often unexpected results.

NEGOTIATING "GOOD": USING WAW TO FIND COMMON GROUND AT A FIRST-YEAR WRITING JOURNAL—MATTHEW BRYAN

In 2009, our FYC program formed a new student magazine, *Stylus: A Journal of First-Year Writing*, for which I served both then and now as faculty editor. Released twice a year online, *Stylus* was developed to "provide a forum for the exemplary writing and research produced by students" in FYC *(Stylus: A Journal of First-Year Writing* 2015). Because more than 3,000 students enroll in composition classes taught by as many as forty different instructors in our program during any given semester, we wanted to be able to share some of the stellar work students were producing.

It was also in 2009 that some instructors in our program piloted the WAW curriculum. This presented an interesting challenge for the student and faculty editors who reviewed submissions to *Stylus*: how do you determine what constitutes "exemplary writing and research" when the types of writing you're considering look so very different? This question would drive much of the discussion around *Stylus* in the coming years, even after our program had transitioned fully to the WAW approach. Proponents of WAW focus less on the kind of writing students produce and more on the knowledge about writing they're leaving with. With dozens of instructors teaching in our program, students produce a wide range of writing, from literacy narratives to more analytical arguments to multimedia projects. Every semester, the faculty and student editors working with *Stylus* find themselves again trying to answer the question "What, exactly, are we looking for?"

The faculty committee charged with launching *Stylus* decided on a two-stage editorial process: student reviewers would read all of the submissions and then pass on their top selections to the faculty committee for a final decision. To facilitate this process, the committee designed a simple rubric that included criteria such as "Does the essay provide a clear focus?" and "Does the author fully develop his or her ideas clearly and cogently?" that student reviewers could use to evaluate submissions (see appendix 26.A for the original rubric and appendix 26.B for the most recent). This rubric marked the faculty committee's first attempt to describe what it saw as successful writing emerging from FYC.

For every issue after the first, we've invited past contributors to serve as editors, and they've formed the majority of the journal's volunteer staff. We have also recruited a mix of university writing center tutors and former composition students suggested by their instructors. Few if any of these students are English or writing majors; instead, they come from disciplines as diverse as hospitality management, biology, and legal studies. The student editors working with the journal thus reflect the population of students in our composition classes and their broad set of perceptions and experiences about what writing can do and be. If the goal of WAW was to get students to write like writing studies scholars, a team of faculty could select the pieces that most represented that. But, instead, WAW asks students to consider ideas about writing that resonate with and can be useful for them. Who better to select the pieces that do that than other students?

Not surprisingly, the student editors frequently did not agree, and our editorial discussions often mirrored some of the conversations about writing with faculty in other disciplines that Kevin and Nichole describe below. As the WAW approach developed in our FYC classes, however, the student editors began to come in with a common language for talking about writing. What they valued in writing continued to differ, but they became more self-aware as to why those differences existed. Student editors began to link their comments to concepts like audience or what a piece was contributing to scholarly conversations, and away from grammar or idiosyncratic preferences. As the conversations with and between student editors became richer, they relied less on the rubric (which grew simpler over time), and their own commentaries and general rankings of submissions were used to determine which submissions would move on.

The composition program's work around *Stylus* prompted useful self-examination at the right time. Questions about what WAW looks like in the classroom and student writing persist, but these are generative questions for a writing program to consider. We hope that *Stylus* helps faculty to answer these questions on occasion, but we should be wary of getting too rigid in our expectations of what this curriculum looks like. The varied perspectives of student editors coming from a variety of disciplines remind us that the question "What makes it good?" is always a negotiation. The WAW curriculum provides some common language and metaknowledge about writing that serve as an inroad to discussions that can move past "good" or "bad." These conversations allow students to acknowledge and value their own developing disciplinary perspectives while also reminding them that possessing different views on writing is always a possibility.

LEARNING TO TEACH: EXTENDING GRADUATE STUDENTS' DISCIPLINARY IDENTITIES INTO WAW—KEVIN ROOZEN

As director of first-year composition, I oversee the preparation of the graduate students who will serve as teaching assistants in the first-year writing courses grounded in a curriculum that immerses students in using key concepts from the study of writing and rhetoric to identify and analyze complex, real-world rhetorical situations that animate their academic, professional, civic, and personal lives. Like the undergraduate student editors of *Stylus*, these stakeholders hail from a variety of disciplinary worlds. The four or five students enrolled in the department's MA program have taken a few graduate courses in rhetoric and composition and worked in the university writing center during their initial semester. The majority of the students, however, hail from the university's MA programs in literary and cultural studies and TESOL, the MFA program in creative writing, or PhD program in texts and technology. Not only will these teachers-in-becoming guide their own first-year writing students through the WAW approach, they also serve as important connections between the WAW curriculum and faculty, other graduate students, and even undergraduate students from their respective departments and disciplines.

No matter which disciplines graduate students have claimed as their own, these backgrounds figure prominently in their identities as teachers and the pedagogical practices they develop. Acknowledging the significance of the histories that people bring to their teaching, Deborah Britzman describes learning to teach as "a struggle for voice and discursive practice amid a cacophony of past and present voices, lived experience, and available practices. The tensions among what has preceded, what is confronted, and what one desires shape the contradictory realities of learning to teach" (1991, 31). Teachers don't just inhabit a curriculum; rather, they inhabit a curriculum in ways that resonate, and perhaps conflict, with the discourses and practices that animate their lives. In this sense, teachers' efforts to navigate their disciplinary histories and what they encounter in a somewhat new disciplinary space can powerfully transform and even disrupt their classroom identities and practices. In the same way that students' histories with writing and identities as writers beyond school shape their learning, teachers' disciplinary histories can play a crucial role in shaping their identities and practices.

The variety of disciplinary backgrounds graduate students bring to their composition teaching presents a number of challenges to their preparation for teaching. Perhaps the most pressing challenge involves helping graduate students, persons at a pivotal stage in developing their disciplinary trajectories, extend themselves into a WAW approach in ways that respect the disciplinary identities they claim for themselves and that allow them to productively extend their disciplinary histories into their teaching.

One of the most crucial moves we have developed involves fostering long-term interactions between these soon-to-be teachers and faculty who share their disciplinary backgrounds. We've accomplished this by pairing each student with a volunteer departmental faculty member who shares the student's disciplinary orientation and has found innovative and effective ways of weaving that background into his or her own pedagogy. In addition to providing these students with feedback over the summer as they plan their composition courses and prepare their teaching materials, these mentors also offer concrete advice about what it means to envision and enact a WAW approach from the perspective of someone working, say, toward an MFA specializing in poetry or creative nonfiction, an MA emphasizing literary studies or TESOL, or a doctorate in texts and technology. In interacting with these mentors throughout the summer and during their entire first year of teaching, and in many cases beyond, these graduate teaching assistants come to view the heterogeneous resources and social identities that they bring to their teaching as fertile grounds for constructing and reconstructing disciplinary worlds and identities, disrupting dominant power relationships, illuminating the affordances and constraints of various kinds of knowledge, practice, and discourse, and, ultimately, transforming classrooms spaces and practices.

Mentors with a background in writing studies, for example, help the graduate students in rhetoric and composition understand how the topics and research methods they encounter in their coursework are useful for encouraging first-year writing students to explore similar topics using similar methods. Mentors with a history in the study of literature help graduate students from literary and cultural studies view their own experiences learning the rhetorical moves of literary analysis as a productive foundation for helping first-year writing students examine how they have learned the conventions associated with other genres. Mentors with expertise in creative writing encourage graduate students in the MFA program to draw upon their own rich repertoires of writing practices, processes, and rituals as a strategy for getting first-year writing students to investigate their own. Mentors with experience working with English-language learners help graduate students in TESOL recognize their expertise with bilingualism, code-switching, transnational writing, and the globalization of English as productive issues for first-year writing students to research. Mentors with knowledge of digital writing and rhetoric help doctoral students in texts and technology productively immerse first-year writing students in investigating digital writing technologies through conducting digital ethnographies and exploring digital archives.

Helping soon-to-be teachers find their way into the WAW approach in a way that respects their unique disciplinary orientations is a key step toward helping them develop a sense of what the students enrolled in their first-year writing classes will experience as they encounter WAW and how they can encourage those learners to weave together their own disparate voices, identities, and lived experiences from their disciplinary pasts, presents, and anticipated futures.

BRIDGING LANGUAGES AND LITERACIES: WAW AND TEACHING ELLS—NICHOLE STACK

With total international student enrollment nearing 900,000 nationwide in 2013–14 (Institute of International Education 2015), forging relationships with stakeholders focused on teaching English-language learners (ELLs) becomes especially important for WPAs in first-year composition, as the resulting dialog can foster a better understanding of how a WAW curriculum effectively meets the needs of this population. This has become particularly relevant at our university with the emergence of an exciting program initiative for international students, in which students complete one year of study in the program's academy, taking a combination of English-language instruction and credit-bearing modules (including ENC 1101 and 1102, the two courses in our yearlong FYC sequence) before moving on to their respective degree pathways. As our department's acting liaison to the program, I work with the academy to create a smooth transition for students progressing from the English-language courses to ENC 1101.

In summer 2014, soon after the program began, I was asked to collaborate with three of the academy's teachers and its director to develop the curriculum for two English-language courses: English for Academic Purposes (EAP) 1 and 2, reading and writing courses that, at the time, focused heavily on grammar and mechanics and primarily used modes for writing instruction. The program discovered early on that this approach was not best suited to prepare students for the credit-bearing modules (which was cause for initiating contact with our department). I was excited to have the opportunity to apply my experience with WAW and teaching ELLs, and although designing a curriculum with stakeholders from different disciplines—in this case, TESOL, education, and business—would prove to be challenging, the main goal was to reach a common understanding of WAW as an effective and desirable approach for these students.

In our first couple of meetings, we aimed to learn more about each program's goals. I shared our first-year writing program's guiding principles, which draw from a number of WAW concepts (see appendix 26.C). Much time was spent discussing the meaning and purpose of these principles, especially those addressing revision and genres (the members of the working group asked many questions about the pragmatic application of these in 1101 and 1102 courses, which was very encouraging). This led to more detailed conversation about the students, our primary stakeholders. Where are they from? What are their educational experiences? What is their English-language proficiency (as determined by standardized tests like TOEFL, TOEIC, and IELTS, since these scores determine entry and placement into the program)? What are their needs and expectations? We held several meetings over the summer, with our remaining rounds of collaboration spent brainstorming ideas for EAP 1 and 2's scope and sequence and working out potential curricula. This included further discussion of materials central to our first-year writing program, namely, 1101 and 1102 course outcomes, Wardle and Downs's (2014) *Writing about Writing*, texts on multilingual learners and FYC (one piece that especially stood out to the members was Canagarajah's [2014] "ESL Composition as a Literate Art of the Contact Zone"), WAW-based readings for students (mostly from *Writing Spaces*), and student work from *Stylus*. By summer's end, the EAP 1 and EAP 2 teachers had developed final versions of their classes to implement in the upcoming semesters.

Dialog had opened, and we continued to have regular communication about relevant program updates, needs, and ideas. Our latest collaboration (summer 2015) began when our department was asked about possibly adding more WAW-oriented readings and assignments into the EAP 1/2 curriculum. Now, as of fall 2015, EAP 2 includes several *Writing Spaces* readings, a literacy narrative project (adapted from Catherine Ramsdell's [2011] "Storytelling, Narration, and the 'Who I Am' Story"), and a final portfolio. These new incorporations show an increase in the valuing of learning over product, a pillar of WAW.

WAW requires a shift in our thinking and values so that we're asking questions like "How does writing work? What do students need to know *about* writing that will help them succeed in later coursework?" This shift is ongoing, and it is encouraging for our department to see the changes taking place in the program's understanding of how a WAW approach in English-language instruction can more effectively prepare students, as evidenced by the revised curricula of their EAP courses. Working with a variety of disciplines represented in the program acts as a reminder that WAW is itself interdisciplinary in nature, and thus affords opportunities for conversations about writing and the teaching and learning of writing that reach across disciplinary and programmatic lines. Surely *interdisciplinarity*, our own hodgepodge of backgrounds, works much like an alloy, and in this case is working to help solidify our university community to better meet the needs of the growing number of ELLs.

CONCLUSION

As WAW continues to grow and transform, a continual next step will involve forging connections with the wealth of stakeholders occupying the institutional landscape. Our administrative efforts at the intersections of multiple disciplines have allowed us to invite others to productively engage with WAW. These invitations across disciplinary lines are made possible by WAW's fundamental emphasis on what students learn about writing and the work it does in the world rather than on the particular kind of writing students generate. If we all had to agree on what effective writing actually looks like, we might never get anywhere. But WAW reminds us that there are, in fact, some overarching principles about how writing works, and these principles inform the shared language about writing that makes conversations with stakeholders from different disciplines productive.

Moreover, these interactions have begun to feed back into how we think about student writing and learning about writing ourselves. Matt's work with the student editors of *Stylus* has created a space for genuine conversation about how best to represent the kinds of learning WAW occasions, which has, in turn, led to ongoing discussions within our program about what student learning might look like and where in the curriculum it might appear. Kevin's interactions with graduate students from a wealth of disciplinary histories and identities have helped us to assemble an approach to WAW that speaks to the wide-ranging interests of the more than 5,000 students enrolled in first-year writing each year. Nichole's efforts with teachers and administrators working with ELLs have generated a dialog based on a mutual respect for everyone's perspectives of and investments in student learning. As a result, we've been able to invite some of those individuals to participate in our faculty's ongoing professional development and thus benefit from their perspectives and expertise. This sort of work would not be possible without close collaboration between the FYC program director and the two coordinators. Within any FYC program, it is imperative that everyone work together and share what they are learning as they collaborate with and try to describe to different groups of stakeholders what it is they do. It has been our experience that, just as the WAW curriculum invites students to find a place for their own experiences and perspectives in the FYC classroom, discussions around the curriculum with other stakeholders create opportunities for generative discussions about what writing and writing instruction can be, opportunities to learn as well as to share.

APPENDIX 26.A

Stylus: A Journal of First-Year Writing Original Rubric

Stylus rubric: After you're done assessing the paper, add up the total number of points you've allotted for each question.

- Does the essay meet all MLA standards and requirements, i.e., formats, citations, works cited and bibliography pages?
    - Circle the number that best answers the above question:
    - 0: Meets very few or does not meet any MLA requirements
    - 2: Meets some MLA requirements
    - 5: Meets all (or almost all) MLA requirements
- Does the essay provide a clear focus, offering an original voice, approach, and perspective on the topic?
    - Circle the number that best answers the above question:
    - 0: Does not provide a clear focus or argument
    - 2: Provides a focus, but it does not offer an original voice, approach, or perspective
    - 5: Provides a clear focus and offers an original voice, approach, and perspective
- Does the essay have a clear audience and rhetorical context?
    - Circle the number that best answers the above question:
    - 0: No attempt to address a specific audience
    - 2: Attempts, with some success, to address a specific audience and rhetorical context
    - 5: Clearly and effectively addresses a specific audience
- Are sentence patterns sophisticated, varied, fluent, and succinct—free of grammatical and mechanical problems?

Circle the number that best answers the above question:

0: Very few patterns are sophisticated, varied, fluent, and succinct

2: Some patterns are sophisticated, varied, fluent and succinct

5: Almost all of the patterns are sophisticated, varied, fluent, and succinct

Does the author fully develop his or her ideas clearly and cogently?

Circle the number that best answers the above question:

0: Many ideas are unclear and undeveloped

2: Some ideas are clear, cogent, and well-developed

5: Almost all ideas are clear, cogent, and well-developed

Does the essay exhibit appropriate use of diction?

Circle the number that best answers the above question:

0: Weak or generic diction throughout most of the essay

2: Some effective use of advanced diction throughout the essay

5: Consistent and effective use of advanced diction throughout the entire essay

Choose *either* question A or B to assess the paper, not both. (A) Is the quality and credibility of any research referenced and/or quoted in the essay at a high level? (B) Is the quality of any evidentiary support well crafted?

Circle the number that best answers the above question:

0: Research/evidence is severely lacking or of very poor quality

2: Some of the research/evidence is at a high level

5: Almost all of the research/evidence is at a very high level

Depending on the type of essay, choose *either* question A or B to assess the paper, not both. (A) Does the essay demonstrate a high level of synthesis between the writer's ideas and any research/topic? (B) Does the essay demonstrate a high level of synthesis between the writer's ideas, details, and evidentiary support?

Circle the number that best answers the above question:

0: Little to no effective synthesis between research/evidentiary support and writer's ideas

2: Some effective synthesis between research/evidentiary support and writer's ideas

5: Clear and effective synthesis between research/evidentiary support and writer's ideas

APPENDIX 26.B

Stylus: A Journal of First-Year Writing Current Rubric

Stylus Manuscript Assessment Rubric

Project #: _____   Total Score: _____

Editor Name: _____

Additional Comments:

Does the project engage the audience through a fresh approach/voice/perspective and/or genuine inquiry into a subject?
- 0–3: Does not engage the audience
- 4–7: Somewhat engages the audience
- 8–10: Successfully engages the audience

Does the project seem valuable/useful for a particular audience and/or in response to a significant exigence/problem/need?
- 0–3: Holds little value/use or value/use is unclear
- 4–7: Somewhat valuable/useful
- 8–10: Very valuable/useful

Are the author's ideas fully developed and well organized?
- 0–3: Few ideas are fully developed and well organized
- 4–7: Some ideas are fully developed and well organized
- 8–10: Almost all ideas are fully developed and well organized

What is the quality of the author's research (primary and/or secondary) and/or other evidentiary support (examples, details, reflections, etc.)?
- 0–3: Research/evidence is lacking or of poor quality
- 4–7: Some of the research/evidence is at a high level
- 8–10: Almost all of the research/evidence is at a very high level

Does the project demonstrate a high level of synthesis between the writer's ideas and any research/reflection/details/evidentiary support?
- 0–3: Little to no effective synthesis between research/evidentiary support and writer's ideas
- 4–7: Some effective synthesis between research/evidentiary support and writer's ideas
- 8–10: Clear and effective synthesis between research/evidentiary support and writer's ideas

Does the project reflect the author's use of effective language for its targeted audience?
- 0–3: The project reflects inadequate register and ineffective sentence structure for its audience
- 4–7: Some of the author's diction and sentence structures are appropriate for their audience, but the language could be revised in some areas
- 8–10: The project demonstrates consistent and effective use of language and sentence patterns

APPENDIX 26.C

Principles of ENC 1101 and 1102 Curricula

Writers need both declarative and procedural knowledge about writing. That is, they need to know how to use language effectively and how to adjust their writing processes to be most effective given the rhetorical situation in which they are writing. But they also benefit from a deep understanding of writing-related concepts such as rhetorical situation, genre, plagiarism, error, incubation, discourse community, and so on. Thus, the composition courses include instruction in drafting and revising, but also have a clear content drawn from writing studies research and theory about composing.

Writers need to engage in sustained drafting and revision in order to write most effectively. Student writers respond best to comments about their writing when they have time and opportunity to incorporate suggestions into revised drafts. Thus, the composition courses are based on a process approach to writing instruction that requires students to engage in substantive global revision over time, in addition to careful editing at the sentence level to produce thoughtful and polished final drafts.

Writers write most effectively when their writing is purposeful, transactional, communicative, contributive, and rhetorical. Thus, the composition courses encourage students to understand and write for specific audiences to achieve clear purposes that are meaningful to the student.

Writing instruction should strive to teach transferable practices and concepts. Thus, the composition curriculum is rooted in research on knowledge transfer that suggests students should learn flexible concepts about writing rather than rigid rules, and they should engage in continual reflection on their writing practices to encourage mindfulness.

Particular genres are best learned in the contexts where they mediate activity. Thus, the composition curriculum focuses on purpose and content first, in the belief that form follows function. Students in ENC 1101 and ENC 1102 will write in a variety of genres appropriate to their rhetorical purposes and learning goals. Genres specific to various disciplinary activity systems (for example, lab reports or philosophy essays) should be taught within the classrooms where those genres mediate meaningful work and learning. Genres or "modes" will not be taught acontextually in ENC 1101 and ENC 1102.

REFERENCES

Bazerman, Charles. 2011. "The Disciplined Interdisciplinarity of Writing Studies." *Research in the Teaching of English* 46 (1): 8–21.
Britzman, Deborah. 1991. *Practice Makes Perfect: A Critical Study of Learning to Teach.* Albany: SUNY Press.
Canagarajah, Suresh. 2014. "ESL Composition as a Literate Art of the Contact Zone." In *First-Year Composition: From Theory to Practice*, edited by Deborah Coxwell-Teague and Ronald F. Lunsford, 27–42. Anderson, SC: Parlor.
Downs, Doug, and Elizabeth Wardle. 2007. "Teaching about Writing, Righting Misconceptions: (Re)Envisioning 'First-Year Composition' as 'Introduction to Writing Studies.'" *College Composition and Communication* 58 (4): 552–84.
Institute of International Education. 2015. "Press Release: Open Doors 2014." http://www.iie.org/Who-We-Are/News-and-Events/Press-Center/Press-Releases/2014/2014-11-17-Open-Doors-Data.
Lowe, Charlie, and Pavel Zemliansky, eds. 2011. *Writing Spaces: Readings about Writing*, vol. 2. Fort Collins, CO: The WAC Clearinghouse.
Ramsdell, Catherine. 2011. "Storytelling, Narration, and the 'Who I Am' Story." In *Writing Spaces: Readings on Writing*, edited by Charlie Lowe and Pavel Zemliansky, 2:270–85. Anderson, SC: Parlor.
Stylus: A Journal of First-Year Writing. 2015. http://writingandrhetoric.cah.ucf.edu/stylus/.
Wardle, Elizabeth. 2015. "Intractable Writing Program Problems, Kairos, and Writing about Writing: A Profile of the University of Central Florida's First-Year Composition Program." In *Ecologies of Writing Programs: Profiles of Writing Programs in Context*, edited by Mary Jo Reiff, Anis Bawarshi, Michelle Ballif, and Christian Weisser, 91–120. Anderson, SC: Parlor.
Wardle, Elizabeth, and Doug Downs. 2013. "Reflecting Back and Looking Forward: Revisiting 'Teaching about Writing, Righting Misconceptions' Five Years On." *Composition Forum* 27. http://compositionforum.com/issue/27/.
Wardle, Elizabeth, and Doug Downs, eds. 2014. *Writing about Writing: A College Reader.* 2nd ed. New York: Bedford/St. Martin's.

27
DIGITAL COMPOSING IN WAW
What Students Learn through Infographics

Christy I. Wenger

> INSTITUTION TYPE AND SIZE: 4,000-student public liberal arts university
> COURSE CONTEXT: Second course in two-course FYW; required general education
> STUDY DESIGN/METHODOLOGY: Qualitative case studies of author's last two sections of second-semester FYW
> WAW PROGRAM OR NOT: Stand-alone WAW course in FYW
> WAW COURSE OR SINGLE ASSIGNMENT/UNIT: Final assignment of course: discourse community ethnography infographic set
> INSTRUCTOR TYPE/POSITION: Assistant professor and director of writing and rhetoric program
> KEY TERMS: Infographics; composition; first-year writing; multimodality

ABSTRACT

This chapter explores the benefits of composing digital genres to engage students, using a study of WAW pedagogy in a specific context. Using student examples of infographics and reflective testimony, I argue that when students can draw on the digital literacies of their lives outside of the FYW classroom and put them to use within that classroom, they are left to rethink what counts as writing and writing expertise. They in turn become reflective producers and consumers of both essayistic and digital texts, developing what Stewart Selber (2004) calls a "postcritical" stance to technology and meta-awareness or mindfulness of the composing process.

INTRODUCTION

As the WPA of my small, mid-Atlantic liberal arts university, I approached the last program workshop I led with excitement; the writing faculty and

DOI: 10.7330/9781607328421.c027

I were using our professional development day together to talk about digital pedagogy in the first-year writing (FYW) classroom.[1] Frank discussion a short half-hour into our workshop, however, showed me that my excitement was met by instructor trepidation. When I mentioned how digital pedagogy presented students new opportunities to compose the kinds of texts that surround them today, my instructors replied, "But then how will they learn the academic essay?" And when I pressed the need for students to encounter real-world communication problems that require them to engage in both face-to-face and online response, they countered, "What will the other faculty think of us and what we are doing to prepare students for their university careers?" While no one denied that digital genres were changing mass communications in the world, my instructors were more concerned about a particular short view of writing as it served students through their college careers and revolved around alphabetic literacy.[2]

While this chapter does not focus on professional development, I begin with this short anecdote because I believe it illuminates what can be a problematic trend: because FYW is beholden to so many curricular expectations, much discussion regarding digital literacy and pedagogy remains focused on advanced writing students and not first-year writers. While it is not my aim to elaborately examine FYW's service mission, I am interested in exploring how we might move around the stalemate of "service" in order to discuss what we can do with digital pedagogy in FYW and why we might do it. I suggest here that we start by linking digital composing practices to the writing about writing (WAW) movement. Like WAW, digital pedagogy has struggled against the service mission of FYW to teach a universal version of academic discourse promised by alphabetic literacy. Yet, with its focus on exploring "how writing works" through a study of genre and activity theory, WAW pedagogy, I argue, provides FYW instructors a means of resolving this struggle and navigating the "digital turn" meaningfully.

My digital WAW pedagogy supports students to become reflective consumers and producers of the digital genres that mark both their college careers and their lives beyond the university by giving them purchase on the topic of digital literacy and practice composing digital genres like blogs and infographics.[3] After outlining the theoretical and practical context for my course in what follows, I will focus on its culminating project, the discourse community infographic set, which asks students to synthesize their ethnographic findings with a pair of infographics, each targeted to a different audience. Using examples of infographics and students' reflective testimony, I argue that when students can draw on the digital literacies of their lives outside of the FYW classroom and put them to use within that classroom, they are invited to rethink what counts as writing and writing expertise. They, in turn, become reflective producers and consumers of both essayistic and digital texts, developing what Stewart Selber (2004) calls a "postcritical" stance to technology, as well as increased awareness, or mindfulness, of the composing process.

THE LURE OF EXPERTISE

In the modern history of the debate over the FYW requirement in universities nationwide, the course has been decried as primarily serving a gatekeeping function (Crowley 1995; Smith 1997) and a service mission (Crowley 1991; Bartholomae 1986), purporting to teach a universalist conception of academic discourse for students who need to navigate the discourse structures of the university (Downs and Wardle 2007; Downs 2013). And while WAW effectively critiques the service mission of FYW and provides an alternative, it can become trapped by the notions of expertise to which it marries itself, notions that can make this pedagogy slow or resistant to accommodate digital composing practices. WAW's trappings of expertise are most evident in the academic genres of writing studies it asks students to practice, prevalent in the first edition of Wardle and Downs's (2011) textbook, *Writing about Writing: A College Reader*. None of this text's suggested assignments include composing with digital genres, and all of the sample student writings reproduce fairly standard academic genres. For a pedagogy that claims to help students develop a conceptual and not just procedural framework that will lead them to approach writing rhetorically and flexibly so they can adapt to new writing contexts and rhetorical situations, this is a glaring omission. Indeed, Jason Palmeri argues that "if we limit students to only alphabetic means of invention and revision, we may unnecessarily constrain their ability to think intensively and complexly about their work" (2012, 44). While the second edition of this textbook (Wardle and Downs 2014) does include a more robust section on multimodal composing, the emphasis remains on reading about this topic to the end of writing conventional alphabetic texts and not digital compositions.

The favoritism shown to nondigital academic genres in FYW may have been necessary to situate WAW as a legitimate approach for our field in 2011 when its first textbook was published, but we have more options today. An alternative WAW approach can be inspired by the recent attempts of multimodal pedagogy to take hold within our courses—a struggle since digital genres have complicated what "counts" as writing and have destabilized what we think we ought to teach. Adopting a postcritical stance in the FYW classroom requires us to change our understanding of expertise, untying it from the moorings of alphabetic literacy and academic discourse. Tarez Samra Graben, Colin Charlton, and Jonikka Charlton offer an alternative version of expertise in the context of digital pedagogy, valuing a flexible and rhetorical approach to digital technology where invention and reflection are the goal, creating a process-based approach that is more invested in students developing rhetorical dexterity and awareness than arriving at expertise (2013, 250). What this means for my digital WAW approach is that I don't have to be an expert of the technology or genres I ask students to use, but nor should I take for granted that my students' preexisting ability to use a technology is akin to their expertise, or that they can think critically about their production without my guidance. As with the use of various digital tools, a collaborative relationship is necessary for critical consciousness of how digital composing impacts our literacy and writing habits. This is why I begin my course with an essay that asks students to investigate their relationship with technology by exploring their functional literacy as well as their awareness of how technology shapes their communication. A second essay, written as several blog entries, asks students to log all of their interactions with technology with the end goal of redefining just what literacy in the digital age means to them. The goal of my course, then, is to get students thinking metacognitively about their digital writing; greater fluency with certain digital tools like blogs or genres like infographics isn't enough. Course assignments don't just ask students to produce digital writing but push them to also reflectively investigate themselves as digitally mediated writers. This means that my course shares the impulse with more traditional WAW approaches to investigate writing as a topic of inquiry, not just a matter of production or presentation.

A benefit of integrating digital composing in my WAW approach is that it destabilizes my complete authority as teacher to determine the effectiveness of a text. For example, when discussing digital genres like infographics for our final discourse ethnography, I ask students if a model graphic is something they would "click on" in their news feed on Facebook (see appendix 27.E). This challenges conventional expertise and brings us to closer to the ways Peter Elbow (1995) has argued we maintain tension between the role of the writer and that of the academic in the FYW course, which remains a useful benchmark.[4] Digital WAW pedagogy guided by principles of rhetorical dexterity and flexibility rather than more fixed notions of expertise invites more opportunities for us to engage with our students as collaborators who are open to listen and learn.

THE VALUE OF INFOGRAPHICS IN FYW

The final project in my course is a digital discourse community analysis that asks students to research and write about concepts such as conflict within activity systems and multiliteracies with texts that address digital writing and visual argumentation. To examine the importance of visual argument in today's culture, we watch the TED talk *The Beauty of Data Visualization* by David McCandless (2015). McCandless argues that data visualization to turn complex data sets into well-designed images can help us to better understand our modern "data jungle" and to find connections we might otherwise miss. He notes that while his expertise is more experiential than conventional, "we are all visualizers now," as our continual exposure to media gives us a profound sense of what works and is persuasive in data design.

If the goals of this project and others like it in my classes aren't driven by expertise, they are instead motivated by the principles of mindfulness. If students are to develop a postcritical stance to technology and an increasingly complex understanding of writing, they need to become mindful writers, perceptive and aware of their processes and able to monitor their changing understandings and how those impact their production and consumption of texts. Both Wardle (2009) and Beaufort (2007) explore mindfulness, what the latter defines as the self-monitoring of awareness about writing (186) and the former notes must be present to encourage the transfer of learning (771). As I am a yogi and avid meditator, the flexibility and awareness promised by mindfulness resonates with me. I understand mindfulness as simply a process-orientation to the present, an active mode that counters our tendency to automatically complete an activity without our full, engaged attention, relying instead on old scripts or unchecked habits.

The promise of digital composing to help students become more conscious of their writing behaviors and to begin a process of mindful monitoring is great, in part because of the ways digital writing asks students to create new composing scripts and to communicate with real audiences for genuine purposes. Composing infographics (see appendix 27.A for the assignment) helps students become more mindful of the multimodality of all writing, one of the threshold concepts identified in the collection *Naming What We Know: Threshold Concepts of Writing Studies* (Adler-Kassner and Wardle 2015). My students examine within the context of the New London Group's (NLG) five modes: linguistic, aural, visual, gestural, and spatial (Ball and Charlton 2015, 42). Infographics also reinforce the threshold concept of audience and how it is related to genre and purpose (Lunsford 2015, 20). In my class, students work to develop mindfulness about their composing processes as they remain constant or become variable depending on what genre and for what context, community, and purpose they are writing.

THE CASE OF ROBERT AND ADELE

I'd like to take a closer look at the evolution of two students' infographic sets in order to trace these writers' growing mindfulness, particularly related to their metaknowledge about audience and multimodality.[5] Starting with the creation of his infographic mini-proposal (see appendix 27.B), Robert was immediately certain that he was going to focus his project on the Boy Scouts of America (BSA) so that he could use our project as a platform to discuss the merits of joining and maintaining membership throughout a lifetime. Having achieved the highest honor of Eagle Scout, Robert was eager to eventually use his infographics (see figures 27.1 and 27.2) as promotion materials for his home troop, which shaped his audience choices: young boys who might be interested in joining BSA and their parents. Robert's final infographics are a version of his planned "matching set," both designed with a rustic feel, with a woodlike background and bold black text to echo the BSA's emphasis on crafts and outdoorsmanship.

Despite his general excitement, Robert faced several challenges when grappling with his two audiences. He met with me several times to brainstorm how he might make each infographic "different enough" so that he could persuade both targeted generations to consider BSA as a viable youth activity yet keep the two graphics related so that his core message was the same. Robert used design to help him focus the two graphics, noting in his designer's note (the mandated reflective description of his process—see appendix 27.A) that he purposely chose "a rustic wooden board appeal to help [emphasize] the amount of exploring and nature that one would experience in scouting." But he remained stumped about what information to provide on each, especially the parent version, since he felt more removed from that audience. After presenting his mini-proposal to the class and receiving feedback from his peers, Robert "decided to divide [the Scout version] in half (top and bottom) so that the top was more of a fun informative journey or trail though the infographic, and the bottom having the Scout Law and Oath" to hint at

Figure 27.1. BSA for young troops

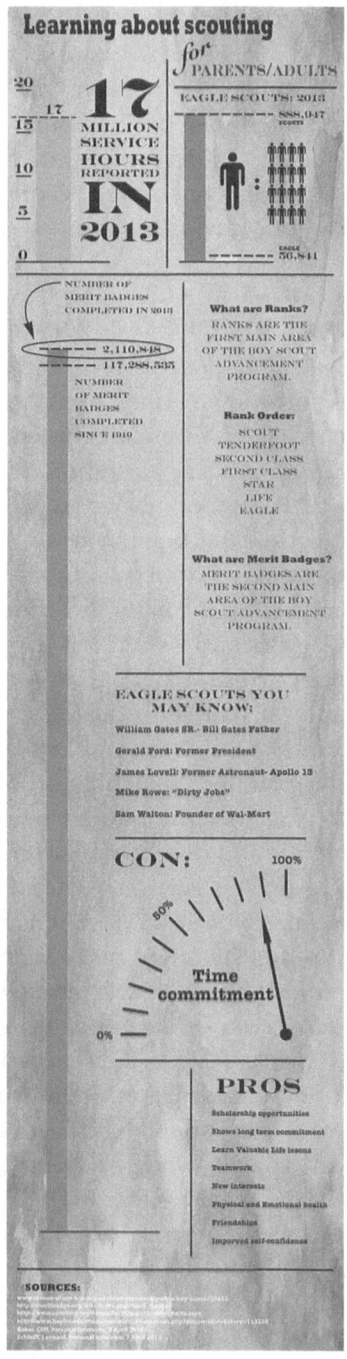

Figure 27.2. BSA for parents

the fun and adventure boys who joined could have while also making the graphic a "learning tool" foreshadowing Scout responsibilities.

Upon my urging him to talk to some parents as part of his primary research, to see what might persuade them to get their children involved, he interviewed his father, who ultimately became a source for the parent graphic. When I followed up with him after this interview, Robert was bursting with ideas about including a section on famous Scouts "to help parents think their kid could be like that too" and a list of skills Boy Scouts developed that would resonate with parents. Robert's final explanation of the parent version in his designer's note is that "it is much more informative . . . about the organization by showing facts, famous people who are Eagle Scouts, explaining some of the aspects of the scouting, and how their child would work through the Trail to Eagle." While Robert was a strong writer throughout my class, the learning gains represented in these reflective comments and his progression toward them are significant for the ways they demonstrate how digital writing pushed him to explore a more conscious and reflective understanding of audience. Because Robert understood the infographic assignment as contributing meaningfully to the kinds of writing he often read online and because he believed his project could be used for a future purpose within his troop—a purpose that extended beyond the more specialized audience of academic discourse reproduced in a conventional academic essay—he better recognized the persuasive aim of his graphic to move an audience.

When Robert completed his in-class final reflection on this project (see appendix 27.F), written after handing in his infographics for assessment, he was conscious of his development of audience awareness, which became increasingly important to him as a writer as a result of our digital project. He noted, "I don't think I ever thought about audience so much as I did for this project . . . maybe because I had to be very careful about what information I could include?" Robert cited a class workshop where he realized that his infographic should examine the negative aspects of being a Scout, "kind of like a counterargument in a regular essay." Slowly understanding how certain composing heuristics can transfer from alphabetic to digital texts, Robert explained that while he initially thought the infographics would be "easier" to compose than a traditional research paper, he later recognized that "this would be just as difficult" because "though the method is different and more visual, there are a lot of the same elements . . . like the need to have a purpose and to convey that to a specific audience."

Robert's recognition and his careful consideration of how his infographics' content is related to each of his audiences show his developing hold on the threshold concept of audience that was prompted by the creation of his infographics. Doug Downs and Liane Robertson comment that in WAW approaches, mindful reflection on what is being learned in a course "is likely to occur near its end or after the course is over because of the time required to build critical mass against any ineffectual prior knowledge and to reflect on new explanations" (2015, 116). Robert's growth seems to point to the accuracy of such a statement. Robert's ability to create a useful heuristic about the importance of counterpoints to persuade an audience by developing one's *ethos* illustrates a postliminal stage in his learning where he has begun to think like a writer and to reflect on his composing process in ways that enable him to transfer his learning to new projects and different genres (Meyer and Land 2006, 23). At this stage, his learning became more conscious and counterarguments became less a formula followed for a well-written essay and more an observation of what persuades audiences.

Adele didn't share Robert's initial enthusiasm for the infographic project and was vocal from the beginning, asking me after class why she couldn't "just write a research paper instead." In our first conference, she worried repeatedly that she would say the "same thing" on each infographic. She admitted that despite my directions to focus on various audiences for our previous assignments, she hadn't before given much thought to an audience beyond her teacher, conceding that "just won't work this time." Rebecca Pope-Ruark notes that while students become adept assessing the instructor-as-audience in schooling, they often cannot translate these skills to other "dynamic and transactional contexts" (2011, 3). Adele's struggle thus brings her to a point of disjunction, a useful dissonance between her old beliefs of audience and a transactional view of audience as driven by her exposure to writing studies and prompted by the specifics of our infographic assignment.

Adele ended up working though this state of disjunction from what she thought she knew about audience to new understandings by choosing her workplace, an upscale consignment store, as her discourse community. Taking a different approach than Robert's tightly themed set, Adele chose to create one infographic for potential buyers and sellers, to inform them of the consignment process and its advantages, and another for those individuals who might be interested in owning a franchise to consider her store as a viable investment and business opportunity (see figures 27.3 and 27.4). Between this early conference and her final infographics, Adele and I met several times and had many lengthy conversations about the importance of audience and how design and content were interrelated. Like Robert's, her learning illustrates how the threshold concepts of audience and multimodality are interrelated and manifested in digital assignments like the infographic.

Adele's designer's note testifies to how her mindfulness of both concepts grew together as a result of our project: "Creating infographics made me a better writer because I am now aware of the language I am supposed to use when talking to a certain audience." While all of my class projects explicitly asked students to address particular audiences, Adele claimed that "more than any other paper we wrote this semester, I think this project helped me to see just how important it is to think about your audience when you write . . . [since] content and design were equally important in this infographic I didn't want to include unnecessary information and lose the attention of my audience." It is not unusual for students like Adele and her classmates to recognize the importance of a key element of the rhetorical situation like audience as a result of working on this digital project, since "many classical rhetorical principles of communication . . . may be more difficult to ignore in audio and visual compositions" (Takayoshi and Selfe 2007, 5), lending importance to students' work on such projects in FYW.

Adele said in her final in-class reflection on the process of completing her infographic that she "sorta understood now why we talked about multimodal writing in this class, before this project . . . since just like how our writing essays can use layout and pictures to help the words to make an argument, infographics are like that in reverse." I hear Adele saying in this reflection that she is beginning to understand how all writing is on a kind of continuum where style, design, visuals, and text are used and are important, but that some writings draw different foci for readers and therefore merit different attention from authors. Adele goes on in her reflection to say

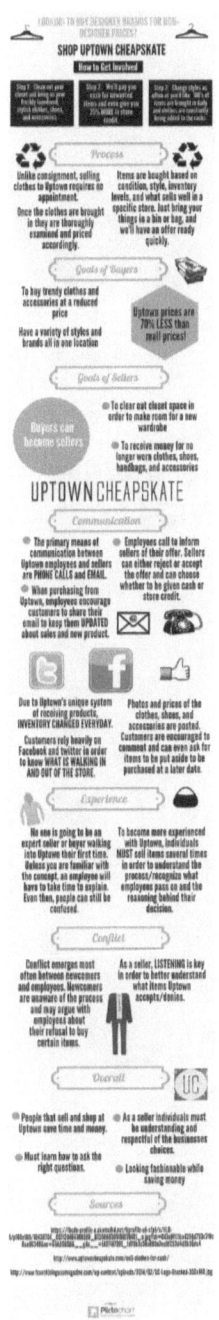

Figure 27.3. Consignment for buyers and sellers

Figure 27.4. Consignment for franchise owners

why infographics work in "reverse" because "everyone uses electronic devices, so being able to represent so much data in such a visual way will make it noticed by so many more people," further illustrating her learning as resulting in mindfulness of genre and multimodality as opposed to her desire to universalize writing.[6] Adele's statements represent mindfulness about how audience, purpose, and genre are interrelated and context-specific.

Adele and Robert's experiences suggest that their WAW course's focus on threshold concepts is dependent on "explicit, extensive reflection on what's being learned . . . interrogating one' knowledge and deliberately trying to compare different ways of thinking" (Downs and Robertson 2015, 116). Consequently, as I develop my digital WAW approach in FYW, I will continue to use designer's notes to accompany students' digital projects. Though Ball, Bowen, and Fenn note that such reflections are pseudo-transactional genres (2013, 28), the insights contained in them help me to monitor students' development in ways I may not be able to otherwise access. If we are aiming for mindfulness and not expertise as our end goal, these reflective writings are key to helping students engage in the kinds of reflection that helps them articulate their metaknowledge and helps instructors assess the value of our pedagogies and projects.

NOTES

1. It is challenging to talk about digital pedagogy in the field today because of the ways this term has yielded to the more comprehensive term *multimodal*. While this latter term may provide a more inclusive pedagogical frame because it isn't limited to the production of digital texts and the use of digital tools in our classes, in this essay I am concerned primarily with the digital; my goal is to discuss WAW pedagogies focused on expansion of students' digital literacy skills and critical consciousness. Even so, my own terminology will necessarily move back and forth to accommodate both the "digital" and the "multimodal" because of the complicated ways these terms are used in our field. Often these terms are used interchangeably, even if they are distinct. See Shipka 2011 and Ball and Charlton 2015.

2. My instructors aired other fears as well, including questions of student access to technology and instructor expertise with various digital platforms and tools, but the service refrain was the loudest and seemingly the most daunting obstacle facing digital pedagogy within my program.
3. While infographics, or visual representations of information and data, have been around for ages, they are experiencing a renaissance, and a corresponding evolution, in contemporary online communications. Current use of social media as a news medium can be attributed to their rise in popularity (see Crooks 2014 and Fogel 2013).
4. In his classic argument, Elbow notes that he wants his "first year students to be saying in their writing, 'Listen to me, I have something to tell you' not 'Is this okay? Will you accept this?'" (1995, 82).
5. All student names are pseudonyms and all student writings and comments are drawn from formal and informal student writings and contributions, including conferences and discussions I recorded in my class journal for later reference. Students self-selected to be a part of my study, and all permissions are IRB approved.
6. A less generous take might see her trying to equate all writing so she can exert some measure of control. But for a first-year writer, I believe the ability to reflect on similarities between various genres and to become mindful of the rhetorical elements at play in them is a great step toward thinking about writing *as a writer*—and not just as a student trying to pass a class, the motivator for her earlier inattention to anyone but her instructor as a reader.

APPENDIX 27.A

Discourse Community Infographic Set

Once you have compiled findings about your chosen discourse community, you will create a *pair* of infographics, each targeting a different audience of your choosing. The aim in each infographic is to forward a central claim based on one specific topic related to your discourse community; that claim is the purpose for your infographic. Your audience should be able to easily understand your purpose even if you never explicitly state your claim in a sentence on the graphic, which is not necessary. Because you're forwarding that claim in response to other texts, you need to cite your primary research as well as additional research from texts in class and any outside sources within your infographic.

INFOGRAPHIC TOOLS

You can use any tool you'd like that exists on the web, but listed below are a few I recommend. Easel.ly and Cava allow you to upload your own images to customize your infographic and allow PDF downloads, which is helpful for project submission. All of these are *free* tools (free, but you will need to sign up for an account), and are linked on our course website and/or can be found easily through a Google search:

Easel.ly

Canva

Piktochart

Others?

Additional sites to create images to add to infographics created with the above tools:

Wordle

Pixlr

Chartle

The Noun Project

Open Clipart

Others?

DESIGNER STATEMENT

Just like the "director's cut" of your favorite movie, you write a designer's statement for this project. The design statement must be three or more Times New Roman double-spaced pages that detail your decisions for all four parts of *each* infographic in your pair. This statement must include:

- A clear statement of what your claim for the infographic is and an explanation of how you supported that claim through all four elements of your infographic.
- Reflection on the choices you made to develop the four elements of your graphic and the reasoning for those choices.
- Reflection on the process of creating an infographic, relating it to our class discussion of digital literacy and how a project like this both resembles and deviates from the standard research essay.
- Note what this project taught you as a writer and any problems you encountered or elements you'd like to tweak if you had more time.
- **No infographics will be accepted without their accompanying design statements.

ASSESSMENT

Your infographics will be assessed using the same qualities of effective writing that all of your papers are assessed by: thoughtful ideas; claim with support; effective organization; relationship between ideas; style; and, attention to conventions. Additionally, for this project, we will add *design*: how effective the visual presentation supports the overall purpose/message and how visually appealing the overall product is; as well as *rhetorical awareness*: meaning, how well you reflect on the process of creating your infographic in your design statement.

The best infographics will not simply present information about a discourse community, but will argue for a way of looking at/understanding that information. They will therefore answer a research question that is revised and made more and more specific through a genuine research process that gets more complex as more data is collected. The best infographics will also present their findings in clear and organized ways that guide the reader toward interpretation and understanding.

APPENDIX 27.B

Infographic Mini-Proposal

    The program/tools I think I'll use:

    Anticipated topic:
        The "so what" of my topic, or what I hope readers will learn:

        Notes, facts, stories, statistics I'd like to include:

        My two audiences will be:

        And, I will alter my infographic in these ways to address the rhetorical situation each audience presents:

Ideas about how I will address all four components of infographic:

    Visual: including the graphics, colors, and images that make up the design of the infographic. My ideas are:

    Content: the information presented, or all the various components that make up the message or argument of the infographic. My ideas are:

    Purpose: a central message: a claim or argument supported by both the content and the visuals that is clear to readers. My ideas are:

    Sources: like the works cited page of an essay; sources should be professional and/or credible. My ideas are:

My questions to the class include:
    1.
    2.
    3.

APPENDIX 27.C

Infographic Peer Review

1. What is the central claim of each infographic? Is it small and manageable, or can it be made smaller and more manageable? Explain your answer.
2. How is each *claim* (just focus on that right now) represented by all four components of an infographic?
   a. VISUAL: how do the visuals relate to the claim?
   b. CONTENT: is the content appropriate for the claim? Why/why not?
   c. PURPOSE: what is the purpose? How is it connected to the claim?
   d. SOURCES: how well do the sources support the claim?
3. Talk more comprehensively about the four components of the infographic now.

   VISUAL: all the graphics, colors, images that make up the design of the infographic

   Look at the graphics/images: are they appropriate to the content? Any that could be changed for more impact? How? Why?

   Look at the colors: do they make the infographic visually appealing? How might color be better utilized for persuasive impact?

   CONTENT: the information presented, or all the various components that make up the message/argument of the infographic

   Look at the text (writing): are you overwhelmed with words? How can the graphic be made easier to consume? What parts of text need to be visually represented and/or what visual representations need to be spelled out with text?

   PURPOSE: a central message, a claim or argument supported by both the content and the visuals that is clear to readers

   What is the purpose of this infographic? How could each infographic's purpose be made clearer? Give specific suggestions.

   SOURCES: like the works cited page of an essay; sources should be professional/credible

   Does each infographic have a source list? Is there a convincing mix of sources used? Could the graphic benefit from another primary or secondary source; if so, which and why?

APPENDIX 27.D

Design Statement Peer Review

1. How clearly is the claim /purpose (so what?) of the infographic explained? How might this be made both clearer *and* more detailed?
2. How clearly does the author describe *each* of the four elements of the infographic? Remember, you need a clear statement of what your claim for the infographic is *and* an explanation of how you supported that claim through all four elements of your infographic.

   What more might the author say about his/her choices for the visual (all the graphics, colors, images that make up the design of the infographic)?

   What more might the author say about his/her choices for the content (the information presented, or all the various components that make up the message/argument of the infographic)?

   What more might the author say about his/her purpose (a central message, a claim or argument supported by both the content and the visuals that is clear to readers)?

   What more might the author do for effective source use (like the works cited page of an essay, sources should be professional/credible)?
3. Describe the draft's organization. Could it be improved? Why? How? Are like themes placed with like, or does it ramble? Give specific suggestions for improvement.
4. What more might the author say about the process of creating an infographic, specifically discussing the audience for each infographic and the ways audience shaped the choices made for each?

APPENDIX 27.E

Peer Response to Infographic In-Process Presentation

Peer Response to Infographics
Presenter: _____

Please use the following questions to respond to your classmates' infographics—complete one sheet for each infographic. Be fair and provide constructive criticism.

***

On a scale of 1–5, how clear is the main claim, audience, and purpose of the infographic?

    1   2   3   4   5

What is the main claim, audience, and purpose of the infographic?
How could the infographic be improved to more directly illustrate this?

On a scale of 1–5, how effective is the visual design of the infographic as a whole?

    1   2   3   4   5

What are some of the strongest examples of visual design in the infographic?

What jumps out as really striking?

What are some of the weakest examples of visual design in the infographic?

What needs a little more work? What might be done?

On a scale of 1–5, how likely would you be to click on this infographic for a better view if it popped up in your Facebook news feed?

    1   2   3   4   5

Explain your numerical answer here:

APPENDIX 27.F

In-Class Infographic Reflection

1. How does creating an infographic ask you to use the same sorts of skills you might for a conventional paper? Concepts from this semester that you might want to discuss include: audience awareness, awareness of how language is used differently in different communities and in different genres, purpose and constraints (both positive and negative) of different forms of writing.
2. How does creating an infographic ask you to build upon and expand those skills you use for more conventional papers?
3. What did you learn about yourself as a writer and the process of writing by creating an infographic?
4. What did you learn by creating not just one but two infographics for difference audiences? How did audience awareness impact your design choices?

REFERENCES

Adler-Kassner, Linda, and Elizabeth Wardle, eds. *Naming What We Know: Threshold Concepts of Writing Studies*. Logan: Utah State University Press.

Ball, Cheryl, Tia Scoffield Bowen, and Tyrell Brent Fenn. "Genre Transfer in a Multimodal Composition Class." In *Multimodal Literacies and Emerging Genres*, edited by Tracey Bowen and Carl Whithaus, 15–36. Pittsburgh: University of Pittsburgh Press.

Ball, Cheryl E., and Colin Charlton. 2015. "All Writing Is Multimodal." In Adler-Kassner and Wardle 2015, 42–43.

Bartholomae, David. 1986. "Inventing the University." *Journal of Basic Writing* 5 (1): 4–23.

Beaufort, Anne. 2007. *College Writing and Beyond: A New Framework for University Writing Instruction*. Logan: Utah State University Press.

Crooks, Ross. 2014. "Are Infographics Still Effective as Part of Your Content Strategy?" *Forbes*, January 14. http://www.forbes.com/sites/rosscrooks/2014/01/14/are-infographics-still-effective/.

Crowley, Sharon. 1991. "A Personal Essay on Freshman English." *Pre/Text* 12 (3–4): 155–76.

Crowley, Sharon. 1995. "Composition's Ethic of Service, the Universal Requirement, and the Discourse of Student Need." *JAC* 15:227–39.

Downs, Doug. 2013. "What Is First-Year Composition?" In *A Rhetoric for Writing Program Administrators*, edited by Rita Malenczyk, 50–63. Anderson, SC: Parlor.

Downs, Doug, and Liane Roberston. 2015. "Threshold Concepts in First-Year Composition." In Adler-Kassner and Wardle 2015, 105–21.

Downs, Doug, and Elizabeth Wardle. 2007. "Teaching about Writing, Righting Misconceptions: (Re)Envisioning 'First Year Composition' as 'Introduction to Writing Studies.'" *College Composition and Communication* 58:552–84.

Elbow, Peter. 1995. "Being a Writer vs. Being an Academic: A Conflict in Goals." *College Composition and Communication* 46:72–83.

Fogel, Becky. 2013. "Show, Not Tell: The Rise of the Infographic." *Science Friday*, October 18. http://www.sciencefriday.com/blogs/10/18/2013/show-not-tell-the-rise-of-the-infographic.html?series=20.

Graben, Tarez Samra, Colin Charlton, and Jonikka Charlton. 2013. "Multivalent Composition and the Reinvention of Expertise." In *Multimodal Literacies and Emerging Genres*, edited by Tracey Bowen and Carl Whithaus, 248–81. Pittsburgh: University of Pittsburgh Press.

Lunsford, Andrea A. 2015. "Writing Addresses, Invokes, and/or Creates Audiences." In Adler-Kassner and Wardle 2015, 20–21.

McCandless, David. 2015. *The Beauty of Data Visualization*. TED talk. http://www.ted.com/talks/david_mccandless_the_beauty_of_data_visualization.

Meyer, Jan H. F., and Ray Land. 2006. *Threshold Concepts and Troublesome Knowledge*. London: Routledge.

Palmeri, Jason. 2012. *Remixing Composition: A History of Multimodal Writing Pedagogy*. Carbondale: Southern Illinois University Press.

Pope-Ruark, Rebecca. 2011. "Know Thy Audience: Helping Students Engage a Threshold Concept Using Audience-Based Pedagogy." *International Journal for the Scholarship of Teaching and Learning* 5 (1): 1–16.

Selber, Stewart. 2004. *Multiliteracies for a Digital Age*. Carbondale: Southern Illinois University Press.

Shipka, Jody. 2011. *Toward a Composition Made Whole*. Pittsburgh: University of Pittsburgh Press.

Smith, Jeff. 1997."Students' Goals, Gatekeeping, and Some Questions of Ethics." *College English* 59:299–320.

Takayoshi, Pamela, and Cynthia L. Selfe. 2007. "Thinking about Multimodality." In *Multimodal Composition: Resources for Teachers*, edited by Cynthia L. Selfe, 1–12. Cresskill, NJ: Hampton.

Wardle, Elizabeth. 2009. "'Mutt Genres' and the Goal of FYC: How Can We Help Students Write the Genres of the University?" *College Composition and Communication* 60:765–89.

Wardle, Elizabeth, and Doug Downs, eds. 2011. *Writing about Writing: A College Reader*. New York: Bedford/St. Martin's.

Wardle, Elizabeth, and Doug Downs, eds. 2014. *Writing about Writing: A College Reader*. 2nd ed. New York: Bedford/St. Martin's.

28
Student Voice

PODCASTING AND PROTOCOLS
An Approach to Writing about Writing through Sound

Christian Smith with Gabrielle Frick and Patrick Siebel

> INSTITUTION TYPE AND SIZE: Regional public liberal arts university with just over 10,000 undergraduate students
>
> COURSE CONTEXT: Upper-level Advanced Composition and Rhetoric course primarily for English majors and included, as an elective, in a four-course cluster on language and theory
>
> STUDY DESIGN/METHODOLOGY: Mixed-methods study
>
> WAW PROGRAM OR NOT: Stand-alone WAW course for English majors
>
> WAW COURSE OR SINGLE ASSIGNMENT/UNIT: WAW course
>
> INSTRUCTOR TYPE/POSITION: Assistant professor
>
> KEY TERMS: Podcasting; protocols; defamiliarization; sound; affect

ABSTRACT

This chapter demonstrates the benefits of podcasting assignments in the context of an upper-level writing about writing course—specifically, podcasting assignments using student writers' own recorded think-aloud protocols in order to gain a better understanding of pre-identified threshold concepts in writing studies. Further, it seeks to theorize the results of these assignments using Steph Ceraso's (2014) notion of *multimodal listening* and the important role sound can play in defamiliarizing the writing process.

INTRODUCTION

In a recent article, "(Re)Educating the Senses: Multimodal Listening, Bodily Learning, and the Composition of Sonic Experiences," Steph Ceraso (2014) argues that "sound is playing an increasingly important role in a wide range of texts, products, environments, and experiences," and therefore writing instructors should work to "help students cultivate a heightened sensitivity to sound in different contexts" (103). Further, Ceraso makes clear that listening is more than simply taking in sound through the ears or the act of interpreting those sounds; rather, listening is an embodied experience irreducible to one sense organ or mental process and, as such, affects multiple sites and bodies across many registers. To nuance the act of listening, Ceraso introduces the concept of *multimodal listening*, which works to encompass the many ways that sound is composed and experienced. Pedagogically, for Ceraso, multimodal listening offers "a way to teach students to be more capable and sensitive listeners during the production of multimodal compositions, and in their experiences with various sonic texts, products, and environments" (120).

Multimodal listening, I would argue, holds much potential for WAW pedagogies when used to enable students to become more attentive to their own writing processes. What I propose here are ways to develop listening practices that, when used to *defamiliarize* the embodied process of writing and *make strange* students' habitual writing routines, can be an effective way to teach some threshold concepts in writing studies. As an approach to WAW pedagogy, multimodal listening is especially useful, as it aims to increase students' understanding of their own writing processes while simultaneously giving them a vocabulary to communicate what they have learned. While this is a single-authored piece, I have incorporated extended reflections from two students, Gabrielle Frick and Patrick Siebel, whose words highlight general conclusions arrived at by the class regarding the value of pairing podcasting assignments with an upper-level WAW course.

COURSE DESIGN AND ASSIGNMENT RATIONALE

This course, which took place at Coastal Carolina University in spring 2015, asked eighteen students to compose a three-episode podcast series throughout the semester. Each of the episodes was to correspond to three of the four major units in the course: literacy, process, rhetoric, and a fourth unit focusing on "multimodality" that gave students an opportunity to synthesize and reflect upon the digital composing practices they had worked with all semester. Episodes were also to center on possible threshold concepts that we had collectively identified from course readings and class discussions. Much like Linda Adler-Kassner and Elizabeth Wardle (2015) observe in *Naming What We Know*, the work of identifying threshold concepts must first concede that knowledge in the field is contingent and can reflect only "final-for-now definitions of *some* of what our field knows" (4). Similarly, as a class, we worked to find the common concepts and provisional arguments running through multiple course readings as a way to talk about the content of writing studies and to anchor the production of podcast episodes.

While many of the episodes ran longer, students were asked to compose five- to eight-minute podcasts using sound effects, music, field recordings, interviews, and their own voice. Students were encouraged to compose using the audio editor Audacity and to gather their assets from the Free Music Archive and Freesound.org. As a model podcast, students were asked to listen to several episodes of Mary Hedengren's *Mere Rhetoric*—a series that promotes the aims of our course through both content and form. While *Mere Rhetoric* focuses on an individual figure or concept relevant to the rhetorical tradition, it is produced in a way that is both accessible and enjoyable for undergraduates new to the study of rhetoric and composition as a discipline. Additionally, as is true of most popular podcast series, the consistency of Hedengren's "on-air" personality works to create a sustained sense of unity from episode to episode. Students were encouraged to think about how their own favorite podcasts work to maintain a unified identity and how this can be expressed through rhetorical concepts, particularly *ethos*. As Dickie Selfe observes in Dangler, McCorkle, and Barrow's (2007) "Expanding Composition Audiences with Podcasting," "The primary value of podcasting seems to be the commitment to systematically broadcast media over time. One has to plan carefully enough to take advantage of what Louie Ulman calls 'serial writing' or in this case, serial composing. To imagine yourself as the author or one of the authors of a podcast, you have to think about projects that deserve a serial and long-term organization and the commitment that goes along with it." Further, assigning a podcast *series* provoked the kind of consistency of form—or "brand," as we eventually defined it in class—necessary to shape and refine just who students' audiences were. Two of the three podcasts of their series were more conventional podcast assignments—the kind that Ceraso (2014) notes are "quite similar to writing a textual essay" (113), thus serving the same kinds of interpretive meaning-making that typify the semiotic purposes of text, and therefore not necessarily the kind of embodied use of sound that *multimodal listening* attends to. The second episode, the assignment I focus on here, stood out for its use of a think-aloud protocol technique within the framework of a podcast episode and how recording protocols work to defamiliarize the student writer with her own writing process.

Focused on the student-identified threshold concept that writing is a process involving many actors, this podcast assignment asked students to record two thirty- to forty-five-minute think-aloud protocols as they wrote a short, formal assignment. Weeks before the podcast's due date, the class discussed Paul Prior's (2004) chapter "Tracing Process: How Texts Come into Being" in order to introduce both the concept of think-aloud protocols and writing as an *embodied* activity. Concerning this, Prior suggests, "If we look at actual embodied activity, we also see that writers are doing many other things as well—drinking coffee, eating snacks, smoking, listening to music, tapping their fingers, pacing around rooms talking to themselves, and so on" (171). During their task-based protocol recordings, I encouraged students not only to verbalize what they were thinking—how they interpreted the assignment prompt, how they reread the text in light of the prompt, how they planned to begin, and so on—but also to verbalize other, *seemingly* unconnected activities and objects circulating through their writing spaces. Once recorded, students were to listen to their protocols in order to begin shaping and making sense of the material, the objective being to incorporate those raw recordings within an accessible podcast episode. It was important for the assignment and to the threshold concept it was meant to engage that students present selections of their recorded protocols to a public—in our case, the rest of the class—as it demonstrated the many actors involved in the seemingly solitary act of composing.

Though the technologies have changed, the value of recording and sharing protocols has remained the same as those argued for in previous scholarly collections such as Flower et al. (1990) and Penrose and Sitko (1993). In many ways, the use of digital audio editing software and the ease of sharing files present a contemporary version of the ways protocols were distributed in those collections. Rather than transcribing protocols and making hard copies for the class, students simply uploaded their files to SoundCloud and tweeted a link using a common hashtag.

Both Linda Flower et al.'s (1990) collection *Reading-to-Write: Exploring a Cognitive and Social Process* and Penrose and Sitko's (1993) *Hearing Ourselves Think: Cognitive Research in the College Writing Classroom* demonstrate the benefits of a socially oriented protocol practice for writing instruction. Penrose (1993) suggests that recording and listening to informal think-aloud protocols on "tape recorders while working at home" can grant students insight into their own writing processes, but *sharing* those protocols with others can garner a fuller understanding of the writing process more generally. As Penrose notes, "Discussing their findings with others (and analyzing others' transcripts if time permits) can be an eye-opening experience for students as they discover the wide range of responses that a seemingly straightforward assignment elicited"

(63). I would argue that this is particularly effective within the context of a WAW pedagogy as students are together beginning to identify the same threshold concepts, the same terminology, and the same unfolding of disciplinary history. In other words, not only will they be able to verbalize their individual writing during protocol recordings, they will be able to do so using a common language and set of assumptions grounded in writing studies. While I had anticipated the value of protocols for podcast production when planning the course, what I had not expected was the *defamiliarizing* effects students reported after the first round of think-aloud assignments. Specifically, students repeatedly mentioned how jarring it was to hear their own unrecognizable voice report back to them something as intimate as their own writing process. Many reported that it was like hearing another person discuss something they clearly wrote.

This effect can be partly explained by the audible differences between hearing one's spoken voice from one's mouth versus hearing one's spoken voice played back from a recorded source. The shock of hearing the sound of one's own voice on a recording has been well documented and researched. Particularly relevant to the study of electroacoustic devices for the hearing impaired, there is a noticeable difference between hearing one's own spoken voice in person and hearing it on a recording. The difference is so great, in fact, that early studies concluded that most of us could not recognize the sound of our own voices in test situations. This phenomenon, I would argue, is interesting in light of Ceraso's (2014) concept of *multimodal listening* and the increased attention to the affective, embodied, and material activities of listening at work alongside the conscious act of *hearing*. It is not unreasonable to assume that the affective experience of hearing one's voice describing the writing process through a think-aloud protocol may be a productive means to *other* the act of composing enough to defamiliarize it in ways essential for learning. Further, I would agree with Ceraso that it is an instructor's duty to create opportunities for defamiliarization to occur when designing courses and assignments. As Ceraso notes, "Just as poets and writers use defamiliarization techniques to heighten readers' awareness of language, teachers of multimodal listening practices must design opportunities and assignments that give listeners a chance to experience sound in new and surprising ways" (113).

THE PROTOCOL PODCAST ASSIGNMENT

As discussed, the second unit culminated with a podcast assignment that asked students to return to their two recorded protocols in order to say something about the writing process that could be publicly meaningful in some way. Based on the reading-to-write assignment prompts discussed by Flower and others in the early 1990s, the writing prompts arrived on students' desks folded and stapled in a way that would prevent their preparing for the task beforehand. For the recording, students were instructed to have read the assigned texts—Peter Elbow's (2012) "The Need for Care" and Donald Murray's (2013) "The Maker's Eye"—and be prepared to sit down and write.

Although space is limited here, I would like to share two student reactions from this particular podcasting assignment. The first is from the second episode of Patrick Siebel's podcast series, *Aristotle's Armchair*. This episode begins with the host discussing the felt frustration of sitting in front of a computer attempting not only to write an assignment but also to vocally record his thoughts during the writing process. Says Siebel, "All the things I did, said, and thought—to prompt awareness. So much is hidden in tacit knowledge." What Siebel did bring into awareness through this process, he reports, was largely brought about by simply having his writing process quantified for the first time: the time it took to record was a living record of how long it took him to write. In this way, like the many apps and wearables that have emerged from the "quantified life" movement, Siebel's realization was centered on the tension between time and production: "I recorded myself for forty-five minutes, and weeks later, listening back to transcribe, . . . I noticed something interesting: for the entire length of my recording, what ultimately constituted about 20 words of a paper I spent forty-five whole minutes [on]; that's almost 2.5 minutes per word—*per word!*" Siebel goes on to analyze the time spent during his drafting process (brought to his awareness by the verbalized protocol) through the vocabulary of Elbow's notions of care and carelessness while writing. In a reflection written for this chapter, Siebel discusses the value of the assignment and returning to it months later while attending graduate school:

> I opened up my recording software, pressed the little red button, minimized it. I opened a Word document. For forty-five minutes, I worked on a 350-word assignment for my Advanced Composition and Rhetoric class while simultaneously speaking into my laptop microphone, voicing my thoughts on the writing process—everything from choices made to rationales for choices made to my various frustrations regarding these choices made. Nothing was left unsaid.
>
> In the end I discovered both significant benefit and drawback to these think-aloud protocols. While helping me understand my own writing process, mainly as something byzantine and recursive, it also posed the threat of interdicting the natural flow of thought. Several times I was preoccupied

with explaining an idea that took only a moment to process cognitively to proceed forward in the text. What is lost is the immediacy of thought, the naturalness of more organic prose. What is gained—and what is perhaps the most important insight possible—is awareness.

These protocols seem practical—perhaps compulsory—for writers seeking to identify problems, weaknesses, and/or habits in their process. I cannot say the same for, in my case, an assignment requiring a cohesive draft: it is simple to lose the thread of a developing idea, and it is nearly unavoidable not to do so. Its limitations should not, however, understate its importance. One year later, having done several more of these since our freewriting efforts, I still listen back to that recording when a draft refuses to move forward.

Similar to these insights discussed by Siebel, Gabrielle Frick's podcast series *Life's Passions, Rules, and Literacy* demonstrates another aspect of writing as an embodied activity involving many actors. Specifically, in Frick's case, the integral role of her children's presence as she wrote came to light through the recording of protocols. As Frick's reflection below notes, much of her writing was dictated by the breaks in concentration necessary to take care of her children. Far from being a hindrance to her writing processes, however, taking time out from writing to tend to her children allowed her to come back to the process with "fresh eyes":

> This project allowed me to take a more in-depth look at my personal writing process. It showed me how much time I actually spend writing versus other tasks that help me to complete my writing. For me it takes a lot of time to even get started. There are many steps that go into my process. For example, one of the first things I must do is find an activity that can entertain my children in another room. This gives me some quiet time to at least get started. Next I gather all of the materials I need to sit there for a long time, such as notes, text, pen, paper, and something to drink. Then I scan all the texts and notes. I will take notes from that information that I think are relevant to the chosen topic. If there are quotes that I feel are useful I will try to frame my sentences around them. I also note my own thoughts on the topic that I feel will help further my argument. Of course throughout this process there will be many times that I must get up to help my kids with things. In this podcast you can hear my children in the background. These distractions will get my mind off of the task at hand and sometimes be helpful, allowing me to come back with fresh eyes on what I have just written. Overall this helped me really look into what I was trying to accomplish with my writing.

CONCLUSION

As both Frick's and Seibel's work demonstrates, students' recording of protocols can be an effective tool for the learning of threshold concepts. This works, I would argue, largely by defamiliarizing student writers with their own writing process. Much as Jennifer Bowie's (2012) discussion of the value of podcast assignments for "learning through listening" shows, listening to a voice is fundamentally different than reading a text as it allows us to *hear* things—diction, intonation, cadence—that provide for a richer, more meaningful experience. This is particularly poignant when discussing how student writers benefit from listening to the sound of their own voices discuss their own writing processes.

As Elizabeth Wardle mentions in a comment on Douglas Downs and Wardle's (2007) article "Teaching about Writing, Righting Misconceptions," the goal of WAW approaches is to "*empower students to understand better how writing works in the world and in their lives*," and there are "many means (methods and activities) by which to achieve this goal" (2008, 176). One such means, I have discovered, is through the implementation of think-aloud protocols within the context of a shared podcast series. This is beneficial not only because sound plays an increasing role in our disciplinary identity through sound studies, as Ceraso (2014) suggests, but also because aurality, particularly in a WAW approach to our teaching, allows us to be more holistic teachers. As Cynthia Selfe (2009) has noted, students "need opportunities to realize that different compositional modalities carry with them different possibilities for representing multiple and shifting patterns of identity, additional potential for expression and resistance, expanded ways of engaging with a changing world" (645). A WAW approach to sonic composing can provide such opportunities by encouraging a *defamiliarizing* shift in both the modes of writing and the tools used to inscribe. Such shifts aim to invite students not only into an understanding of the threshold concepts of writing studies more generally, but also into an understanding of one particular threshold concept: that there is a connection between writing practices and identity construction.

REFERENCES

Adler-Kassner, Linda and Elizabeth Wardle, eds. 2015. *Naming What we Know: Threshold Concepts of Writing Studies*. Logan: Utah State University Press.

Bowie, Jennifer L. 2012. "Podcasting in a Writing Class? Considering the Possibilities." *Kairos: A Journal of Rhetoric, Technology, and Pedagogy* 16 (2). http://kairos.technorhetoric.net/16.2/topoi/bowie/index.html.

Ceraso, Steph. 2014. "(Re)Educating the Senses: Multimodal Listening, Bodily Learning, and the Composition of Sonic Experiences." *College English* 77:102–23.

Dangler, Doug, Ben McCorkle, and Time Barrow. 2007. "Expanding Composition Audiences with Podcasting." *Computers and Composition Online*. http://www2.bgsu.edu/departments/english/cconline/podcasting/index.htm.

Downs, Douglas, and Elizabeth Wardle. 2007. "Teaching about Writing, Righting Misconceptions: (Re)Envisioning 'First-Year Composition' as 'Introduction to Writing Studies.'" *College Composition and Communication* 58:552–84.

Elbow, Peter. 2012. "The Need for Care: Easy Speaking onto the Page Is Never Enough." In *Vernacular Eloquence: What Speech Can Bring to Writing*. London: Oxford University Press.

Flower, Linda, Victoria Stein, John Ackerman, Margaret J. Kantz, Kathleen McCormick, and Wayne C. Peck. 1990. *Reading-to-Write: Exploring a Cognitive and Social Process*. Oxford: Oxford University Press.

Murray, Donald. 2013. "The Maker's Eye: Revising Your Own Manuscripts." In *Language Awareness: Readings for College Writers*, edited by Paul Eschholz, Alfred Rosa, and Virginia Clark, 194–98. Boston: Bedford/St. Martin's.

Penrose, Ann M. 1993. "Writing and Learning: Exploring the Consequences of Task Construction." In *Hearing Ourselves Think: Cognitive Research in the College Writing Classroom; Social and Cognitive Studies in Writing and Literacy*, edited by Ann M. Penrose and Barbara M. Sitko, 52–69. New York: Oxford University Press.

Penrose, Ann M., and Barbara M. Sitko, eds. 1993. *Hearing Ourselves Think: Cognitive Research in the College Writing Classroom; Social and Cognitive Studies in Writing and Literacy*. New York: Oxford University Press.

Prior, Paul. 2004. "Tracing Process: How Texts Come into Being." In *What Writing Does and How It Does It: An Introduction to Analyzing Texts and Textual Practice*, edited by Charles Bazerman and Paul Prior, 167–200. London: Routledge.

Selfe, Cynthia L. 2009. "The Movement of Air, the Breath of Meaning: Aurality and Multimodal Composing." *College Composition and Communication* 60:616–63.

Wardle, Elizabeth. 2008. "Continuing the Dialogue: Follow-up Comments on 'Teaching about Writing, Righting Misconceptions.'" *College Composition and Communication* 60:175–81.

29
PLAY THE GAME BUT REFOCUS THE AIM
Teaching WAW within Alternative Pedagogies

Katie Jo LaRiviere

> INSTITUTION TYPE AND SIZE: Public R1 Research University; 24,000 students
> COURSE CONTEXT: First or second course in a two-course FYW; required general education sequence
> STUDY DESIGN/METHODOLOGY: N/A
> WAW PROGRAM OR NOT: Non-WAW program, stand-alone course in a FYW program
> WAW COURSE OR SINGLE ASSIGNMENT/UNIT: Non-WAW course
> INSTRUCTOR TYPE/POSITION: Graduate teaching fellow/graduate student now doctoral candidate and Writing Center director
> KEY TERMS: Open/closed outcomes; double pedagogy; argumentative essay model

ABSTRACT

This chapter explores the critical differences between programs open to WAW practices and those that are not conducive to WAW pedagogy and that restrict pedagogical approaches outside of the argumentative essay model. It identifies and analyzes these writing programs' respective closed and open outcomes and their implications. The chapter then offers a set of guiding principles for implementation of WAW values into non-WAW composition programs, resulting in a "double pedagogy" that serves to benefit students with the virtues of WAW even while, programmatically, WAW may not be a viable pedagogical approach.

INTRODUCTION

This chapter describes my experience as a WAW-trained instructor teaching FYC in a program that is not conducive to WAW pedagogy and that restricts the freedom of its teachers to explore pedagogical approaches outside of the argumentative essay model. After nearly a decade of college-level teaching and substantive training in WAW pedagogy, I reflect on a mid-career adjustment to a new set of pedagogical guidelines required by the argumentative essay (AE) model, based strictly on John Gage's (2005) *The Shape of Reason*. The model frames an approach to first-year composition that has one kind of writing and one rhetorical situation in mind for its students. Yet while I am not able to change the program in which I work, I have found productive ways to weave WAW pedagogy into my FYC courses. I've realized that even in institutional settings that are not set up to support WAW pedagogy, an instructor's careful assessment of WAW's values and desired outcomes can enable her to implement them in programs with pedagogical approaches that seem counter to the WAW ideal. This essay will explore some principles through which WAW pedagogy can be incorporated into programs that are not set up to support it, resulting in an approach that is effectively a "double pedagogy." I argue that WAW pedagogy can be more flexible than an "all or nothing" strategy for FYC and, when faced with an unsupportive institutional approach to FYC pedagogy, it is better to incorporate some of its values than none at all.

BACKGROUND

Over the past six years in a new writing program, I've made an adjustment from my WAW training to the AE approach, and the transition required me to investigate my own clear preference for teaching WAW. I had to understand why I was so "attached" to WAW in order to do my best teaching another pedagogy with which I was admittedly uncomfortable. As a result, I set out to closely analyze both AE and WAW approaches, working to understand the AE model and finding that it was exactly the kind of approach that WAW theory directly criticizes. In fact, Downs and Wardle's (2007) work on the mistaken beliefs "that suffuse expectations for FYC" explains the kinds of misconceptions about writing that disciplinary research has consistently "call[ed] into question" (553), but that various pedagogical approaches continue to promise: "that academic writing is generally universal, that writing is a basic skill independent of content or context, and that writing abilities automatically transfer from FYC to other courses and contexts" (554). My analysis revealed that the AE model clearly participates in these misconceptions.

As I call these misconceptions about writing to the surface, I hear my new colleagues whispering in my ear, arguing that the AE pedagogy doesn't *intend* to teach these mistaken beliefs. In the required course text, *The Shape of Reason*, Gage (2005) is clear that all writing situations require the writer to address a particular discourse community (chapter 4). The course's required design emphasizes practice in the form of repeating essay cycles wherein students write essays addressing two or three various questions at issue from their readings and practice formulating and arguing enthymematic essays; the emphasis on practice should convey that writing is not an easily acquired "skill." Yet in practice, teachers at my institution have one ten-week term to introduce these concepts and work with students to practice them. This short time frame limits the positive aspects and intentions of AE pedagogy and can reduce essay writing to a formula for one kind of paper with one goal. Students write a five-page essay based on a topic of the instructor's choice (usually a social justice–based issue) with what amounts to a checklist of features that are clearly designated on grading rubrics.

Thus, both the content and design of the course emphasize all three misconceptions by reducing "writing" for the college freshman to a set of skills determined by course outcomes that become a checklist for "success" rather than markers of student thinking and learning. These outcomes are measured by teachers and then submitted for overall program assessment, and they are also basic guidelines for grading individual essays, which means they appear as categories on grading rubrics. Students' ability to achieve these outcomes affects not only each individual essay grade but also their standing in the course. In this way, this list of outcomes affects both students and teachers on every level of the pedagogy. Let us examine the official course outcomes more specifically:

Upon completion, students should be able to achieve the following outcomes:

> Write essays that develop and respond to a significant question that is relevant to the context in which it is written and appropriate for the audience to which it is addressed.
>
> Provide logical answers to questions at issue and develop lines of reasoning in support of those answers, while taking into account and responding to objections or competing answers and lines of reasoning.
>
> Write an essay that is unified around a main claim, proceeds in a logical way, and consists of cohesive paragraphs that separate and connect ideas effectively.
>
> Produce written work that displays adherence to the conventions of academic writing, including control of grammar, spelling, word usage,

> syntax, and punctuation; appropriate tone, style, diction, and register; proper formatting, use, and documentation of sources.
>
> Improve the content and organization of an essay draft in a revision process, both by reevaluating the reasoning and context of the essay and by responding to critiques from peers and instructors. (University of Oregon n.d.)

At first glance, these may seem rather innocuous. But they are what I shall call "closed" outcomes rather than "open" ones. That is, they direct students and teachers toward evaluation based on a checklist of skills, rather than on how students have developed their thinking about writing as a rhetorical practice and attempted to implement that thinking in their work.

"Closed" outcomes ask, "Has the student achieved X?" and allow only one path to success in writing. They contribute to the misconception that writing can be taught as a skill. Has the student written at least one passable argumentative essay in this course? Check. Does it have what we could call an enthymeme or reasoned thesis in or near the introduction? Check. These kinds of questions, in other words, suggest that successful writing results from this singular track; they perform an evaluation that pretends "that FYC can do what nonspecialists have always assumed it can: teach, in one or two early courses, 'college writing' as a set of basic, fundamental skills that will apply in other college courses and in business and public spheres after college" (Downs and Wardle 2007, 553). Indeed, these kinds of outcomes cannot appear innocuous for long because the moment the student steps outside my classroom, she learns that these goals for learning "how to write" in fact apply only to my humanities-based "English" class, and not to the full range of other classes she is taking. These are outcomes for learning *one* kind of writing and *one* kind of rhetorical situation (to which the first outcome passively alludes). The problem with this "one way" message is that it conflates the goals of one type of writing with program outcomes that are supposed to represent "college writing" as a whole. Closed outcomes, then, are a problem not only with AE pedagogy but with any writing program that offers the "one way" impression *through* its pedagogical approach. Ultimately, the biggest mistake of pedagogies like this one is not that their goals are directed toward only one kind of writing, but that they absolutely fail to be explicit about that fact and its implications.

Alternatively, "open" outcomes ask, "How has the student changed or developed her thinking about X?" and call into question the "unsupportable assurances" of skills-based knowledge transfer composition programs too often make (Downs and Wardle 2007, 553). They are the kind of outcomes WAW suggests are more helpful to students as the pedagogy strives to "shift the central goal from teaching 'academic writing' to *teaching realistic and useful conceptions of writing*—perhaps the most significant of which is neither basic nor universal but content- and context-contingent and irreducibly complex" (557–58). In this way, the outcomes of WAW pedagogy are less a matter of neatly assessing students' discrete skills and more a matter of assessing how and what they have learned about writing as a concept, a strategy, a mode. Kristen di Gennaro's chapter in this volume exhibits some excellent examples of open outcomes that aim for this kind of assessment. To this end, WAW tends to focus its energies on helping students to discover its grounding principles via its open outcomes rather than developing certain closed skills. As a matter of principle and practice, WAW simply asks different kinds of questions because its values are different: it evaluates outcomes that stem from questions like these: How has the student developed his or her thinking about what writing is or does? What has changed over the course of the term in the way a student defines "good" writing? How have students developed their ability to analyze writing rhetorically and apply those analyses to their own work? WAW's greatest virtue is that it values students' thinking about writing and so requires students to think via the methodology of these open outcomes. The pedagogy simultaneously prompts students and teachers not only to see writing as a practice *and* a discipline but, as its greatest virtue, it also actively and consistently promotes metacognitive thinking.

SUGGESTIONS FOR A DOUBLE PEDAGOGY

The result of my analysis of AE and WAW pedagogies has affirmed my commitment to WAW principles and to incorporating those principles into the AE pedagogy that I am required to teach in my institution. I consider my commitment to WAW's "grounding principles" (Downs and Wardle 2007, 559) an ethical one, and for this reason, I have shifted the terminology of "principles" to "virtues." I have worked to found my AE course upon those virtues, such that they inform my pedagogical attitude toward the requirements of the argumentative essay and its constitutive assignments. In this way, I believe I am able to maintain the values and outcomes of the AE pedagogy, to which I am formally committed, along with the virtues of WAW pedagogy, to which I am ethically committed. For this reason, it is perhaps more helpful to think of my pedagogical approach as a layered one, rather than an attempt to teach both in one term. In service of this approach, I have developed some suggestions for implementing WAW virtues that help me to maintain the underlayer of WAW virtues as a foundation for AE outcomes and assignments; they are ways to put WAW's virtues into action. And they can be adapted to other pedagogical requirements besides the AE approach; I can imagine particular success in the genre-based approach and multilingual courses taught by my colleagues at other institutions. Di Gennaro's chapter offers specific examples for teaching WAW in a multilingual classroom, for example, and her course design concretely demonstrates all of the forthcoming suggestions.

One of the most obvious ways to organize another pedagogical approach upon the virtues of WAW is to *plan readings that topically focus on writing* if at all possible, even if they cannot be readings directly from composition scholarship. This principle makes my following suggestions much easier to implement and, significantly, "contravenes the typical assumption that first-year writing can be about anything [and that] somehow the content is irrelevant to an instructor's ability to respond to the writing" (Downs and Wardle 2007, 559). Yet in cases like mine, using readings with a topical focus on writing can be difficult or impossible. One of the greatest constraints on teachers in my program is that we must choose from a set of preapproved readers for use in our classroom, with the option of adding up to two readings from outside one's chosen reader. Most of the readers in our program focus on social justice issues because the "questions at issue" are easy to identify, and arguments can be relatively straightforward for students to consider, plan, and write (Gage 2005, 58). Yet the use of topical readers implicitly communicates that writing itself is secondary to the course topic. For this reason, I choose a reader with essays that can also be discussed easily in terms of rhetorical strategy, audience, and discourse community. I also take full advantage of my two allowed "outside" readings, which I build into my course strategically, as we shall see. With these two readings, both grounded in composition scholarship, students see what writing about writing actually looks like, and we think about composition theory alongside the topical choices from the reader.

The combination of composition theory and topical readings requires my next suggestion: *be explicit.* While working under the constraints of another pedagogy, it is impossible to institute the kind of "radical change" proposed by Downs and Wardle in their initial essay on WAW (2007, 553). However, we should still be realistic about what our institution's pedagogy can and should accomplish, and we should be explicit with students about its aims and limitations. Building on the virtues of

WAW means that, many times, the lessons we would ideally have them discover via WAW-specific assignments have to be stated outright in my classroom. For example, the AE approach helps students to think critically about texts and to develop logically reasoned arguments in response to a set of "questions at issue" in a particular kind of discourse. In theory, the approach could remain rather open to letting students explore these processes in writing across the disciplines. However, because the "parts of an essay" reflect the stated course outcomes, they can be taught as a checklist or formula. More troublingly, however, the parallel between such an approach and the stated learning outcomes gives the impression to both teachers and students that the argumentative essay *is* writing, that we are "'teach[ing] students to write' in general" (559) with this checklist of essay components.

Instead, if we are honest with our students about what the FYC course can accomplish, and about what our particular institution's pedagogical approach can teach them, then we can at least uphold the WAW-inspired virtue that promises to be "forthcoming about what writing instruction can and cannot accomplish" (Downs and Wardle 2007, 559). More than that, we can be honest about why their "writing class" requires something completely different from what their chemistry labs require, why their journalism courses don't ask for explicit arguments and MLA formatting, or why and how they should sometimes write for a tightly specific audience and sometimes their writing is allowed to address a broad readership.

In practice, being explicit with students sets their expectations to fit what we can accomplish in one term, and it also helps them to better understand the nature of writing as communication. It means admitting that, in this class, we will practice one kind of writing, and we will focus on some narrow sets of ideas about writing. It means being clear about the kind of writing we will be working on, and the fact that it is *just one kind* of writing. And finally, it means writing an explicit *caveat emptor* into my syllabus as well as repeatedly pointing out, verbally and sometimes on assignment sheets, that what we are learning in any given unit is part of a specific idea about writing that creates argumentative essays.

Next, *use what you have to create more awareness* about writing concepts and ways to think about writing. For me this means that I emphasize the concept of discourse community beyond its iterations in *The Shape of Reason*. While the AE approach uses the concept as a way for students to relate to their classmates around a set of course readings, I expand this concept in my course using James Paul Gee's (1989) "Literacy, Discourse, and Linguistics: Introduction." We discuss Gee's concept of

Discourse as it applies to the argumentative essay, but also as a way to discuss the ways in which different kinds of writing must adapt to different audiences and accomplish different goals. Written assignments surrounding our readings of Gee's essay ask students to think about the nature of their primary Discourse, how they've learned various secondary Discourses, and what they'll need to learn about the Discourse of their respective academic disciplines; I am explicit about the fact that their various majors are going to require them to adapt to different Discourses. As a class, we work to understand the features of our own course, the academic discipline of writing, and our class culture as a specific Discourse community.

The virtue behind my approach to the concept of discourse might also be seen as one specific way to frame my next suggestion: *build WAW practices into as many appropriate moments as possible.* Specifically, whenever we encounter an idea about writing that can be made into a "metamoment," we capitalize on that moment. Practically this means that if we are learning any given component of the AE pedagogy that I can refocus onto students' processes, habits, or ideas about writing, we take the time to reflect and discuss the fruit of that reflection. The concept of Gee's "Discourse" communities is one of the most fruitful of these discussions, but we can also discuss questions at issue, stasis, audience, exigence, and arguments this way. Merely asking them to evaluate whether they think that all (their) writing contains an argument is one way we can begin to analyze the tasks of the course as *one idea* about writing among many. We can also be honest with each other about the fact that different kinds of writing require different processes and that these differences are available for study as part of a unique academic discipline.

Thus, in many ways, building in WAW practices, and specifically reflection, whether as part of class discussion, informal homework assignments, freewriting exercises, or as part of comments on student work, is often a task of many small iterations throughout the term. Whether implemented formally or informally, WAW practices require students to analyze their own ways of thinking about writing *as they are doing it.* Results from these practices often show students realizing that writing isn't the one-shot product or general skill they had learned or assumed it was.

Ultimately, with each of these suggestions, I *play the game but refocus the aim.* For example, students are required to write two "essay cycles" as part of the AE approach, each practicing the enthymematic essay on a new set of readings. My classes maintain the required cycles and process from reading to essay, but the readings for my third cycle include Keith

Grant-Davie's (1997) "Rhetorical Situations and Their Constituents." Then, the task for their final formal essay is slightly different from the other cycles because I propose the "question at issue": what is good writing? Students must use one of our theory texts (essays by Gee or Grant-Davie) and a proof text (one topical reading from our reader) to prove their answer, or thesis, to my question. I ask students to provide examples of the theoretical principles of "good writing" alongside examples of texts that they think actually achieve those principles in practice. In this way students think metacognitively about what the term *good writing* could actually mean and how they would define it based on our disciplinary theory. Additionally, they practice rhetorically analyzing their proof text and arguing its merits on the basis of rhetorical theory, rather than what "English" has taught them about good writing.

As a result, students accomplish the outcomes required by the AE approach, but must also use the virtues of WAW to arrive at those outcomes. I'll venture that in most pedagogical situations, if students must achieve mastery of a closed set of skills, it is ideal that they do so *by means of* engaging the values that open outcomes explore and promote. As the final project in the course, this assignment employs the open outcomes proposed by WAW in the process of achieving the institutional outcomes I am required to observe; the suggestions I've described transform the course from a progression through a closed checklist to an exploration of open questions from which students benefit in many ways, one of which is the achievement of discrete skills articulated in the official course outcomes.

CONCLUSION

Reflecting on and strategically implementing WAW's methodology and pedagogical virtues helps me to remain true to my pedagogical values and best teaching practices in the service of students as I continue to teach composition in an alternative pedagogy. By implementing WAW virtues in these ways, I can offer the best to my students, even if I cannot take advantage of the WAW ideal. Additionally, the ways I have found to incorporate WAW into my institutional requirements keep me passionately engaged in teaching composition. I am personally committed to the honest nature of this pedagogy because it has realistic and research-based expectations for students; it is challenging and rewarding for teachers and students alike; it combines discipline with pedagogy in ways that reflect the modus operandi of other academic disciplines and legitimize our discipline's principles and goals. Perhaps most important from a pedagogical standpoint, it presents a most productive method for students to think about, research, and practice writing not only in college but also in the real world. It may be that writing about writing makes its "radical change" from the inside out for teachers who face the limitations of alternative pedagogies, but situations like mine may also be one of its most inspiring footholds for the future of first-year composition.

REFERENCES

Downs, Doug, and Elizabeth Wardle. 2007. "Teaching about Writing, Righting Misconceptions: (Re)Envisioning 'First-Year Composition' as 'Introduction to Writing Studies.'" *College Composition and Communication* 58:552–84.

Gage, John. 2005. *The Shape of Reason*. 4th ed. New York: Longman.

Gee, James Paul. 1989. "Literacy, Discourse, and Linguistics: Introduction." *Journal of Education* 171 (1): 5–14.

Grant-Davie, Keith. 1997. "Rhetorical Situations and Their Constituents." *Rhetoric Review* 15:264–79.

University of Oregon. n.d. "Learning Outcomes." *Composition Program.* http://composition.uoregon.edu/requirement/learning-outcomes/.

Conclusion
AFTERWARDS AND FORWARDS

Barbara Bird, Doug Downs,
I. Moriah McCracken, and Jan Rieman

When this project began, we set out to collect voices that together would extend representation of this "thing" that has come to be called writing about writing. We knew a growing number of teachers and writing programs were experimenting with WAW in a wide variety of forms, and we heard in the multiplicity of their stories affirmation that *there is not "one" way to do WAW.*

The curricula described by authors in this resulting volume demonstrate the wide inclusivity of WAW. In each chapter, we see a focus on helping students to, at all levels and with all kinds of preparations, think about how writing works in all kinds of situations. This inclusivity means that no chapter discusses *the way* to teach students *the way* to do writing; there is no single set of practices to which each author conformed. Rather, each chapter addresses a common set of concerns that seem to bracket WAW approaches. Each, in different ways, focuses on helping students become adaptive writers, individuals who can combine metacognitive strategies with rhetorical awareness to demystify writing *for themselves*. Though these authors each emphasize different concepts, they all center their courses on what we know about writing as well as the core focuses that WAW courses usually incorporate: identity, process, and engagement. While we've organized the book by which of these themes an author principally engages, each author addresses all three in some way. Additionally, the outcome and purpose that *all* authors embrace at some level is transfer of learning. Through focuses on identity, process, and engagement, each of these authors at least touches on transfer as a goal.

Yet while we see learning transfer through identity, process, and engagement as connected themes in the WAW courses discussed in this volume, we also know, because we see WAW in the plural, approach*es*, that there are new directions in which WAW is heading, or could head.

DOI: 10.7330/9781607328421.c030

If the preceding observations are where we are "afterwards," what about *forwards*? Where to from here?

NEW DIRECTIONS IN RESEARCH

First, we hope readers will mine the data. We see this collection and its accompanying website neither as simply a teaching resource nor a collection of scholars reflecting on writing pedagogy, theory, and research, but as a deep repository of images of student learning through contemporary WAW approaches. We mean this book to be itself a research tool, so that readers can investigate across methods and approaches, contact other instructors whose work they're interested in hearing more about or approaches they'd like to try, and develop research questions that one or more of the methods described in this book can make a start at answering. As one example, we are fascinated by which particular writing studies texts trend across the widest variety of programs. What does it tell us—about the nature of writing, the nature of student learning, and/or the nature of writing instructors' instincts—that certain texts circulate so heavily and are seen by so many teachers as being instrumental to students' learning? So much awaits scholars who take this collection as a large data set (even as we acknowledge that "data" is not the plural of "anecdote") and explore what can be inferred and interpreted from it.

As we and other readers continue to find common threads with each other within the realm of WAW, this book and accompanying website provide a space to make those commonalities visible. Here are just a few examples we found among the contributing authors in this collection:

Many feel a sense of isolation.
Many express a sense that they feel a permission to interrogate their writing instruction practices.
Many feel a significant sense of authenticity when teaching writing from a WAW stance.

We would love to see teachers and researchers collaborate on research, teaching, and program development work with others who share similar goals for student learning. As editors, we have benefited greatly from our own contacts with all the contributors, and we imagine this collection can facilitate the formation of a stronger and more interactive community of teachers and scholars who believe that students more deeply learn and effectively transfer writing knowledge when they study, discuss, and write about that knowledge. Strengthening community is paramount.

Those working with graduate teaching assistants or relatively inexperienced instructors seem to have an easier time of such community building since collaboration and mentorship are at the heart of such relationships. To many new writing teachers, WAW seems intuitive. As some of the authors here relate, for many who have been teaching for decades, WAW has become a welcome grounding to what they have already observed is true about how novice writers learn. New demands from student, culture, and economic realities make us eager to share our wealth of knowledge with co-learners of this approach that emphasizes writing knowledge.

While contributors were writing and revising for this collection, the field's interest in writing our knowledge, and in learning transfer, became even more pronounced with the publication of *Naming What We Know: Threshold Concepts of Writing Studies* (Adler-Kassner and Wardle 2015). *Naming What We Know* contributes critically important ideas to our field, and articulates well the epistemic assertion underlying writing about writing instruction: our field has developed knowledge about the nature of writers, writing, discourse, and rhetoric that is valuable to veteran and novice writers alike. Instructors who have been working with WAW approaches have been thinking about how to teach many of the very concepts articulated by contributors to *Naming*. While our own collection comprises a significant contribution to accounts of how to do such teaching, it also shows us where more research is needed—both about *what* we teach and about how we're teaching it.

We think the same of the learning-transfer question. Contemporary WAW approaches have from the first been part of the field's current wave of self-conscious inquiry on and analysis of learning transfer and how to teach for it explicitly. As Downs and Wardle suggest at the end of "Teaching about Writing, Righting Misconceptions," "Teaching students what we know about writing and asking them to research their own writing and the writing of others encourages this self-reflection and mindfulness, thereby improving the possibility that students will maintain a stance of inquiry toward writing as they write in other disciplinary systems. Only with additional implementation of the pedagogy and longitudinal studies to assess students' later writing experiences will we be able to tell whether this theory bears out in practice" (2007, 577).

This collection contributes to the growing body of research on transfer, including those in the Teaching for Transfer (TFT) curricular conversation (Yancey, Robertson, and Taczak 2014) and the significant work that has (and will continue to) come out of the Elon Transfer Project, notably Jessie Moore and Randall Bass's 2017 collection *Understanding Writing Transfer*. These newer voices have joined the sometimes more quiet voices of the instructor-scholars who have been using WAW approaches to contend that deliberate, direct engagement with disciplinary knowledge is the most efficient way to prepare students to be flexible, adaptive writers. We see research on WAW and other approaches like TFT as centripetal, not centrifugal, forces. Although there are pedagogical and (some) theoretical differences between these two approaches, both are asking our discipline to refocus on what we know—to make the content of writing the content of our courses.

We are pleased with how this collection incorporates not just contemporary scholarship on learning transfer but voices from long past. We are reminded again, for example, of George Jardine, who in teaching working-class, first-generation college students noted the importance of engaging students in rich reading, writing, and discussion of rhetoric and writing principles: "The student must not be allowed to act the part of a mere recipient. On the contrary, he must be taught to ruminate on what he hears; to pass it through all the channels of his own mind; to arrange and digest it; to write on it, to reason on it; and finally, to make it his own by combining it with his own thoughts and reflections" (1825, 522). Jardine reminds us that students rarely transfer processes or concepts that are not in some way integrated into their sense of self, their identities. We may in fact be wiser to understand "learning transfer" not as the transportation of knowledge but as the transformation of *people*. Writers here describing WAW approaches observe that students will learn writing concepts more deeply, engage them more holistically, and integrate them into their identities more fully fitting who they are and want to become when these students read, ruminate on, and write about these concepts.

Such theoretical, curricular, and scholarly connections between WAW pedagogy and other movements in the field, present as well as past, demonstrated across the work of contributors here are one of the most helpful aspects of this collection, and there is significant value in continuing to return to work of the past, and to network WAW research into the field's continuing knowledge making.

NEW DIRECTIONS FOR EMPOWERING WRITING TEACHERS

Most of the teaching experiences conveyed in this collection demonstrate that students engage well with research-driven texts on the subject matter of our field. The students discussed here—as well as the students *writing* here—who read, write, and discuss concepts of writing often do so within the realm of their contemporary practices as composers. The study of writing need not be dry and disengaged from the "popular" or contemporary topics that many writing instructors feel are necessary to hold student interest. We read this as empowering to teachers. We hope the evidence of student learning, and the student voices themselves, in these pages gives writing teachers who are new to or considering WAW approaches more confidence that students, including "basic" and multilingual writers, have far greater capabilities of engaging with texts about writing—including those that are viewed as difficult for freshmen, as Bartholomae and Petrosky (2008) argue—and have far more *interest* in engaging writing concepts that can empower them as writers than our field has assumed in the past. Composition studies may be the only discipline in the entire academy that has been built on self-effacement of its own expertise. Our discipline's roots imbibed the university's insistence that there is so little *there* there that our subject could be sufficiently taught by faculty spouses. Is it any surprise that such denial of expertise, of a research-derived content meaningful to students, by all quarters—including our own English departments—would disempower instructors through the decades? We are thus unsurprised, in the presence of the opposite assertion of a disciplinary content and expertise valuable to students, to read the empowerment that arises throughout this collection—notably, among all ranks and among all institutional types.

We see in this collection instances of empowerment arising as writers give themselves permission to use approaches other than the default of a specific context. Ours is the latest collection to demonstrate how important it is for writing instructors to have "permission," time, and support to examine what they are doing in their classes and what they are being asked to do in their programs. We see the same even of our own paths to WAW approaches. Before using a WAW approach, Jan, for example, never felt that she had the opportunity to question what she was doing in her first-year composition courses. A process-based approach was assumed, and while she knew there was value in process-focused knowledge, she knew that asking students to write formulaic compare and contrast or definition papers as part of that process was a false representation of writing. She knew that exploring Rogerian or Toulminian forms of argument was reductive. Like many of us, her colleagues turned to creative nonfiction as a substitute, and others followed the lead of their programs and turned to literature in their second required writing course as a way to fill the "content gap." We don't think Jan's story and experiences are unique. We know her reaction isn't. Like many of the faculty teaching in our programs, she had *no idea* what to replace her previous content with or even that she might have "permission" to use different content.

In an academy ever more industrialized to minimize expenses and academic freedom while increasing student throughput and workforce preparation, we are at increasingly greater risk of writing programs settling curricula without input from ever more contingent faculty. Maybe even when curricular discussions are happening in a program, a given instructor simply isn't a part of the conversation. In either case, bringing WAW approaches to discussions of curricular content can open spaces for exploration and help faculty and students become stronger advocates for program and professional development. As writing teachers and writing program directors, we *all* need to engage with what we are doing in the classroom and why. We hope the experiences described in this book give readers permission to examine their own approaches to writing instruction; we hope this book encourages teachers and students and stakeholders to start such a conversation or join one that is already ongoing. In particular, we hope this book could help the *thousands* of writing teachers who were not trained in our discipline to knowledgeably choose disciplinary readings that help students engage with their identities as writers and with their complex writing processes. That is, we hope this collection can serve as an entry point for engaging with composition scholarship and as a rationale for why it's important to do so.

The community-building and advocacy potential of this book appeals to us as editors precisely because the voices gathered here suggest that after more than ten years, some instructors using WAW approaches still feel alienated from their programs and each other. We suspect some of this alienation relates to perceptions (we would argue, misperceptions) of what WAW is, especially its inclusiveness, and what it does. If evidence were needed that WAW approaches are widely diverse and make a broadly inclusive and welcoming pedagogical community possible, this collection should offer it. If instructors wants to use their disciplinary and firsthand knowledge about how writing works in their classrooms by having students write and reflect on both the knowledge the instructor introduces them to and students' own experiences as writers, then they are using a WAW approach. In "Reflecting Back and Looking Forward: Revising 'Teaching about Writing, Righting Misconceptions' Five Years On," Wardle and Downs (2013) revisited the reception of WAW by the field, reflecting on assertions they made in their first articulation of writing about writing. One point they reconsider is the staffing of WAW courses. In the intervening years, they had learned that it *is* possible "*to invite willing faculty members* to learn about writing studies research while *bringing their own expertise to bear at the same time*" (emphasis added).

We take it as axiomatic that inclusion is empowering; we also recognize that *true* inclusion must welcome the existing identities and values of all a community's members. This collection demonstrates openness to and inclusion of colleagues with literature and linguistic and cultural studies backgrounds and continuing commitments. We are all writers; we all have valuable perspectives on what it is, and means, to write. Our students benefit from mindful and deliberate engagement with all those perspectives.

NEW DIRECTIONS FOR PROFESSIONAL IDENTITIES

Given this collection's demonstration that WAW is a truly inclusive pedagogy—both in its welcoming of all students as agentive writers, and in the access and agency it offers to instructors—welcoming as diverse a mix of instructors and backgrounds as possible is vital to avoid establishing our own dogmas.

Doug's writing program at Montana State offers an example of how the flexibility and multiplicity of WAW approaches can build inclusion. The program includes a mix of highly experienced, traditionalist instructors and less experienced instructors who were trained in more contemporary approaches to writing instruction. The newer instructors have found it relatively easy to explore WAW approaches, while for a number of years more traditional instructors largely opted out. In spring 2015, the program offered a salon series for instructors who were choosing not to use a WAW approach, so they could see firsthand a variety of ways it could be configured in their own classes. What enabled instructors in the salon to explore aspects of WAW approaches was the realization that "WAW" means not a single, forced curriculum, but simply a broad set of principles that lead to an explosion of reading and assignment possibilities. They could use WAW as much or as little as they liked; they could add an assignment, or just a reading, or they could design a whole course to look like some courses already used in the program, or they could design a whole course that was their own. They could say, "I don't teach WAW like you do, but I've noticed that students *really* connect with X reading." Or they could (and did) say, "I don't know why students revise so much more effectively when I teach this way, but I *like* it." They just have to be able to see themselves "in" this.

And here is where the world lights up a bit: these instructors aren't necessarily doing WAW to the same extent, or in the same directions, as other instructors, but they feel *included* both as professional writing instructors and in the *profession* and the *conversation*, in ways unimaginable a few years ago. Something is happening here. More would be good—for our students, for us as instructors, and for our field. The one thing that *no* WAW approach can be a comfortable fit with is a writing program that can't imagine its instructors as *members of a profession of writing instructors*. If a program wants to employ writing instructors who have no communication with, input into, responsibility toward, or recognition from the profession that builds and teaches the knowledge such a program purportedly hires its instructors to profess, it will likely have little interest in, and in fact be profoundly unhappy with, WAW approaches to writing instruction. Again, our field's historical roots in the university's denial of a teachable subject make the preceding sentence an unimaginable statement in any other field. But in composition, our need to advocate for this professional inclusion and connection continues.

As Downs and Wardle (2007) argued, no other composition pedagogy fronts this challenge more starkly—but as the chapters in this collection also demonstrate, no other composition pedagogy offers a greater opportunity *for* that professional inclusion and conversation. WAW approaches offer students, instructors, and our field professional identity. Students in WAW courses or in classrooms with WAW assignments begin to view themselves as having a scholarly identity. Instructors incorporating *their* version of WAW can gain a greater sense of professional identity, both from creating their own WAW course that reflects their teaching/writing strengths and institutional context and also from a sense of teaching their disciplinary expertise (whatever discipline they call home—writing studies, rhetoric, literature, linguistics, creative writing—since all of these disciplines have writing concepts connected to the discipline). Finally, our own field of comp/rhet gains a clearer professional identity among our colleagues across all disciplines. And we gain expanded collaborative discussions with each other as we deliberate which writing concepts we focus our courses on, how we teach those concepts and, most important, what our students teach *us* about writing. For it is here that the ethos of WAW lies: teaching writing concepts to empower our students while simultaneously learning *with* and *from* our students the inexhaustible content of our field, writing.

REFERENCES

Adler-Kassner, Linda, and Elizabeth Wardle, eds. 2015. *Naming What We Know: Threshold Concepts of Writing Studies*. Logan: Utah State University Press.

Bartholomae, David, and Anthony Petrosky. 2008. *Ways of Reading: An Anthology for Writers*. 8th ed. New York: Bedford/St. Martin's.

Downs, Douglas, and Elizabeth Wardle. 2007. "Teaching about Writing, Righting Misconceptions: (Re)Envisioning 'First-Year Composition' as 'Introduction to Writing Studies.'" *College Composition and Communication* 58:552–82.

Jardine, George. 1825. *Outlines of Philosophical Education, Illustrated by the Method of Teaching the Logic Class in the University of Glasgow; Together with Observations on the Expediency of Extending the Practical System to Other Academical Establishments, and on the Propriety of Making Certain Additions to the Course of Philosophical Education in Universities.* Glasgow: Glasgow University Press.

Moore, Jessie L., and Randall Bass, eds. 2017. *Understanding Writing Transfer: Implications for Transformative Student Learning in Higher Education.* Sterling, VA: Stylus.

Wardle, Elizabeth, and Doug Downs. 2013. "Reflecting Back and Looking Forward: Revisiting 'Teaching about Writing, Righting Misconceptions' Five Years On." *Composition Forum* 27. http://compositionforum.com/issue/27/.

Yancey, Kathleen Blake, Liane Robertson, and Kara Taczak. 2014. *Writing across Contexts: Transfer, Composition, and Sites of Writing.* Logan: Utah State University Press.

CONTRIBUTORS

LINDA ADLER-KASSNER is professor of writing, Director of the Center for Innovative Teaching, Research, and Learning, and Associate Dean of Undergraduate Education in the College of Letters and Science at UC Santa Barbara. Her research and teaching focus broadly on how literate agents and activities—such as writers, writing, writing studies—are defined in contexts inside the academy and in public discourse. She also examines the implications and consequences of those definitions and how writing faculty can participate in shaping them. She frequently works with faculty across disciplines on articulating threshold concepts and making them more accessible for students. She is author, coauthor, or coeditor of nine books, including *Naming What We Know: Threshold Concepts of Writing Studies*, co-edited with Elizabeth Wardle, and *The Activist WPA: Changing Stories about Writing and Writers*. Adler-Kassner and Wardle's new edited collection, *Reconsidering What We Know: Learning Thresholds in Rhetoric, Composition, Writing, and Literacy*, will be published by Utah State University Press in 2019.

OLGA AKSAKALOVA is an associate professor of English at LaGuardia Community College, CUNY, where she teaches basic writing, first-year composition, and writing through literature courses. Her research in rhetoric and composition focuses on writing pedagogy in global contexts, civic engagement in composition courses, and bilingual practices at the writing center.

JOY ARBOR is an independent researcher based in southeast Michigan. Her primary research areas are talking and listening across difference. She is currently studying rhetoric and listening in the Israeli-Palestinian conflict. Her work has appeared in *Silence and Listening as Rhetorical Arts*, *Jewish Rhetorics: History, Theory, Practice*, and *Thinking and Practicing Reconciliation: Teaching and Learning through Literary Responses to Conflict*. Her poetry chapbook, *Where Are You From, Originally?* was published by Finishing Line Press in 2016.

BARBARA BIRD is dean of faculty development and professor of English at Taylor University. She directs Taylor University's Bedi Center for Teaching and Learning Excellence, leads the new faculty orientation program, and teaches basic writing. Currently, she is researching the threshold concepts of faculty; her prior scholarship examined the influence of WAW on writer identity and dispositions. She was awarded the Teaching Excellence and Campus Leadership award at Taylor in 2010.

MATTHEW BRYAN is an associate lecturer in the department of writing and rhetoric at the University of Central Florida. He holds an MFA in creative writing, and in addition to writing fiction and nonfiction, he is interested in how teachers find their way into WAW approaches and how student publications can act as sites for learning about writing beyond the classroom. Since its founding in 2009, he has served as editor of UCF's journal of first-year writing, *Stylus*.

SHAWN CASEY is an assistant professor in the department of English and the writing center coordinator at Columbus State Community College, where he also serves as a faculty fellow for dual credit. His teaching and research interests include the study of literacy and the writing curriculum across institutional contexts.

CONTRIBUTORS

GABRIEL CUTRUFELLO is an assistant professor in the professional writing program at York College of Pennsylvania. He teaches first-year writing and courses for the professional writing major. His current research investigates the use of visuals in scientific papers written by physics graduate students at Johns Hopkins University in the late 1800s.

JENNIFER DEWINTER is an associate professor of rhetoric and director of the interactive media and game development program and a professor in the professional communication program at Worcester Polytechnic Institute. Her work focuses on digital rhetoric and international circulation. Further, she builds and consults on a number of games that translate STEM fields for education as well as games to promote social change and empathy.

DOUG DOWNS is an associate professor of writing and rhetoric at Montana State University, where he founded the English Department's Writing major and served for five years as director of the Core Writing Program. His research interests include public conceptions of writing, undergraduate research, and student reading habits. With Elizabeth Wardle, he is coauthor of the textbook *Writing about Writing* and of a 2007 *CCC* article that became a foundational argument for WAW approaches.

KRISTEN DI GENNARO is associate professor of English and director of composition at Pace University in New York City. Her research addresses current issues in writing assessment and pedagogy with a particular focus on second-language learners and Generation 1.5 writers. Her work has appeared in various journals, including *Assessing Writing, Writing & Pedagogy, Language Testing,* and *Journal of Basic Writing*.

EMMA GAIER graduated from Purdue University in 2016 with a bachelor's degree in history. She is currently beginning a Transition to Teaching program with the hopes of teaching eighth-grade United States history.

CHRISTINA GRANT is pursuing a PhD in secondary education with a writing specialty at the University of Alberta. She was lead instructor for the all-multilingual Bridging Program version of Writing Studies 101—Exploring Writing, which received a CCCC Certificate of Excellence (2014–15), from its inception until she began doctoral studies. Her research and teaching interests include writing knowledge transfer in multilingual students, deaf education, experiential learning, internationalized classrooms, and indigenous pedagogies. Her coauthored play, *As Long as the Sun Shines*, a dramatic reenactment of the signing of Treaty 8, appears in *Staging Alternative Albertas* (2002). Her creative nonfiction work *D-Day*, about the language journey of her profoundly deaf son, won the Cecile E. Mactaggart Award for Narrative Writing in 2014.

GWEN HART is an associate professor of English at Buena Vista University in Storm Lake, Iowa, where she teaches composition and creative writing. Her second poetry collection, *The Empress of Kisses*, won the X.J. Kennedy Poetry Prize from Texas Review Press.

KIMBERLY HOOVER is a PhD student at the University of Pittsburgh. Currently, she is studying the rhetoric of Western medicine, placebo effect, and the reification of mind-body-dualism, and therefore, the two-pain problem as it relates to healing modalities in the west. Kim has been teaching college composition since 2013 both as a graduate student and as adjunct faculty. She has taught course arcs based on waw pedagogy, ecological rhetorics, and gender/race studies.

REBECCA JACKSON is professor of English and director of the MA program in rhetoric and composition at Texas State University. She has published numerous articles and book chapters on issues in writing center studies and writing across the curriculum, TA preparation, and graduate curricula. Her book (with Nicole Caswell and Jackie Grutsch McKinney), *The Working Lives of New Writing Center Directors*, was published by Utah State University Press in Fall 2016 and received the International Writing Centers Association Best Book Award in 2017.

FRANCES JOHNSON is a professional associate professor at Texas A&M University, Corpus Christi. Her research interests include the discourse conventions of the IMRaD formatted journal article, first-year composition, and ways to introduce students to the discourse-specific knowledge of scientific communication while fostering the transfer of writing skills. She designed and continues to teach the discipline-specific FYC writing course for science majors and an upper-level introductory technical writing course focusing on designing a survival manual for the zombie apocalypse. Her research has been presented at local, state, regional, national, and international conferences.

ELIZABETH KLEINFELD is professor of English and writing center director at Metropolitan State University of Denver. Her research focuses on multimodal composition and pedagogy, writing center studies, and student source citation practices. Her work has appeared in *Computers & Composition Online* and several edited collections. She is the coauthor, with Amy Braziller, of *The Bedford Book of Genres*.

KATIE JO LARIVIERE is a doctoral candidate in medieval literature and instructor of writing at the University of Oregon. Her research investigates the intersection of religion, identity formation, and selfhood in the late Middle Ages. Teaching writing is a "twin" love for her, as she sees her first-year composition students participate in processes of self-negotiation and development similar to those she sometimes sees in her favorite texts. She has facilitated several trainings in WAW practices and given an invited talk on the principles of WAW as a framework for equitable writing program assessment. Katie Jo has been recognized for teaching excellence in the English departments of both Montana State University and the University of Oregon.

ANDREW LUCCHESI is an assistant professor of writing studies at Western Washington University, where he teaches courses in basic writing, technical communication, composition theory, and disability studies. His research examines the history and politics of disability access programs in public higher education. He recently edited a special issue of the *Journal of Interactive Technology and Pedagogy* titled "Disability Studies Approaches to Pedagogy, Research, and Design."

CAT MAHAFFEY is a senior lecturer and former associate director of first-year writing in the university writing program at the University of North Carolina, Charlotte. Her research interests include online writing instruction, digital literacy, and digital design. In addition, she is currently a PhD student in the Technical Communication and Rhetoric Program at Texas Tech University.

I. MORIAH MCCRACKEN is an associate professor of writing and rhetoric and director of the General Education Writing Program at St. Edward's University in Austin, Texas. Her research interests include writing about writing pedagogies as well as the shared threshold concepts of writing studies and information literacy.

MICHAEL J. MICHAUD is an associate professor in the English department at Rhode Island College. He teaches courses in professional writing, digital and multimedia writing, public writing, argument, and advanced composition. His current research with Sarah Read investigates the multimajor professional writing course. He is writing a book on the history of the University of New Hampshire English department.

REBECCA S. NOWACEK is an associate professor of English at Marquette University, where she directs the Ott Memorial Writing Center. Her publications include *Agents of Integration: Understanding Transfer as a Rhetorical Act*; *Literacy, Economy, and Power*; and *Citizenship across the Curriculum*. Her work has also appeared in *College Composition and Communication, College English, Research in the Teaching of English,* and *the Journal of General Education*. She was a Carnegie Scholar with the Carnegie Academy for the Scholarship of Teaching and Learning, and the 2012 recipient of Marquette University's Robert and Mary Gettel Faculty Award for Teaching Excellence.

CONTRIBUTORS

ANDREW OGILVIE is an assistant professor of business communication at the University of Southern California. His primary research interests are writing development, knowledge transfer between school and work, and communication curriculum in higher education.

SARAH READ is an assistant professor and director of technical and professional writing at Portland State University. She teaches professional and technical writing and rhetoric as well as writing courses for science students. Her current research investigates technical documentation and reporting processes at a federally funded supercomputing center for scientific research. She is also, with Michael Michaud, conducting a national survey of instructors in order to assess the status of the introductory professional writing course across all institutional types.

JAN RIEMAN is a senior lecturer and former director of first-year writing in the university writing program at the University of North Carolina, Charlotte. She currently serves as associate director of the university writing program and coordinates the Writing, Rhetoric and Digital Studies minor. Her research interests include writing program administration and assessment, faculty development, and ePortfolio pedagogy.

REBECCA ROBINSON is a doctoral candidate in writing, rhetorics, and literacies at Arizona State University and an assistant professor of English at Brigham Young University–Idaho. Her current research uses Kenneth Burke's poetic frames as a heuristic for reflection and situated theory-building. Additional research interests include WAW, collaboration, disciplinary discourse communities, and conceptual metaphors for writing. She's also very keen on backyard chickens and *Doctor Who*.

KEVIN ROOZEN is a professor in the department of writing and rhetoric and former director of composition at the University of Central Florida. Kevin's research examines relationships among persons' multiple engagements with literate activity and the implications those linkages have for the extended development of literate persons and practices. With Joe Erickson, Kevin is the co-author of *Expanding Literate Landscapes: Persons, Practices, and Sociohistoric Perspectives of Disciplinary Development*, published in 2017 by Computers and Composition Digital Press. Kevin's work has also appeared in *College Composition and Communication, Enculturation, Journal of Basic Writing, Text and Talk, Kairos, Research in the Teaching of English, Written Communication,* and a number of edited collections as well.

MYSTI RUDD is an instructional associate professor of English at Texas A&M University at Qatar (TAMUQ), an international branch campus granting engineering degrees in the Middle East. Although she ultimately earned her PhD in composition/TESOL from Indiana University of Pennsylvania, she began her college studies as a chemistry major at St. Olaf College and therefore enjoys working with STEM students. Her research interests include the impact of composition pedagogy on first-year student retention. She has also examined issues of academic integrity as well as cultural factors affecting academic resilience, particularly of first-generation students. In addition to her faculty appointment, she serves as director of Student Learning Support in the Center for Teaching and Learning at TAMUQ.

CHRISTIAN SMITH is an assistant professor of English at Coastal Carolina University, where he teaches advanced composition and rhetorical theory. His work has appeared in *Computers and Composition, Literacy in Composition Studies,* and *College Composition and Communication.*

NICHOLE STACK is instructor and first-year composition coordinator in the department of writing and rhetoric at the University of Central Florida. Her research interests include literacy as a translingual practice, transformative learning, and pedagogy focusing on multilingual learners.

Contributors   285

SAMUEL STINSON is a lecturer of English at Shepherd University and has regularly taught first-year, professional, and science writing courses. His research interests include multimodal and algorithmic pedagogies, gaming rhetorics, writing centers, and writing program administration. His creative nonfiction has been featured in *Alimentum*.

HIROKI SUGIMOTO, from Tokyo, is a graduate student majoring in aerospace engineering at Embry-Riddle Aeronautical University in Daytona Beach, Florida. His passions are life sciences, space exploration, and art. He was part of Crew 160 at Mars Desert Research Station, and his research was on the influences of natural sunlight and going outside on the stress level of humans. He will continue further education and research in space-related fields, which he hopes will lead to becoming an astronaut.

LISA TREMAIN is the director of the First-Year Composition and Rhetoric Program and assistant professor of writing practices at Humboldt State University. Her research considers the intersections of composing processes, writing knowledge, student dispositions, assessment, labor, and teaching practice. She is currently leading the Writing-Enriched Curriculum pilot with faculty across three disciplines at HSU.

VALERIE VERA, originally a Brownsville, Texas, native is a recent graduate of Texas State University, where she received a BA in English and a minor in international studies. During her time at Texas State, Valerie participated in various research projects around Latinx studies and the investigation of *nepantla*—or the state of being "in between." Growing up on the border, Valerie has firsthand experience of nepantla, and this has given her a passion for cross-cultural engagement and inclusion. In an effort to further her boundaries and cross-cultural exchanges, Valerie is currently preparing to go to Vietnam to teach English as a second language.

MEGAN WALLACE graduated from Taylor University in 2017 with a Bachelor of Arts degree in psychology. She is currently enrolled in the Transition to Nursing Program at Indiana Wesleyan University and will graduate in April 2019 with a Bachelor of Science degree in nursing. After becoming licensed as a registered nurse, Megan plans to work in the area of labor and delivery.

ELIZABETH WARDLE is professor of English and director of the Howe Center for Writing Excellence at Miami University in Oxford, Ohio. She has directed first-year writing programs at the University of Dayton and the University of Central Florida, where she also served as department chair. Her research interests include transfer of writing-related knowledge and threshold concepts of writing studies. With Doug Downs, she is the coauthor of *Writing about Writing*, and with Linda Adler-Kassner she is the coeditor of *Naming What We Know: Threshold Concepts of Writing Studies*. With Doug Downs, she published a 2007 article in *CCC* that became a foundational argument for WAW approaches.

CHRISTY I. WENGER is an assistant professor of English at Shepherd University, where she teaches first-year writing, advanced composition and rhetoric seminars, and directs the rhetoric and writing program. Her recent publications include *Yoga Minds, Writing Bodies: Contemplative Writing Pedagogy*. Her work has also appeared in *WPA: Writing Program Administration* and *Journal for the Assembly of Expanded Perspectives on Teaching*. She serves on the executive board of the Assembly of Expanded Perspectives on Teaching and edits the organization's professional blog. Her research considers the intersections of contemplative mindfulness, multimodality, and writing for both students and teachers alike. Her recent research advocates for mindfulness as an administrative practice that cultivates well-being.

NANCY WILSON is an associate professor of English and director of lower-division studies at Texas State University. Her scholarship focuses on developing writing center programming and composition pedagogies that challenge systemic racism. She is the author of "Coming in from the (Binary) Code: Deconstruction in the Composition Classroom"; "Making Space for Diversity"; "Stocking the Bodega: Towards a New Writing Center Paradigm"; and "Bias in the Writing Center: Tutor Perceptions of African American Language."

DOMINIQUE ZINO is an associate professor of English at LaGuardia Community College, CUNY, where she teaches basic writing and first- and second-year composition courses and works with LaGuardia's learning communities. Her research interests include writing programs, the culture of writing on college campuses, student writing processes, and interactive technology and pedagogy.

INDEX

Activity
  cognitive, 28
  literate, 142
  rhetorical, 28
  social, 144
  writing as an, 7, 15, 27, 36, 38, 44, 58, 60, 63, 77, 84, 98, 125, 157, 218
  writing as an embodied, 255, 258
Activity systems, 42, 44, 63, 232, 238
Activity theory, 235
Adler-Kassner, Linda, 5, 45, 57, 205, 254
Advanced composition, 150, 257
Algorithm, 182–183
Alumni, 10, 187–196
Analysis, analyses, 32, 40, 43, 48, 54, 58, 69, 117, 166, 167, 178, 190, 191, 194, 207, 262, 265
  audience, 183
  content, 173, 175
  corpus, 144, 145
  course, 189
  empirical, 116
  discourse, 35, 36, 38 (*see also* Discourse)
  literary, 104, 114, 225
  of learning transfer, 273
  of peers as writers, 9
  rhetorical, 182, 187, 188, 190, 192, 265
  of scientific discourse, 9
  stylistic, 195
  textual, text, 4, 38, 41, 42, 44
Analytics, 193
  data, 192
Argumentative essay (AE), 125, 261, 262, 264, 265, 267, 268
Aristotelian, 165
Artifact, 9, 36, 38, 174
Assessment(s), 28, 31, 32, 117, 124, 137, 166, 241, 262, 265
  committee, 167
  course-level, 32
  entrance-level, 59
  formative, 61
  group, 184
  longitudinal, 32
  participatory, 189
  portfolio, 131
  program, 11, 131, 263
  rubric, 231

Assignment
  annotated bibliography, 117
  auto-ethnography, 62–63, 174
  autobiography, 117
  blog(s), 152, 235, 237
  brochure, 165
  content analysis, 175, 173
  design statement peer review, 249
  designer statement, 246
  game creation, 183
  genre guide, 152
  grant proposal, 44, 152
  incident report, 165
  infographic(s), 245–250
  instructions, 153, 165, 168
  interview(s), 37–40, 77, 118, 138, 141, 157, 162
  job application, 166
  lab reports, 150, 152
  letter, 78–79, 82–83, 157, 162, 168, 178, 187
  literacy narrative, 62, 63–65, 140, 222, 227
  literature review, 150, 152
  peer review infographic, 248
  podcast, 254, 256–259
  portfolio(s), 32, 65, 72–73, 76, 131, 210, 214, 227
  presentation, 104, 118, 153, 157, 180, 182, 196, 247
  proposal, 72, 108, 152–153, 168, 196, 239, 247
  recommendation report, 156–158
  reflection, 39, 50, 61, 63–65, 72, 105, 114, 120, 157, 160, 204, 205, 214–215, 237, 241, 242, 243–244, 250, 257, 273 (*see also* Reflection)
  report, 72, 73, 153
  research-based, 72, 173
  style analysis, 195
  website, 152
  work order, 165
  writer's memos, 72–73
Audience awareness, 72, 81, 82, 152, 183, 232, 239–243, 267
Authority, student, 82, 141
Authorship, 177–78

288   INDEX

Bakhtin, Mikhail, 145
Bartholomae, David, 16, 17, 77, 79, 275
Basic writing
　See Writing, developmental
Bawarshi, Anis, 205
Bazerman, Charles, 221
Beaufort, Anne, 16, 59, 62, 63–64, 66, 77, 144, 203, 205, 238
Bilingual, 93
Bilingualism, 88, 89, 225
Blaauw-Hara, Mark, 139
Borderland, 146
Bourdieu, Pierre, 204
Brandt, Deborah, 90, 185
Brent, Doug, 202
Butler, Paul, 194

Canagarajah, Suresh, 227
Carr, Nicholas, 147–148
Carroll, Laura, 182
Conference on College Composition and Communication (CCCC), 15
Ceraso, Steph, 252–253, 254, 265, 259
Charlton, Colin, 90, 237
Charlton, Jonikka, 237
Citation Project, 178
Close reading, 139
Code meshing, 94
Code switching, 89, 91, 94, 225
Coding
　of transcripts, 58, 59
Collaborate, collaboration, collaborative, 138, 193, 237, 278, 229
　assignment work, 39
　authorship, 177
　student, 4, 91, 154, 238
　inquiry, 131
　instructors, 124, 127, 132, 272
　with texts, 178
Communication
　professional, 72, 73–74, 155, 168
　scholar-to-scholar, 14
　strategies, 191, 195
　styles, 69, 70
　technical, 188
　tool, 173
Communication across the curriculum (*See* WAC)
Community college, 139–141, 170 (*See also* Two-year college)
Community service, 189
Community, communities, 27, 49, 52, 148 (*See also* Learning, community)
　of learners, 6, 99
　of practice, 31, 36, 42

of students, 119
scholarly, 171
Composing, multimodal, 110, 140, 243
　(*See also* Multimodal, multimodality)
Concurrent enrollment
　See Dual enrollment
Confidence
　student, 48
　in writing, 57–60
Construct(s)
　belief, 57, 66
　of writing, 58
Context(s),
　transnational, 103, 104
　(for) writing, 58, 59, 64, 158, 236
Contingent faculty, 168, 276
Conventions (of writing, of genre), 27, 62, 69, 68–70, 116, 195, 151–152, 225
　cultural, 69–70
Copyright, 177
Creative repurposing, 202
Critical literacy, 89–90, 138–142
Critical race theory, 92
Critical transitions, 202
Culture(s)
　academic, 93, 137
　difference, 68
　first-year composition, 5
　home, 7, 82, 93, 98–99, 105
　Japanese, 69
　Latinx, 89, 93
　programmatic, 123, 126, 129, 165, 168
　transition, 76
　writing varies across, 116
Current-traditional, 150, 154, 168–169

Data
　alumni, 191
　from instructors, 128, 160
　programmatic, 188, 193
　student-gathered, 62–63, 118, 152, 174–175
　on student outcomes, 105, 139
　used for teaching, 92, 108
　visualization, 238, 244
Database(s), 116
Declarative knowledge, 4, 16, 79, 181, 183, 206
Design
　course, 31–32, 59, 65
　game, 180–185
　participatory, 189
　student research, 107, 108, 153, 174
　studio, 151
　thinking, 152

Development
  awareness, 117, 241
  professional, 28, 124, 126–128, 166, 229, 276
  of threshold concepts, 26, 32
  writing, 29, 56–57, 59, 62–66
Developmental
  reading, 90
  writing, 16, 90, 97, 138
Devitt, Amy, 157, 166
Dew, Debra, 17
Digital, 180–181, 226, 235–239, 241–244, 253, 255
Disciplinary
  discourse conventions, 66, 143, 151, 170, 195, 206, 232
  first-year composition (FYC), 17, 43, 140–141
  identity, 23, 25, 36, 223, 256, 259
  teacher knowledge, 221, 224–226
  writing studies expertise, 36, 140–41, 144, 193, 195–196, 262
Discourse
  academic, 65, 115–116, 140, 145, 235–237
  analysis, 36, 40, 44, 144
  community, 16, 25, 38, 49, 53–54, 59, 77, 144, 173–175, 205, 238, 266–268
  conventions, 31–32, 114
  student study of, 63, 68–70, 128, 143, 151, 235, 237–238
Disposition(s), 57, 146, 204–205
Diversity
  curricular, 18
  linguistic, 89, 94, 119
Donahue, Christiane, 204
Downs, Doug, 18, 28, 103, 125, 151, 190, 206, 242, 262, 276
Draft(s), drafting, 7–8, 40, 104–105, 140, 147, 213–214, 216, 257–258
Driscoll, Dana Lynn, 204
Dual credit
  See Dual enrollment
Dual enrollment, 47, 49–51, 137–138, 142

Editors, student, 220–224, 228
Elbow, Peter, 15, 77, 82, 257
Elon transfer project, 130, 278
Email, 116, 147–148
Employer, employment, 36, 71, 196
Enculturation, 144–145, 212
Engage, engagement (with)
  academic conversations, 48, 51
  communities of practice or discourse communities, 31, 48, 54, 128
  texts, 79, 80, 102, 117, 160, 274
  threshold concepts, 25, 28, 32, 36, 38, 41, 44, 65, 193, 255
  writing studies research, 129, 133, 173, 221, 228, 274
Engaging, 50, 82, 98, 114, 181, 184
Engineer, engineering, 71, 74, 102–110, 150–154, 162, 188–195
English, AP, 48
English language, learning, 68–69, 76–80, 83, 94, 97, 102, 105, 225–226
Ethnography, ethnographies, 58, 128
Expectations
  community, 27, 29–31, 66, 76, 114, 116, 120, 212
  student, 58, 99, 139, 164–169, 227, 267

First-generation, 61, 92, 146, 274
First-year, student(s), 17, 30–31, 41, 75, 104, 225
Focus group, 88–92, 198–91, 209
Freewrite, freewriting, 61–63, 78, 80, 153, 213, 258, 268
Freire, Paolo, 138

Game, gaming, 107, 180–185, 192, 195
Gamification, 180
gateway (course), 193
Gee, James Paul, 41, 144, 181, 267–269
Genre(s), 16, 35, 72–74, 144–45, 156–158, 173, 237
  acquisition, 70, 108, 152
  digital, 234–37
  features and conventions, 27, 117, 151, 161–162, 165–168, 191, 225
  knowledge, 29, 36, 59, 62–64, 77, 114, 129, 143–144, 150–152, 194, 204–207, 244
  non-school, 50, 108
Gorzelsky, Gwen, 140
Graben, Tarez Samra, 237
Grammar, 15, 78, 80, 83, 193, 223, 226, 263
Grant-Davie, Keith, 269

Habits
  of mind, 204, 210–213, 218
  writing, 152, 237–238, 258, 268
Hedengren, Mary, 254
Heuristic, 48, 108, 151, 241–242
Howard, Rebecca Moore, 178
Human participants, human subjects, 174
Hybrid, 6, 77, 123, 143, 162

Identity, identities
  disciplinary, 23, 26, 36, 221, 224–225, 259
  negotiation, 84, 89, 92, 94, 226, 259

as scholars, 44
social or cultural, 89–90, 225, 277
transitions, 76, 78, 180, 203, 274
as writers, 3–8, 25, 57, 60–66, 80–81, 109, 217, 276
as writing teachers, 132, 278
IMRaD, 107–108, 110, 174–175
Information literacy, 191
Informed consent, 174, 209
Inkshed, inkshedding, 15, 77–80, 82–83
Interdisciplinarity, interdisciplinary program, 192
WAW, 119, 132, 229
Intertextuality, 107, 178
Introduction, writing an, 59, 73, 118, 173–175
Invention, 14, 177–178, 236–237

Jardine, George, 17, 274

Kantz, Margaret, 107
Katz, Steven, 192
Knowledge transfer, 119, 166, 170, 232, 264 (*See also* Transfer, learning)
Kozol, Jonathan, 141

L2, 75, 110
Lamott, Anne, 147, 216
LaRiviere, Katie, 144
Latin@, 97
Latinx, 88–90, 94, 144
Learning, learner
community, 173–174
deep, levels, transformed, 25, 26, 30–31, 32, 73, 108, 104, 119, 158, 165, 170, 181, 201–207, 242, 271
English, 64, 69, 91, 93
literacy (*See* Literacy, experiences or development)
outcomes, objectives, 25, 68, 130, 150, 180, 232, 267
prior, 203, 256
process (*See* Process, learning)
student, 23, 24, 26, 32, 43, 49, 57, 68, 71–73, 83, 125, 141, 142, 147, 184, 207, 216, 227–228, 241, 259, 263, 272, 275, 278
threshold concepts, 23–32, 45, 180, 215, 258
to teach, teachers, 224–225, 228–229
transfer (*See* Transfer, learning)
writing concepts and genres, 23, 28, 38, 48–50, 61, 69, 70, 73, 98, 99, 104, 110, 157, 162, 163, 165, 170, 184, 193, 196, 213, 221, 228, 244, 264, 267

Lefevre, Karen Burke, 178
Leydens, Jon, 191
Linguistics, 112–114, 119, 121, 195, 278
Literacy, literacies
concept or theories of, 13, 17, 18, 61, 103, 138–140, 142, 253
experiences or development, 58, 61, 63, 65–66, 126, 128, 138, 141, 142, 161, 182, 185, 221
information, 191
narrative (*See* Narrative, literacy)
skills, 89, 90, 110, 119, 138–140, 193, 235–237
Literature
body of work in composition studies, 32, 118, 189, 190, 191, 193
discipline, 113–114, 119–120, 124, 178, 193, 194, 225, 275, 277, 278
fiction, 48, 172
review, 115, 195
Luo, Michael, 147

Markel, Michael, 157
McCandless, David, 238
McCrimmon, Miles, 138
Mechanics, 184, 207, 227
Metacognitive, metacognition
awareness, thinking, 41, 109, 119, 148, 152, 156, 178, 203–205, 210, 218, 269
skill, 102, 110, 173, 214, 218, 271, 204, 211, 237, 265
students or assignments, 41, 84, 108, 156
Metadiscourse, 116–117
Metaknowledge, 63–64, 181–82, 233, 239, 244
Michaud, Michael J., 72, 73, 156, 157, 159, 170
Mindful, mindfulness
of learning, 242–244
thinking, 72, 74, 109, 214, 232, 238, 244, 273, 277
of writing, 16, 72, 214, 234, 236, 238–239
Minor (curricular program), 188, 191
Misconception(s)
about a writing course, 206, 263
about writing, 28, 36, 190, 206, 262–263
Model(s), modeling
as a curricular type, 59, 108, 113, 119–120, 138, 154, 158, 162, 190, 221
faculty development, 129, 131, 150
for student learning, 42, 62, 79, 91, 115, 118, 129, 147, 148, 213, 237, 254
genre, 151–152, 157, 173–174, 261–262

Monolingual, 112, 113, 115, 116, 119, 120
Multilingual
  courses, 266
  learners, 75–77, 78, 81, 83–84, 94, 97, 112, 113, 115, 120, 227, 275
Multiliteracies, 238
Multimodal, multimodality
  characteristic, 11, 236, 238, 239, 243, 244, 252, 253
  composing or composition, writing, 18, 110, 140, 236, 243, 253
  listening, 252–254, 256
Murray, Donald, 14, 15, 216

Naming What We Know (Adler-Kassner and Wardle), 24, 27–30, 57, 60, 216, 238, 253, 273
Narrative(s)
  account, 133, 141, 160, 194
  literacy, 62–65, 77, 105, 138, 140, 222, 227
Network
  making connections, 194, 274
  of teachers or teaching, 127, 144, 194
New London Group (NLG), 239
Non-tenure(d)
  in box or profile, 56, 123, 164, 209
Novice
  instructor, 151
  perspective, 36
  status, 38–40, 42–43, 44, 120, 152, 174
  writer, 127, 148, 273
Nowacek, Rebecca, 202, 207, 210

Oliver, Simone S., 147
Online
  assignments, 184, 235
  read, 241
Open enrollment, 137, 177
Outcome(s) (*See* Learning, outcomes and objectives)

Palmeri, Jason, 236
Parker, Paul, 178
Peer response, peer review
  as feedback, 99, 185, 193
  as teaching strategy, 72, 53, 119, 207
Perkins, David, 203
Perl, Sondra, 174
Perspective(s)
  American, 103
  critical, 9, 138, 140–142, 156
  disciplinary, 28, 36, 123, 139, 221, 223, 225
  personal, 49, 60, 91, 94, 102, 128, 139, 223, 228

professional, 37, 128, 225, 228–229, 277
student, 10, 24, 28, 49, 60, 94, 102, 229
Petrosky, Anthony, 16, 17
philosophy, philosophies
  as a discipline, 16, 192, 232
  teaching, 106, 160, 161, 163, 165, 166
  rhetoric, 14
Plagiarism, 107, 115, 117, 118, 120, 177, 178, 190, 193, 232
Porter, James, 106–107, 178
Portfolio
  electronic, 129
  general, 32, 65, 72–73, 76, 131
Portfolio assessment
  See Assessment, portfolio
Portfolio assignment
  See Portfolio
Prewriting, 15, 147
Primary research
  professional, 27, 120, 174
  student, 9, 128, 152–153, 172, 241, 245
Procedural knowledge, 8, 119, 206
Process(es)
  curriculum or course revision, 124–126, 130, 141, 196, 269
  learning, 26, 30, 61, 68, 73
  paradigm, 7–10, 15, 52, 54, 72, 119, 140, 142, 146, 147, 150, 192, 232, 238, 271
  reading, 62–63
  writing 5, 6, 7–11, 15, 16, 28, 32, 40, 48–49, 53, 54–55, 59, 62, 63, 64, 72, 77, 80, 84, 88, 98, 141, 146, 147, 148, 150, 155, 166, 174, 188, 190, 192, 203, 205, 207, 213–215, 218, 225, 229, 232, 234–237, 239, 242, 247, 252–259, 268, 276
Professional development
  See Development, professional
Professional writing (PW)
  course or program, 71–72, 155, 159–161, 168, 170, 187–189, 192, 194, 196, 277
  PW skills or knowledge, 71–73, 156–157, 160, 162, 163
  students, 156, 158, 160, 188–189
Project-based, 188
Proofreading, 139

Ramsdell, Catherine, 277
Read, Sarah, 9, 71, 73, 156, 157, 159, 170, 173
Reader(s)
  as audience, 3–4, 15, 30, 42, 43, 49, 54, 72, 80, 82, 113, 115, 117, 131, 153, 157, 243, 247, 256, 272, 276

student, 4, 62, 64, 105, 108, 173
texts, 266, 269
Reading(s)
  ability(ies) or skill(s), 102, 103, 105, 108, 110, 117, 138, 139, 141, 142, 173
  act of, 7, 30, 38, 40, 41, 51–54, 62, 63, 69, 93, 105, 106, 108, 114, 119, 140, 160, 173, 194, 207, 236, 259, 268
  assignments, 3, 49–50, 89, 102, 110, 138, 257
  concepts, 49, 109, 142
  student practices, 62–63, 69, 90, 102, 105–107, 109, 147, 183, 194, 266
  texts, 3, 6, 12, 17, 29, 49, 53, 60, 63, 65, 79–81, 90, 92, 94, 102, 103, 105–106, 109, 112–113, 117–118, 129–131, 147, 163, 167, 170, 173, 178, 181, 183, 185, 194, 210, 213, 227, 253–254, 263, 266–269, 274, 276, 277
Reflection
  critical, 131, 142, 170, 191, 195, 201, 205
  on concepts, 50, 72–73, 78, 109–110, 157, 162, 182, 185, 244
  curricular, 130
  on experiences, 141, 158, 194, 210
  as a genre or practice, 65, 119, 131, 156, 205, 207, 210, 214, 215, 218, 237, 244, 253, 257, 258, 268
  meta-reflection, 63, 65, 80, 157, 203, 242
  on reading(s), 61, 108, 139
  self- or mindful, 64, 65, 72, 78, 84, 117, 157, 242, 273
  on writing or writing process, 29, 31, 39, 61–62, 64–65, 72–74, 77, 80, 101–103, 105, 108, 114, 120, 141, 156, 160, 178, 181, 203, 232, 241–243, 247, 253
Reflective, 50, 201–204, 214, 234–236, 239, 241
Reflexive, 191
Reiff, Mary Jo, 29, 166, 205
Research method
  longitudinal, 32, 45, 133, 209, 273
  student, corpus analysis, 144–145
  student, ethnography, 9, 62–63, 128, 174, 237
  student, interview, interviewing, 35, 37–44, 73, 77, 118, 138–139, 141, 157, 162, 187, 189, 241, 254
Research question, 53, 172, 175, 193, 195–196, 247, 272
Research
  empirical, 24, 108, 115–116, 118
  interview, 32, 36, 40–41, 58, 160, 192, 209–213, 215–217

  primary, 9
  secondary, 118, 128
  student, data collection, 118, 188–189, 191–193, 195–196
  survey, alumni, 10, 23, 188
  survey(s), 18, 102–103, 105–109, 118, 128, 132, 160, 187, 189, 190–191, 196
  teacher action, 101
Retention, 39, 119
Revise, revising, revision, 30, 32, 73, 76, 98, 104, 108, 130, 153, 214–216, 232, 273, 277
Rhetoric
  classical, 184, 243
Rhetorical awareness, 129, 191, 196, 211–212, 271
Rhetorical situation, 16, 77, 81, 85, 107, 109–110, 184, 206, 212, 224, 232, 236, 243, 247, 262, 264
Rhetorical strategies, 45, 144, 203
Robertson, Liane, 28, 242
Rose, Mike, 141
Rubric, 30, 170–171, 222–223, 231, 263
Russell, David, 16, 173

Sargent, Elizabeth, 15, 77
Scaffold, scaffolded, scaffolding, 31, 61, 79, 115, 118, 128–129, 147
Science
  majors, 71–72, 106, 151–152, 162, 172–175, 191, 194–195, 212
  political, 49, 51
Second language acquisition (SLA), 75, 84
Second language writing (SLW), 84
Self-assessment, 64, 119
Self-efficacy, 6, 56–60, 64–66, 83–84, 92, 94, 104, 204
Shor, Ira, 138
Siebel, Patrick, 11, 253, 257–258
Skills-based, 188–189, 192, 264
Selber, Stewart, 234, 236
STEM, 6, 71, 150, 154, 190, 192, 195
Student
  course evaluations, 193
  graduate, 31, 39, 113, 150, 220–221, 224–225, 228
Student-centered, 110, 151, 164
Style(s), 48, 51, 68–70, 76, 82, 172, 194–195, 207, 213, 215–216, 243, 246, 264
Swales, John, 107, 151, 173–175

Teaching English to Speakers of Other Languages (TESOL), 221, 225
Teaching for Transfer (TFT), 203, 273
Teaching load, 165, 169

Technical writing, 8, 74, 103, 150, 160, 162, 167, 170, 190
Technology, technologies, 17, 28, 137–138, 140–141, 147, 151, 188–189, 195, 224–226, 234, 236–238, 255
Tenure(d), tenure-line, 39, 161, 163–164
Terminology, writing studies, 9, 156
Textbook
  adopting, adoption, 102–103, 109–110, 124, 140, 173
  handbook, 94, 152
  Scenes of Writing, 166
  Shape of Reason, 262–263, 267
  Successful Writing at Work, 164
  Writing about Writing, 176, 227, 236
  Writing in the Sciences, 161
Thonney, Theresa, 40–42, 114–115, 145
Threshold concept(s), 5–6, 9–10, 18, 23–32, 35–36, 38, 41, 44–45, 57, 60–61, 66, 130, 180–185, 205–207, 210, 215–216, 238–239, 242–244, 252–256, 258–259
Transfer, learning, 11, 16, 165, 206–207, 271, 273–274
Transformative, 24–25, 82, 131, 202, 205–206
Transnational, 101–104, 107
  writing, 225
Turkle, Sherry, 147–148
Two-year college, 146 (*See also* Community college)

Visual argumentation, 238

WAC, 31, 158, 162, 192
Wardle, Elizabeth, 3, 5, 18, 57, 103, 129, 132, 139, 151–152, 157, 173, 190, 202–206, 220–221, 227, 236, 238, 253, 259, 262, 266, 273, 276, 278
WAW-PW, 9, 72–74, 159–164, 168–171
Wells, Jennifer, 204
WID, 31, 150, 158, 173
Winsor, Dorothy, 191
Workplace, 27, 30, 70, 71–72, 160, 161, 163, 164–166, 191, 242
Writers, basic, 94
Writing
  business, 9, 155–157, 188, 190–191
  center, 28, 88–89, 92, 188, 189, 223, 224
  developmental (*See* Developmental, writing)
  intensive, 188, 192
  low-stakes, 80, 172
  program, 10, 12, 18, 37, 39, 123–124, 130, 132–133, 155, 188, 192, 223, 227, 261–262, 264, 271, 276–278
  program administration, administrator (WPA), 7, 30, 123, 125–132, 139, 173, 201, 220–221, 234, 276

X, Malcolm, 77, 182, 185

Yancey, Kathleen Blake, 203, 206

www.ingramcontent.com/pod-product-compliance
Lightning Source LLC
Chambersburg PA
CBHW030441090526
44586CB00044B/487